BRAWL

BRAWL

A Behind-the-Scenes Look
at Mixed Martial Arts Competition

By Erich Krauss and Bret Aita

ECW PRESS

Published by ECW PRESS
2120 Queen Street East, Suite 200, Toronto, Ontario, Canada M4E 1E2

NATIONAL LIBRARY OF CANADA CATALOGUING IN PUBLICATION DATA

Krauss, Erich, 1971-
Brawl: a behind-the-scenes look at mixed martial arts competition / Erich Krauss

ISBN 1-55022-517-0

1. Martial arts—Competitions. I. Title.

GV1101.K73 2002   796.815   C2002-902199-5

Acquisition Editor: Emma McKay
Editor: Mary Williams
Design and typesetting: Yolande Martel
Production: Heather Bean
Printing: Webcom
Author photo: Andrew Krauss
Cover design: Guylaine Regimbald
Front cover photos: Susumo Nagoa (top); courtesy Dream Stage Entertainment (bottom left);
courtesy Zuffa Sports Entertainment (bottom middle and right)
Back cover photo: Andrew Krauss

This book is set in Janson and Argo.

The publication of *Brawl: a behind-the-scenes look at mixed martial arts competition* has been generously supported by the Canada Council, the Ontario Arts Council, and the Government of Canada through the Book Industry Development Program. Canada

DISTRIBUTION

CANADA: Jaguar Book Group, 100 Armstrong Avenue,
Georgetown, Ontario L7G 5S4

UNITED STATES: Independent Publishers Group, 814 North Franklin Street,
Chicago, Illinois 60610

EUROPE: Turnaround Publisher Services, Unit 3, Olympia Trading Estate, Coburg Road,
Wood Green, London N22 6T2

AUSTRALIA AND NEW ZEALAND: Wakefield Press, 17 Rundle Street (Box 2066),
Kent Town, South Australia 5071

PRINTED AND BOUND IN CANADA

ECW PRESS
ecwpress.com

Contents

Foreword

Erich Krauss is a young man full of adventure, loyalty, and love of the fighting game. When he wanted to learn about muay Thai, he went to Thailand by himself and trained and bled in the gym for almost half a year. He succeeded in his mission and went on to compete professionally in the arenas of Pataya, Thailand.

We have been friends for several years, and I have watched him continue to grow. He has become a great writer, as you will see. He has trained with me in mixed martial arts, so he knows the fight game from actual experience. He writes from the fighters' point of view, he doesn't just describe things the way he thinks they should be, like so many other sports writers.

The sport of mixed martial arts is growing and will someday be a mainstay in the world's sports diet. Right now, it is in the same position boxing was seventy-five years ago, and I think it will become even bigger than boxing as it encompasses all the phrases of single athletic competition. Not just standup or martial arts or even wrestling—you have to be able to do it all.

Writers such as Erich, who research their material thoroughly—not only to tell of the fights, but also to tell the story of the fighters—are a welcome addition to our sport. Good reading, and follow your dreams.

—Bob Shamrock, father of legendary fighters Ken and Frank Shamrock, and founder of Team Shamrock 2000

PART I

In the Beginning

CHAPTER 1

From the Arena to the Ring

Over two thousand years ago, in the dusty arena of the Greek Olympics, a hero named Arrachion engaged a dangerous competitor in no-holds-barred, hand-to-hand combat before a crowd of thousands. After a lengthy and brutal battle, Arrachion got caught in a crushing choke hold. His pride and valor would not let him submit, however, and even as he found himself fading to black he struggled to put his foe away. When nothing else presented itself, he seized his adversary's toe and wrenched it back. The pain made his opponent submit, but not soon enough. As the fighters were untangled, Arrachion was discovered to be dead, apparently of asphyxiation—but because his opponent had submitted first, the deceased Arrachion was declared the victor, and his memory has lived on through the ages.

* * *

For thousands of years, soldiers have tested their hand-to-hand combat skills in war, transforming their bodies into effective and deadly weapons. Although there were those who survived to become heroes, the blood-stained battlefield was a harsh proving ground, and eventually the ways of war were turned into sport so combatants could test their skills and live to tell the tale. The participants in these man-to-man spectacles were limited to the brave, and a new kind of hero was born. Spectators clamored by the thousands to behold them in action. Images of broken arms, knees to the face, and powerful choke holds spawned daydreams of competition, victory, and glory.

Even in our modern technological world, where battles are won with the touch of a button or the pull of a trigger, the need to experience the rush of hand-to-hand combat persists in both warriors and their fans. In Brazil, they call these competitions vale tudo. In Japan, it's called submission fighting. It sprang up in the United States as no-holds-barred and was later dubbed mixed martial arts. Whether combatants battle it out in cages, rings, back alleys, or warehouses, their reasons are usually the same: to discover what works and what doesn't, to test their personal limits, and to answer the age-old question, "Who is the toughest?"

This anything-goes style of hand-to-hand competition is documented as early as 648 BC with the introduction of pankration, a combination of boxing and wrestling, into the Greek Olympics. "Pankration" means "all-powers," or "all-in-combat," and it originated when fighters in both boxing and wrestling began refining their skills, seeking a new level of competition. This is not to say that these individual sports weren't already vicious. Boxers, unlike today's pugilists, were allowed to punch their opponents unmercifully while they were on the ground. Wrestlers learned various joint manipulations to inflict as much pain upon their opponents as possible. In both boxing and wrestling, there were no time limits, no rounds, and no weight classes. The bouts were decided when a fighter either submitted or was rendered incapable of continuing the match.

The pankratiasts of yore took man-to-man combat one step further. They synthesized the techniques of the boxer's strikes and the wrestler's groundwork into a lethal and individualistic fighting style. The only rules in pankration were no biting and no gouging of the eyes, and the matches were often brutal. Many ended with the champion being permanently disabled and the loser dying. On the upside, however, there was immeasurable glory and honor involved. The victors of these games were treated like mythical heroes, their lives and deeds depicted on pottery and immortalized in stone carvings.

Tales of pankration champions are shrouded in legend and poetic license. One story is of the charismatic Milo of Crotona, who achieved a level of popularity comparable to that of modern-day martial artist Bruce Lee. He engaged in all sorts of public displays of skill, and it was rumored that Milo built up his unusual strength by lugging a calf on his back every day until it became a bull. Stories recount how Milo would tie a cord around his head and hold his breath, creating such a rush of blood to his skull that the pressure would snap the cord.

Unfortunately, Milo's tendency to constantly test himself led to his demise. One day, he happened upon a dying tree that someone had begun to separate with wedges. He got it into his head that he could pull the two halves of the tree apart. As he attempted this, the wedges slipped out and the tree halves snapped together, pinning Milo. Apparently, trapped like this in the forest, the legendary fighter was eaten alive by wolves.

Yet another account is of a pankratiast who would attack his opponents with a straight-hand strike to the gut. His fingernails were hard and jagged, and he used them to cut into his challengers. Once his fingers were under the skin, he thrust his hand deep and proceeded to extract their bowels. Victory in these matches was secured by submission, by knockout, and often by death. Many times, fighters chose to assure their wins by the most conclusive option available.

Perhaps the most famous pankration fighter, however, was Dioxippus. His reputation in battle was so daunting that no one dared fight him. He was a close friend of Alexander the Great, and it is conjectured that through his training of both the Greek and the Roman armies pankration spread throughout Europe and eventually made its way over the Himalayas with Alexander's forces. There is a theory that pankration's deadly effectiveness, mixed with the religious and meditative practices of the Chinese, became the root of Asian martial arts.

Pankration lasted until the height of the Roman Empire. Although it continued on in the Greek Olympics, in Rome it had mutated into a gladiatorial blood sport, for which warriors donned bladed gloves and fought to the death. But in the fourth century AD, when Christianity took over as the official religion of the conquering Roman Empire, both the gladiatorial games and the Greek Olympic games, with their pagan ancestry, were done away with. And so went pankration. It's fortunate that the sport had already been established throughout the known world, sowing the seeds for what would surface nearly three thousand years later as mixed martial arts (MMA).

*   *   *

Submission wrestling competitions began to emerge in America in the late nineteenth century. Traveling carnivals featured "athletic shows," in which brave audience members could take on one of the carnival's wrestlers. If the challenger could last in the ring with this hired gun for a predetermined amount of time, he received a cash prize. But seldom did challengers walk away victorious, and seldom did they walk away unscathed. These nomadic wrestlers were brutal diehards, dedicated to the art of wrestling. They were kings of the ring, and they were far from being the type of men one might imagine today when the words "professional wrestler" are spoken. Their style was called "hooking," named after the submission tactics they used called "hooks" (Sam Chan. "The Japanese Pro-wrestling / Reality Based Martial Art Connection." 15 Feb. 1998. *BJJ.org*. 21 Feb. 2001. <http://bjj.org/editorials/19980215-prowrest/>).

In hooking, there was a hierarchy of skill. Traveling with most carnivals was a journeyman, a somewhat capable wrestler who was pitted against nonthreatening challengers. Above him was the shooter, the more proficient wrestler who took on the difficult opponents. And then there was the master of the art, the submission-wrestling guru known—for better or worse—as the "hooker."

Hookers knew all the tricks of the trade, and the carnival was their domain. They policed the matches of their underlings to ensure that a desperate challenger did not resort to biting or gouging. They settled territorial disputes, and because they were often faced with skilled opponents looking for an easy buck, they had to refine their art continually in order to stay on top of their game (Tony Checcine. "Catch History." *Tony Checcine's Catch Wrestling*. 18 Feb. 2001. <http://www. catchwrestle.com/ catchhistory.htm>). They were experts at administering punishment through spine locks, shoulder locks, neck and face cranks, and an array of arm and leg holds (Tony Checcine. "What is a Hooker?" *Tony Checcine's Catch Wrestling*. 19 Feb. 2001. <http://www.catchwrestle.com/ whatisahooker.htm>). Hookers were considered by many to be the most dangerous men of their time. With the fundamentals of wrestling and countless submission techniques in their arsenal, they could attack an opponent from any angle.

Although the popularity of these athletic shows began to fade in America in the early part of the twentieth century, the art of hooking survived. It was introduced to Japan in 1914, when legendary wrestler Ad Santel defeated a fifth-degree black belt in judo. The Japanese opponent had claimed to be the Japanese judo champion, so after the match Santel crowned himself world judo champion (Chan). His declaration embarrassed the founder of judo so severely that he sent another student to challenge Santel and restore honor to the Kodokan, the world-renowned judo dojo in Japan. But once again Santel was victorious, and a few years later he extended a challenge to the entire Kodokan, daring its members to contest his claim as champ. He went on to secure more victories, and because of these matches, a fascination with Western submission fighting erupted in Japan.

The legendary wrestler Karl Gotch made a further impression on the Japanese with his exceptional hooking talent. Already a European wrestling champion, Gotch had moved to the United States in 1959 to continue to promote his skills. But because he was a reality-based wrestler, he wasn't accepted warmly in America, where pro wrestling had become mostly staged matches known as "works" or "worked" fights (Chan).

Gotch did not adhere to predetermined outcomes, and many American pro wrestlers feared both him and his submission skills. Searching for a new platform, Gotch went to Japan, where he quickly earned the title "God of Pro Wrestling."

Among Gotch's admirers were many of the athletes participating in the Japan Wrestling Alliance (JWA), an organization founded by a former sumo professional and devoted to promoting worked matches. Gotch's hooking style changed their conception of wrestling, and many went on to become his students. Satoru Sayama, Yoshiaki Fujiwara, Antonio Inoki, and Akira Maeda were the most famous of his pupils. Several of these wrestlers were already proficient in a variety of martial arts, such as muay Thai (a form of kickboxing that utilizes devastating elbow and knee strikes), judo, karate, and sumo. Combining their backgrounds with Gotch's hooking, they developed their own hybrid-fighting styles, and each would have a direct impact on contemporary MMA competition.

Japan's most famous wrestler, Antonio Inoki, was kicked out of the JWA in 1971 when it was discovered that he was plotting to take over the promotion. This did not halt his ambition, however, and he went on to form one of Japan's most popular wrestling organizations ever: New Japan Pro Wrestling (NJPW). The first NJPW match was held in March of 1972, and its popularity inspired Inoki's contemporaries Sayama, Maeda, and Fujiwara to join.

NJPW was catapulted into the spotlight in 1976, when Inoki staged a mixed martial arts tournament. It was an extravaganza the likes of which had never before been seen in Japan, and although the fights were, for the most part, worked, the concept of pitting style versus style helped to elevate Japanese pro wrestling still further. For the event, Inoki scoured the globe and rounded up some of the world's most respected fighters, including Olympic judo gold medalist William Ruska, boxer Chuck Wepner, and world kyokushin karate champion Willie Williams (Steve Slagle. "Antonio Inoki." *Professional Wrestling Online Museum.* 3 Feb. 2001. <http://www.wrestlingmuseum.com/homeie.html>.). But the main event was what people came to see—a worked fight between boxing great Muhammad Ali and Antonio Inoki.

The bout did not live up to the fans' expectations, however. Ali's training camp suspected that Inoki would use his submission tactics and try to turn the fight into a real match, so rules were established that barred Inoki from using any hooking techniques or suplexes (Chan). The result was a long and boring fight that ended in a fifteen-round draw. But this tournament, along with the NJPW's adoption of many martial arts techniques, specifically low kicks and judo throws, forever changed pro wrestling in Japan (Chan). Many wrestlers were now inspired to bring more realism to their matches, and their fighting styles became more applicable to MMA combat.

In response to this interest in realism, Akira Maeda left the NJPW and formed the Universal Wrestling Federation (UWF). Sayama, Fujiwara, and Nobuhiko Takada (a student of hooking) quickly followed suit. Although the UWF bouts had predetermined outcomes, making them essentially worked, the techniques applied during the matches were delivered with full force. This became known as "stiff" wrestling. But the UWF did not stop there. Real matches were eventually arranged between certain wrestlers and boxers, moving Japanese pro wrestling still closer to MMA competition.

This evolution was not rapid enough for some wrestlers, who were eager to test their skills in full-on MMA warfare. On September 2, 1985, in a match between Maeda and Sayama, Maeda purposefully kicked Sayama in the groin (Chan). Sayama abandoned any plan for a predetermined outcome and laid into Maeda with full force. The match became violent, and thousands of spectators got their first glimpse of MMA fighting. It was breathtaking.

Sayama was promptly fired from the UWF for his extreme retaliation. For the time being, he was finished participating in staged matches. He founded Shooto in 1987, a completely legitimate organization with no fixed fights, and he brought true MMA competition to Japan. Later, he organized the first Japan open vale tudo (anything goes) tournament, drawing the acclaimed jiu-jitsu tactician Rickson Gracie over from Brazil to fight (Chan).

The same year that Sayama founded Shooto, Maeda, having returned to the NJPW, had another outburst during a worked fight. On November 27, 1987, he once again purposefully kicked a rival wrestler, but this time the damage he inflicted was much more serious. He broke three bones in his opponent's face, and he was fired the following March because no wrestler was willing to enter the ring with him (Chan).

Not to be stopped, Maeda and Takada formed a new UWF in April of 1988. But their organization suffered without a young and dynamic fighter. To solve this problem, they convinced two of the more popular wrestlers, Masakatsu Funaki and Minoru Suzuki, to leave NJPW for the new UWF (Chan). Despite this talent, the UWF ultimately failed, and it disbanded in 1990. Several spin-off promotions stepped in to fill the void. Maeda started an organization called RINGS, which put on half-

Royce Gracie after a brutal UFC bout, surrounded by his brothers and family.

worked, half-real matches. But the most notable of the UWF splinters was Pancrase.

Pancrase was the brainchild of a businessman named Ozaki, who combined forces with Suzuki, Funaki, and wrestler Karl Gotch with the intention of creating the most realistic fighting promotion possible. Although the rules were not as loose as those of the soon-to-emerge Ultimate Fighting Championship in America, it was a far cry from the fixed matches of pro wrestling. There were no weight classes. A competitor could strike his opponent with a closed fist to the body, and an open palm to the head. A fighter could also kick, knee, and elbow—but knocking an opponent out with strikes was not always the choice method of achieving victory. With master submission fighters like Funaki, the emphasis of Pancrase was on technique, with much of the action occurring on the ground. If, however, a fighter found himself in trouble, he could work his way to the edge of the ring and cling to the ropes. The referee would separate the fighters and the match would be restarted standing. This reprieve was called the "rope escape," and it was a remnant of the organization's pro wrestling roots.

To increase the popularity of this new organization, the promoters sought out foreign martial artists who had proven their courage and skill in hand-to-hand combat. One such foreigner was Ken Shamrock, who hailed from the Japanese pro wrestling scene. With his hulking frame and intense personality, Shamrock quickly became a crowd pleaser.

Another foreigner who helped this new organization attain the international-fight-world spotlight was the famed Dutch kickboxer Bas Rutten. Growing up in Holland, suffering from asthma and a rare skin disease, Rutten had no idea that one day he would go to war in a ring before tens of thousands of Japanese fight fans. He was too busy fending off the neighborhood bullies, who had chosen to pick on him because of his handicaps. "I got messed with a lot as a kid, walking around with special gloves," remembers Rutten. "I was called a leper, a homo—everything. Sometimes I would have to stay in bed for three weeks, and I couldn't walk or nothing."

All this abuse wore on the young Rutten, but at twelve years of age, after seeing Bruce Lee in *Enter the Dragon*, he discovered a way to fight back. He enrolled in tae kwon do classes and learned how to kick and punch. Just a few weeks later, he was forced to put his new defense techniques to use in a street fight and broke his adversary's nose. When his parents found out, they yanked him from martial arts training. But those few weeks of instruction stuck with him, and ten years later, when he was out on his own, he picked up where he had left off. "I soon realized that tae kwon do was not it for me," says Bas, "because there were no low kicks allowed, no knees, and no punches to the head. I realized that in a street fight they can hit you to the head. Then I started doing Thai boxing in addition to my tae kwon do. I had my first fight after six weeks of training. I won by knockout with a spinning back kick to the liver."

After winning his first kickboxing bout, Bas decided he wanted to be the best fighter in the country, which was not an easy task in his homeland. "Fighting is like soccer in Holland," explains Rutten. "Everybody does Thai boxing." Despite the fact that he was competing against the toughest in the world, he racked up an impressive kickboxing record of fourteen wins and two losses. Having garnered a reputation as one of the strongest strikers alive, he attracted Pancrase's attention.

In 1993, Rutten traveled to Japan and entered his first Pancrase bout. "I was pretty much a striker," says Rutten. "I came in at two hundred pounds. I came from Thai boxing, where a five-pound difference meant a lot. My first opponent was forty-five pounds heavier than me. I also thought the fight was going to be five rounds of three minutes, but then they told me it was one round of thirty minutes. I told them no problem, because I was in good shape, but in my mind I was thinking, 'Oh my God!' Luckily, it turned out okay."

As a matter of fact, it turned out better than okay for the Dutchman. Rutten won his bout with Ryushi Yanagisawa by way of a knockout. "I caught him right under the jaw with a palm," explains Rutten. "He stood up, and I kicked him in the liver and hit him again in the head. When he fell down, I kneed him in the head and it was over. I won in forty-three seconds, and he was taken straight to the hospital."

By no means was Rutten's debut a fluke. He returned to Pancrase just a few months later and proceeded to knock out Takaku Fuke in the same dramatic fashion. With each victory, he became a more complete warrior. "Pancrase made me a good fighter because of the rope escapes," claims Rutten. "It makes you more of a thinker than a doer. If you are close to submitting somebody and are close to the ropes, you first have to drag them towards the center of the ring. There is more thinking involved than just submitting someone. The only thing I didn't like about Pancrase was the openhand strikes and shin protection. I wished I could have closed my fists."

Even with the openhand rule, Rutten claimed more than his share of victories in the Pancrase ring. With almost thirty bouts under his belt, he experienced only four losses. His superlative strikes and impressive submission skills entertained Japanese crowds of tens of thousands.

Although Rutten and others made Pancrase tremendously popular in Japan, and similar competitions were booming thousands of miles away in Brazil, it wasn't until 1994 that MMA would be reintroduced on a global scale through an unlikely champion named Royce Gracie, and a groundbreaking event called the Ultimate Fighting Championship.

CHAPTER 2

The Ultimate Challenge

With thousands of bloodthirsty fans packed into McNichols Arena in Denver, Colorado, and hundreds of thousands more watching at home on pay-per-view, a train of brothers clad in matching sweat suits emerged from the blue lights and billowing smoke—the Gracie family had come to the first Ultimate Fighting Championship in force. Although their specialized style of jiu-jitsu was virtually unknown in America, the family had been participating in no-holds-barred events for more than fifty years in Brazil, taking on all comers from a variety of disciplines, such as boxing, karate, and kung fu. But tonight's event was more than just another competition in which to test their skills. The UFC had been designed as a platform to introduce the art of Gracie jiu-jitsu to the world.

Now it was up to Royce Gracie, the family's chosen representative, to prove the superiority of his family art. Although he was the smallest competitor in the event, he was expected to defeat his larger opponents in a competition where there were no rules, no weight classes, and no time limits. Tonight, Royce was expected to bring honor to his family name, just as his father, Helio, had done for half a century.

* * *

Born on October 1, 1913, Helio Gracie was the youngest of five brothers growing up on the Brazilian Amazon's wild jungle frontier. Unlike his brothers, Helio was not athletically endowed. He suffered from fainting spells and poor health, and under doctor's orders his family kept a close watch on him, not allowing him to participate in sports of any kind. But that didn't stop the strong-willed boy from pursuing his dream and becoming a fighter who, in his prime, was considered by many Brazilians to be the toughest warrior on Earth.

The Gracie family was introduced to the Eastern fighting arts by Mitsuyo Maeda, a famous Japanese jiu-jitsu practitioner whose hand-to-hand combat skills were unmatched. Much like the hookers in America,

The amazing Helio Gracie backstage at the UCF.

Maeda had begun his career participating in wrestling tournaments sponsored by the carnivals that traveled throughout rural Japan. Eventually, he moved on from his wrestling roots to judo, a sport that combined several Japanese jiu-jitsu styles with an emphasis on throws and strikes. Maeda was fortunate enough to study directly under the founder of judo, Jigoro Kano.

Quickly becoming Kano's favorite student, Maeda was made an official judo ambassador and sent on a worldwide mission to bring recognition to the art. He traveled throughout Europe, the United States, and Latin America. Determined to put judo on the map, he challenged and defeated hundreds of wrestlers and heavyweight boxers alike in no-holds-barred demonstrations.

By the time Maeda's travels brought him to Brazil, he had his art down to a science. As always, he participated in a number of wrestling demonstrations against local challengers; and, as always, he blazed through the competition. His victories, however, caught the attention of some wealthy Brazilian landowners, who were so impressed with Maeda's skill that they rewarded him with property.

The offer was too good to pass up, and Maeda made a new home for himself on the Amazon's expanding frontier. Although he continued to train and perfect his art, the jiu-jitsu master started on another mission: to establish a colony of Japanese immigrants in Brazil. While on this path, he met Gasteo Gracie, a scholar who used his political connections to help Maeda with his colony-building cause. In return, Maeda offered to teach Gasteo's son Carlos the secrets of his fighting art.

Carlos excelled as a student, and then as a teacher. He taught all his brothers jiu-jitsu, except for Helio, who was still considered too weak to participate. When Carlos relocated the family to Rio de Janeiro to open the Gracie Jiu-Jitsu Academy, Helio sat on the sidelines, watching and learning from his brothers' classes, waiting for a chance to follow in their footsteps.

That opportunity came the day Carlos failed to show up for a private lesson with one of his students. Having watched his brother for years, studying the moves, Helio took it upon himself to teach the student. By the time the lesson was over, the student wanted Helio as his instructor.

This so impressed Carlos that he finally permitted Helio to begin his official training. Because he lacked size and strength, Helio relied more on leverage and technique. He constantly searched for ways to make the methods of traditional jiu-jitsu less strength dependant. While accepting what worked and throwing out what didn't, Helio realized the importance of fighting from his back. When bigger and more powerful opponents took him to the ground, Helio learned that he could control them better by using his legs rather than competing against their arm strength. Expending less energy, he could wait for them to make a mistake and then catch them in an arm bar or a choke. Instead of focusing on throws, as one did in Japanese jiu-jitsu or judo, Helio became a master at fighting on the ground. And so Brazilian jiu-jitsu was born.

Helio improved countless techniques, and, knowing they could benefit anyone in a fight, he passed them on to his students and his brothers. To prove the effectiveness of his refinements, now known as Gracie jiu-jitsu, Helio entered no-holds-barred matches against martial artists of other fighting styles. In no time at all, he had chewed through the local champions in boxing, wrestling, and karate.

Soon, word of Helio's effective fighting style and challenge matches had spread throughout Brazil, and, in keeping with Brazil's notorious reputation as a country of savage street fighters, plenty of takers stepped up to Helio's challenge, hoping to knock the Gracie brothers down.

In 1931, at the age of seventeen, Helio climbed into the ring to face a renowned pugilist by the name of Antonio Portugal and defeated him in under thirty seconds. This match, and several other higher-profile bouts, gave the Gracie name national attention. But there were those who didn't acknowledge the effectiveness of Gracie jiu-jitsu, including many judo students who wanted to prove the superiority of Kano's teachings.

Masahik Kimura was the man chosen to do it. An undefeated Japanese judo champion for sixteen years, and an undefeated world champion for five years, he was a living legend. Kimura came to Brazil in 1951 not only to accept the Gracie Challenge, but also to put the family in its place and remind the world that jiu-jitsu and judo came from Japan, not Brazil.

Even though Kimura was ten years younger than Helio, who was now forty-two, and outweighed him by almost fifty pounds, Helio welcomed the fight. While no punching and kicking would be allowed in this grappling match, no holds would be barred. Kimura was confident that he would win the bout, and he went so far as to tell the press that if Helio could last three minutes with him in the ring, then Helio should consider it a victory. In front of twenty thousand spectators at Maracana Stadium, the largest soccer stadium in the world, Helio fought with heart. He would not give up, even when Kimura dislocated his elbow with an arm lock. The fight did not end until Helio's brother Carlos threw in the towel at the thirteen-minute mark.

Helio lost the match, but he had survived in the ring with the world champion for thirteen minutes, something few had ever done. He had proven just how effective his techniques were against a younger, larger, and much stronger opponent, making the Gracie family name and their fighting system even more renowned throughout Brazil.

After his defeat, Helio continued the family challenge. In 1957, at fifty years old, he stepped up to face a former student, Valdemar Santana. Despite Santana being more powerful and a great deal younger, Helio battled it out for a grueling three hours and forty-five minutes. It was an amazing feat for a man his age, and although he lost the match, it was further proof that Gracie jiu-jitsu was an art that demanded skill rather than brawn. This appealed to the masses, bringing droves of students to the already popular Gracie Academy.

That match signaled the end of Helio's career in the ring, but Gracie jiu-jitsu did not fade away. Helio had been teaching all of his sons— Rorion, Relson, Rickson, Rolker, Royler, Robin, and Royce—and they kept the family art and the Gracie name alive.

The Land of Opportunity

Helio's first-born son, Rorion, had ambitious dreams for his inherited fighting system. His first visit to America was in 1969. "My return ticket was stolen, so I ended up staying here for a year," says Rorion. "I spent my time panhandling and sleeping on newspapers." When he finally returned home, he was not bitter about his time abroad. America had actually made a positive impression on him, and, after earning a law degree from a prestigious Brazilian university, he returned to the land of opportunity in 1978 with the intention of establishing Gracie jiu-jitsu in the States. "I always knew that if you make it in America, the whole world is going to know about it," says Rorion.

Rorion's vision of a jiu-jitsu martial arts empire, however, was not realized right away. The American public had no idea what Brazilian jiu-jitsu was, and, even more frustrating for Rorion, they had no desire to learn.

Due to the influence of such movies as Bruce Lee's *Enter the Dragon*, released in 1973, karate and kung fu had taken the States by storm. People began associating flashy moves and whirling kicks with powerful and effective fighting. Rorion knew this was far from realistic; after all, his family had been destroying flashy fighters for more than half a century. But it was tough to change the perceptions of a culture swayed by the romantic mysticism of Hollywood. Americans didn't understand such powerful techniques as arm bars or ankle locks. They didn't realize that a fighter lying on his back could actually be in an advantageous position.

Rorion set about his task by teaching Brazilian jiu-jitsu out of his garage in Hermosa Beach, California, to anyone who was willing to learn. Every time new students would come to his house, Rorion would bring them inside and, after serving them watermelon juice and crackers, show them some tapes he had of his family fighting in Brazil. He had fifteen tapes of different bouts, and each time he showed them he had to explain every fight. One day, he decided to clip the fights together and throw a narrative down on top. When he had a finished product, Rorion marketed the tape, advertising it in martial arts magazines. The tape was titled *Gracies in Action*, and word of his family's fighting style slowly began to spread.

In addition to the *Gracies in Action* tape, Rorion was making tapes of new fights in his garage. "My students would bring in their former instructors of martial arts," remembers Rorion. "For the first ten years, I had people coming in left and right from all different styles."

One such challenge came by way of one of Rorion's more zealous students. The student, thinking the world of his teacher and his system, wandered into a dojo across town and, while chatting with a friend, made the statement that Rorion could beat his buddy's teacher. The instructor of the dojo made the challenge formal, and Rorion, with the intent of making his art more recognized, eagerly accepted. Originally, the prize was to be one thousand dollars, payable by the loser, but the karate instructor who had initiated the challenge reneged on the day the event was supposed to take place. As luck would have it, kickboxing great Benny "the Jet" Urquidez—who claimed to have fought over fifty matches and never lost—was a good friend of the timid sensei. "I had no idea who Benny 'the Jet' was," says Rorion. "I was from Brazil." Urquidez accepted the challenge on his friend's behalf, and the match went on as planned at the North Valley YMCA.

"Every time we squared off," says Rorion, "I closed the distance, got into the clinch, and then took him down. I did that a dozen times." Once Rorion had his opponent on the ground, the fight was over almost instantly. After Urquidez had been submitted several times, he congratulated Rorion on his fighting ability. Rorion quickly corrected the kickboxer by saying, "It's not me; it's what I teach that is good." To prove his point, Rorion pitted one of his new students, who'd had only forty jiu-jitsu classes, with one of the kickboxer's advanced students. The match ended seconds later when Rorion's student wrapped his opponent up in a choke hold and forced him to tap out. "You could see the shock on their faces," says Rorion. "They get into the clinch and suddenly they're on the ground. They had no idea what happened. They thought somebody must have pulled the carpet out from underneath them. The shock that Benny went through is the same shock that all those guys went through when Royce did what he did in the UFC. For me, there's nothing to it. It's just another day at work."

Urquidez was so amazed by the Brazilian's ability and fighting style that he promised to help promote Gracie jiu-jitsu, claiming he had all the connections. But Rorion explains that when he went to follow up with the contact, "Someone said, 'Oh, he's busy. He can't talk right now. So later I called him again, and they said, 'He's busy, he can't talk right now.' So I never called him again." Rorion would have to wait a little bit longer to see Gracie jiu-jitsu attain wider recognition.

A few years later, a filmmaker approached Rorion. He liked Rorion's challenge concept and proposed a match with a kickboxer he knew. "He started painting this picture of this deadly guy," says Rorion. "I asked his name, and he said, 'It's Benny Urquidez.' I said, 'Stop. Tell Benny you're talking to me on the phone. Make sure he wants to do this.'" Knowing he could not beat the Brazilian in a true MMA bout, Urquidez wanted to keep the fight standing as much as possible, and the rules of the match would limit the time on the ground to no more than a minute per takedown. Another stipulation, one that kept the fight from ever taking place, was that Rorion would have to pay Urquidez $100,000, win or lose.

Rorion scoffed at the idea and put forward his own version of the fight rules. "I'll put up $100,000, and Benny puts up $75,000," Rorion told the filmmaker. "We'll make it five rounds of five minutes, and if the fight goes to the ground, it stays on the ground." Rorion felt so confident of winning under these rules that he included a bonus in the deal: if the fight went to a draw, Urquidez would get to keep the $100,000. Obviously, Urquidez knew he couldn't win in a true fight, and he never responded.

Rorion was through with talking. "From that point on, every time something came up I said, 'Put up or shut up.' I'm willing to bet $100,000 against anyone, winner take all." The offer did not spark any challenges, but it did catch the attention of freelance writer Pat Jordan. Rorion told his story to the journalist, and Jordan published an article based on it entitled "BAD," in the September 1989 issue of *Playboy*. Following the publication of the article, Rorion was inundated with both students and challengers. The challengers hailed from a variety of martial arts, and they were eager to prove themselves and their styles against the Brazilian.

It was at this time, almost ten years after moving to the United States, that Rorion brought his seventeen-year-old brother Royce over from Brazil to help out with the family business. Royce, like all the boys in the family, had been studying Gracie jiu-jitsu almost from birth. He arrived just in time to take part in the challenge matches that ensued after the *Playboy* article.

One rival Royce faced was Jason Delucia, a kung fu practitioner who was confident he could dominate the Gracie Challenge with his "five-animal" style. Delucia was so confident, in fact, that he wanted to wager five hundred dollars on the outcome. Rorion did not accept the bet, which turned out to be a good thing for the deadly kung fu expert, who ended up tapping out shortly after the match began. Delucia wasn't alone by any means—a host of other challengers would end up the same way, submitting to the superior style of Gracie jiu-jitsu.

Although the Gracie name was becoming well known within a small network of fighters, Rorion, who was still teaching out of his garage, knew that the general public needed to see it to believe it. Brazilian jiu-jitsu (BJJ) was not flashy, and it would seem to have little pizzazz to someone who associated martial arts with high kicks and dramatized openhand strikes. To make BJJ more accessible to the public, Rorion invited two more of his brothers, Rickson and Royler, into the picture in 1989 to open a school in Torrance, California.

The school helped to promote the family's fighting style, but Rorion did not stop there. Knowing there were people all over the States who would be interested in learning his art, he put together a series of instructional videotapes. To sell the tapes, he employed one of his students, Art Davie, who had marketing know-how.

Art Davie first came to the Gracie Academy in 1992. He had just left a job at an advertising firm and was looking for a new project. Intrigued by Gracie's skill, Davie agreed to help market the instructional videos, along with the *Gracies in Action* tapes, and he began selling them by direct mail. The tapes met with tremendous success, and Davie's mind began to spin with images of an even bigger, more stunning media extravaganza. He wanted to create a show that would capture the reality-based essence of the Gracie Challenge.

This type of tournament was exactly what Rorion had been experimenting with all along, but up to that point he'd never found a way to put it together on a larger scale. Working with Art Davie, Rorion employed the skills of yet another of his students, John Milius, a respected Hollywood director known mainly for his cult classic *Conan the Barbarian*. Milius's role would be to give the show a dramatic edge that would help to sell it to the American public. Things were falling into place. They named the event "War of the Worlds." "We thought of 'War of the Worlds,' because each martial art is its own world," says Rorion.

Davie began pitching a detailed proposal to many of the established pay-per-view companies. The idea was to pit fighters from different martial arts disciplines in a no-holds-barred elimination tournament to see which style would prevail. Unfortunately, most of the pay-per-view programmers could not see the potential popularity and money-generating force behind such a competition—in fact, they couldn't even comprehend it.

Davie's pitch of the groundbreaking show fell on deaf ears until he turned to Semaphore Entertainment Group (SEG). At SEG, the proposal reached the desk of programmer Campbell McLaren, who happened to be searching for new ideas for pay-per-view events.

War of the Worlds struck his fancy from the get-go. McLaren carried it enthusiastically up the corporate ladder to the chief himself, Robert Meyrowitz—the man responsible for the *King Biscuit Flower Hour*, the first syndicated rock-and-roll radio talk show. Although Meyrowitz knew little about martial arts, he trusted McLaren's programming abilities and gave him the go-ahead to move on the idea.

"I went to New York and had a meeting with SEG," says Rorion, "and I played an *In Action* tape. They went crazy. They had never seen anything like it. We did a partnership together, and the rest is history."

The show that would start a revolution in both pay-per-view and the martial arts was well on its way to getting off the ground. But there would still be a few snags.

After Art Davie and Rorion Gracie formed WOW (War of the Worlds) Promotions, they worked with SEG to figure out the details of the event's production. One of the things they had to decide was what kind of ring the bouts would be held in. It had to be not only dramatic enough to capture the attention of the spectators, but also practical. Rorion knew he had to come up with something that would prevent the fighters from escaping the ring, and he started brainstorming. "We thought of everything," he remembers. "We thought about putting Plexiglas around the ring, but that wouldn't work for the cameras because of the reflection of the lights. We thought about a moat with water and alligators, sharks, sand, and electric wire. This was Hollywood. We even came up with something like Mel Gibson's 'Thunderdome,' which would drop from the ceiling with a cable. We thought of everything." When nothing worked, Rorion and Milius came up with the idea of a thirty-foot-diameter octagonal ring surrounded by a five-foot-six-inch chain-link fence—an arena that was both flashy and durable enough to contain two clashing warriors.

The exact name of the event also had to be worked out. "Ultimate Fighting Championship" (UFC) eventually replaced the original name, "War of the Worlds." Along with this came the famous UFC logo: a menacing bald man clasping the letters UFC.

The next question that needed to be answered was which State they should hold the event in. Colorado was ultimately chosen because it didn't have a boxing commission that could create hassles. McNichols Arena, seating sixteen thousand, was picked as the venue. Then the only other thing they had to do to make the show happen was to get the fighters.

Because the whole idea had originated from the *Gracies in Action* tapes, it was only fitting that a Gracie be on the card. Many thought Rickson should be the representative for the Gracie family. He had established himself as a legitimate vale tudo champion while in Brazil, and he was considered by many to be the best fighter in the family. Although Rickson wanted the opportunity, he wasn't given the shot because he had left Rorion's school to teach on his own several years prior.

"Rickson had more experience than Royce, but he'd decided to make his own move," explains Rorion. "I felt that Royce would be a very convincing example of what jiu-jitsu can do for people. Royce was twenty-seven years old, 176 pounds, six-foot-one. You look at Royce, you almost feel sorry for him. He's a little string bean. I felt it would be a much better example of what jiu-jitsu can do, much like my dad did in Brazil at 140 pounds. You see a little guy beating a big guy—that's proof of how effective this stuff is."

Although Royce was chosen to represent the Gracie family, seven other fighters still needed to be recruited. This proved difficult. "The concept was so new that nobody knew anything about it," says Rorion. "I sent faxes to martial arts schools all over the world. I had some contacts in Europe, South America, and the Orient. I got a few guys who responded, and I chased others through the telephone."

Another thing that had to be worked out was how to market the unknown sport. Art Davie decided to take the approach of pumping up the UFC's inherently violent appearance, and it was subsequently marketed as a blood sport. "We never had rules," claims Rorion. "What we had was two restrictions: no eye gouging and no biting. But neither of those were forbidden. I knew from the beginning we could not stop the fight. Once the fighters went in, you could not stop the fight, no matter what. If one guy eye gouges the other and we stop the fight, people were going to say, 'What kind of fight is this?' Everything was permitted. The consequences if you eye gouged the other guy or bit him would be a fine of one thousand dollars, and the money would go to the guy who got bit or gouged."

Another interesting aspect of Art Davie and SEG's early marketing efforts, which eventually fed the fires of opposition, was the decision to not use gloves. Although this may seem more damaging, bare-knuckle brawling is actually less dangerous than gloved punching. The gloves that a boxer wears protect his hands, not the person he hits, allowing him to deliver repeat blows to his opponent's head. However, the SEG marketing team decided to put a spin on this aspect to make the sport appear more dangerous.

With everything in place, all they could do was hope for the best. "The week preceding the UFC," recalls Rorion, "was the most exciting and most intense, and one of the most rewarding weeks of my life. It was a very meaningful moment for me, because it was a way to show the whole world that my old man was the one who made the whole thing happen. If it wasn't for him, we wouldn't be here."

UFC I—The Beginning/December 11, 1993
(Denver, Colorado)

On the night of the show, thousands of viewers watching on their television screens across America were introduced to the Ultimate Fighting Championship by the soft-spoken veteran kickboxer Bill Wallace, who happened to burp into the microphone while welcoming them to McNichols Arena. To Wallace's right sat a confused Jim Brown, the hall-of-fame running back, and to his left was an even more confused Kathy Long, a five-time world kickboxing champion. Despite Brown's knowledge of football and Long's experience in kickboxing, neither of them could offer any worthwhile information on the upcoming event, and so they passed the buck to announcer Ron Machado, who did quite well forewarning the fans about what they might see and who to watch out for—in particular, Royce Gracie.

But Machado's explanations would mean little to those who had a preconceived notion of how this elimination tournament would end up. Many still saw the superior opponent as the one who threw snappy punches and Bruce Lee-style strikes. The next hour and a half forever changed the world's view of the martial arts.

The first fighter to make his way past the aisles of reaching fans and step into the octagon was Telia Tuli, a nervous, six-foot-two, 410-pound sumo wrestler from Honolulu, Hawaii. Not only did Telia Tuli fill the "giant quota" for the event, but he was also quite efficient in his art of sumo. Along with being a top competitor in the Makushita class of the Japanese Pro Sumo Association, the bald-headed Tuli was known for having an incendiary temper. He seemed exactly the kind of fighter to stir things up.

Tuli was shortly joined in the octagon by Gerard Gordeau. Although the confident, slick-headed savate (French kickboxing) practitioner from Amsterdam stood six-foot-five and weighed in at 216 pounds, judging simply by looks, he appeared no match for his hefty rival.

Gordeau had been asked by phone to participate in the UFC. "They contacted many people from Holland," remembers Gordeau, "but nobody had the guts to go. They asked me if I wanted to make the Ultimate fight, and I said, 'Sure, why not?'"

Before the UFC, Gordeau's career had already spanned two decades. He had begun judo at thirteen, and then moved on to karate at the age of sixteen. His professional record was 27-4, which included the 1992 World Savate Championship. He reigned as the Dutch karate champion from

1978 to 1985, and he came in sixth at the Japanese World Karate Championships. Gordeau was tough as nails—for a while, many Dutch nightclubs had paid for his protection services.

Gordeau, having competed in full-contact events much of his life, was a little surprised at what he found when he arrived at the venue. Although the show was well organized, he felt it was an amateur event in many ways. "Nobody knew what they had to do," he says. "They spent two hours on the rules meeting, but there are no rules, so why do you need a meeting? I just signed the paper and then said, 'I leave the building now. I shall see you tomorrow.'"

Gordeau was also surprised to find himself facing Telia Tuli for his quarterfinal bout. His opponent was supposed to be Royce Gracie. "When I arrived at the event, a lot of Japanese reporters were there," says Gordeau. "I was very famous in Japan already. All the Japanese photographers and reporters came to me. Gracie asked them who I was, and they said, 'This is Gerard Gordeau. He has fought many times in Japan.' Then my fight was suddenly changed, and I was to fight Telia Tuli. If it was a fair event, they would have put eight names in a hat. But they did everything in advance."

The bout was a classic match between a David and a Goliath. After Rich Goins made the announcements, the cage was locked tight.

Battle began with the chime of a bell. Tuli danced for a moment around the ring, showing the crowd just how nimble a 410-pound man could be. Then he charged with his arms outstretched. A composed Gordeau simply backed off, launching a series of jabs and crosses that confused the advancing giant. Running out of room, they both crashed into the fence. Gordeau shoved Tuli to his backside, and then he stepped back and to the left, regaining his footing. While Tuli was attempting to rise, Gordeau dropped a solid round kick into his opponent's mouth, sending a tooth flying out of the ring. Just as the tooth was landing, Gordeau finished the job with a powerful right hook to Tuli's dome.

The ref jumped between the two fighters. Tuli tugged himself to his feet using the chain-link fence. Blood drained from a cut under his eye and from his mouth. His smile looked odd. He was not missing one tooth—he'd lost three. The other two would later be found embedded in the foot of Gordeau.

"Kathy Long had a tooth sitting in her lap," says Rorion. "They had never seen anything like it. Telia Tuli was bleeding, and the referee I had brought in from Brazil stopped the fight. I said, 'Wait, you're not supposed to stop the fight! Let him keep kicking. This is the name of the game. Let him kick him in the face.' We brought the doctor in, and we had to stop the fight. It was pretty wild; we were making the rules as we went along."

Although Gordeau was declared the winner and would continue on to the semifinals, the twenty-six seconds it took him to finish off his opponent brought him his share of injuries. "I broke a knuckle and a small bone in my hand," remembers Gordeau. The two teeth embedded in his foot would also cause him some agony—the wound became badly infected. After he returned to his homeland, says Gordeau, he had to go to the hospital every day for nine weeks. This could have been avoided, but the doctors at the UFC had left the teeth in Gordeau's foot to prevent an open wound.

As the fighters made their way out of the octagon, the crowd seemed stunned. No one was sure what to think. One thing was clear, however: they wanted more action, any way they could get it. Several fights erupted in the stands.

Kevin Rosier, hailing from Cheektowaga, New York, was the next warrior to make his way into the octagon. His record looked very impressive on paper. He had participated in numerous underground fighting events, and he'd even been a bodyguard for rocker Billy Idol. Standing six-foot-four and weighing in at 265 pounds, he was announced as having the impressive record of 66-8, all sixty-six wins coming by way of knockout. He was also three-time WKA World Super Heavyweight Kickboxing Champion, and the ISKA North American Super Heavyweight Kickboxing Champion—but no one would have guessed it by looking at him when he stepped into the ring. Sporting white trunks pulled up over a massive belly, Rosier looked more like a man who was entering an ultimate eating challenge.

His opponent, fourth-degree kenpo karate black belt Zane Frazier from North Hollywood, California, was also six-foot-four, but he weighed in at a trimmer 230 pounds. He, too, was announced as an international karate champion and WKA World Super Heavyweight Kickboxing Champion. Frazier had been added to the UFC card after Rorion Gracie and Art Davie had witnessed him in action. They had gone to watch the kenpo fighter compete in a karate tournament, but instead of seeing a point sparring match, they got to watch Frazier in no-holds-barred form as he beat a fellow martial artist down in an all-out brawl that took place in the lobby of the venue. His rival was none other than Frank Dux, the fighter whose tall tales of underground fighting served as the foundation for the movie *Bloodsport*. Although Dux's validity as a fighter was highly questionable, when Frazier came out on top, the promoters knew he was a must for the show.

Unfortunately, their bout did not live up to their titles. Action began as Rosier advanced upon his opponent with his hands down, like a man reaching for a jelly doughnut. Frazier did not capitalize on the opportunity, however, and as a result allowed Rosier to bash him in the head with a huge, telegraphed forearm. After eating several more wild fists, Frazier dropped to all fours. But, with Rosier oblivious as to how to finish a downed opponent, they both scrambled back to their feet.

Frazier finally got to work. After landing several blows, he drove his opponent back into the fence, where he landed a solid knee to Rosier's groin. The dirty fighting didn't stop there. Grabbing a handful of Rosier's hair, Frazier unleashed his right hand, several elbows, and more knees. But, as he did this, the altitude of the Mile High City began to catch up with him.

The tide of battle continued to shift back and forth, but it ended up with Rosier throwing sloppy bombs at his gassed-out opponent, who could barely keep his hands up. Using the last of his own energy, Rosier drove Frazier back into the fence and began pummeling him. It was too much for Frazier, who knelt down to cover the back of his head with his hands. Rosier rained down six punches and two foot stomps to the back of his opponent's head before Frazier's corner threw in the towel.

Royce Gracie was up next. His opponent was the six-foot-one, 196-pound boxer Art Jimmerson, who happened to be the most unprepared competitor in the event. Many arguments had been made (especially with the emergence of such powerful fighters as Mike Tyson) that a world-class boxer could walk through a traditional martial artist. This question needed to be resolved, and Rorion knew that if he could get a top-ranked boxer, he would increase interest in the event. After negotiating with several boxers, he finally managed to get one of the better champions of the time—"King" Arthur Jimmerson. Though the dealings went back and forth, Jimmerson, who was ranked tenth by the WBC with a professional record of 29-5, eventually agreed to participate for an appearance fee of twenty thousand dollars.

After it was decided that Royce should not take on the famed Gordeau in his first bout, Art Jimmerson seemed the best replacement to ensure Royce the victory and keep him from getting tired before the upcoming matches. "There's no doubt Rorion picked Royce to fight Jimmerson because he was a boxer," says John McCarthy, who became the octagon referee for the second show. Jimmerson, who knew nothing of fighting outside of boxing and was guaranteed a substantial purse, win or lose, entered the octagon donning a single regulation glove for show.

As the referee brought the two fighters together in the center of the ring, announcer Bill Wallace apparently forgot his lines and blurted, "I think it's kind of ironic that Royce Gracie will wear his *judo* top," but then he quickly retracted his own statement and began filling in the uninformed public on the benefits of wearing a "gi" in Gracie jiu-jitsu—which included added friction, so an opponent couldn't slip away.

The fight was the most uneventful of the evening. After both fighters had spent a moment circling each other, Royce took the boxer to the mat and mounted him. Jimmerson, not understanding how to fight from his back, clung on for a few brief moments before tapping the canvas. He hadn't been caught in a crushing choke hold or an arm bar. Gracie had simply delivered a single head butt, nothing more. Guaranteed a paycheck of twenty thousand dollars, Jimmerson had no motivation to take abuse.

Royce was declared the winner as the crowd voiced their disapproval. He had advanced without so much as a bruise. However, the competitor he would face in the semifinals, shoot fighter Ken Shamrock, would not tap out so easily.

Ken Shamrock had learned of the event through an ad in *Black Belt* magazine. Although his style of fighting was not well known in the States, Rorion knew that the six-foot-one, 220-pound ex-South Atlantic Professional Wrestling competitor, laden with muscles, would be a crowd pleaser. He was right. And, not only did Shamrock have the muscles and the cool, but he also had the fighting ability to back it up. He would become the future nemesis of Royce, and together the duo would serve as the backbone of the sport. How Shamrock arrived at the first UFC, however, is a tale in and of itself.

CHAPTER 3

Nemesis

Ken Shamrock moved swiftly past the aisles of reaching fans, his eyes pinned on the eight-sided cage where he would unleash his fury. He was no stranger to hand-to-hand combat. Growing up in Georgia, he'd fought for his survival and his pride. He'd proven himself on the streets, in back alleys, in bars, in Toughman competitions, and in the Japanese mixed martial arts bouts of Pancrase. But here, at the first Ultimate Fighting Championship, he had been given the opportunity to prove himself to the entire martial arts world.

In the ring, he stripped down to his fighting trunks, giving the audience their first glimpse of his swelled muscles and chiseled frame. As the women in the crowd swooned over Shamrock's build, kickboxer Patrick Smith made his way towards the octagon, surrounded by his entourage of trainers and friends.

Standing six-foot-two and weighing 217 pounds, Smith was a Denver native and a hometown favorite. He was ranked seventh by the World Kickboxing Commission, and he boasted an unsubstantiated record of 200-0. He held a third-degree black belt in an African martial art called robotae, a first-degree black belt in tae kwon do, and was coming off a championship win at a full-contact karate tournament called the Sabaki Challenge. He was arrogant and brash, and the crowd roared with approval as he entered the enclosure.

With these two intense warriors locked in the cage, many thought this would be the most brutal fight of the night, ending with one brawler lying in a puddle of blood. They couldn't have been more wrong.

Only seconds into the match, Smith shifted his balance to throw an inside leg kick. Shamrock shot immediately in for the double-leg takedown. Although Smith fought hard to keep from getting slammed—dropping a knee to Shamrock's midsection and landing a swift elbow—Shamrock quickly found the leverage to hoist him off his feet.

As the two hit the canvas, Shamrock positioned his muscular frame on top of his opponent, who was now holding on for dear life. To soften Smith up, Shamrock delivered several blows to the temple and midsection. Once Smith's hold was completely broken, Shamrock hooked his arm around the kickboxer's right ankle and dropped backwards. Within seconds, Smith was pounding the canvas in submission. Despite his ridiculous claims of being immune to pain, Smith had tapped out from the agonizing pressure of an ankle lock.

The crowd, wanting to see blood and ignorant of what a submission hold was, began to boo. They wanted more—and, apparently, so did Smith. Although the pay-per-view didn't show it, Smith actually got up and shoved Shamrock. Never having backed down from a fight in his life, Shamrock was ready to go, but the two fighters were separated before any blows could be thrown. "I think that was his way of trying to save face," says Shamrock. "He got up, started screaming. His boys were holding him back, and he was hopping on one leg. He talked a lot of trash before the fight, and then he got in there and ended up getting submitted. One of the things he said was, 'Oh, I can withstand any pain.' And then he tapped out to a heel hook, which is painful."

While Smith was escorted back to the dressing room, Shamrock was kept in the ring. He had won his first fight. Although the crowd thought it fitting to chant "Bullshit!" Shamrock's adopted father, Bob Shamrock, couldn't have been more proud. Ken had come a long way.

*   *   *

When thirteen-year-old Kenneth Kilpatrick first came to Bob Shamrock's group home in sunny Susanville, California, his future did not look bright. He had grown up fatherless in a poor neighborhood in Georgia, and he'd learned life's lessons in the streets. While his mother worked to put food on the table, he had cruised the neighborhood with his two brothers, brawling, shoplifting, and causing trouble wherever they could.

The first time Ken ran away from home, he was only ten. He took refuge in an abandoned car with some fellow delinquents, but he wound up in the hospital after getting stabbed by another child who was also on the run. In the years that followed, he would be ousted from seven group homes, serve time in juvenile hall, and be accused of strong-arm robbery. Although the strong-willed youth weighed only 125 pounds, he had his own way of looking at the world, and he was always ready to protect his pride with his fists.

Ken showed no signs of rehabilitation, and the State grew weary of him. He was given one last chance to turn his life around: he would go to a group home—the Shamrock Ranch—run by Bob Shamrock, a man renowned for working with misguided youths. While Ken had a history of conflict with those in charge of group homes, he fit in quite well at Shamrock's.

Bob had raised more than six hundred boys in his home, and his methods were both unique and effective. In response to the feuds that often arose among prideful boys sleeping under the same roof, he offered an unorthodox method of resolution. If both parties were willing, he allowed them to throw on boxing gloves and duke it out in the backyard. The matches were intended to keep bad blood from developing, and although the scraps were often heated, Bob made sure to keep the mood jovial, serving soft drinks to the boys who gathered to watch.

Ken quickly became the house champion in both boxing and wrestling. Outside of these in-house matches, he also earned a reputation around town as "One Punch" Shamrock. "He'd get into a fight and just knock the guy out," recalls Bob. "He hit them once and they were down. He never picked fights, but he never backed away from them."

One such occurrence happened when Ken was sixteen. On a cold winter afternoon, Bob got a call from one of his boys to get home in a hurry. When Bob arrived at the house, Ken was standing there with his sweater ripped off. Apparently, some baseball players from a nearby college had made the mistake of picking on the young scrapper. Words were exchanged, and when Ken refused to back down, a conflict ensued. In a rage, Ken beat down his attackers and sent them fleeing from the scene.

Another incident took place at a party after a high school football game to which Ken had driven Bob's beloved 1957 Cadillac El Dorado. An older student, quite drunk, accused Ken of making a move on his girlfriend, and he broke a bottle on the hood of Bob's car. Ken was furious, and he hit the drunk so hard he literally went flying out of his shoes.

Recognizing the boy had tremendous athletic ability, Bob redirected Ken's anger into sports. He got him on a weight-lifting program and enrolled him in wrestling and football. Ken quickly excelled. As a senior, he was elected captain of his football team and was climbing the ladder towards the State wrestling championships. He seemed unstoppable. But then an unfortunate accident at wrestling practice landed Ken in a hospital bed. While lifting a fellow wrestler over his head, Ken lost his footing and his opponent crashed down on his head, injuring his neck. Ken was rushed to the hospital. After conducting several tests, his doctors informed Ken that his neck had been broken.

To keep his spine from shifting, they inserted a metal plate at the base of his skull. The doctors told him he could never again be involved in contact sports. This was something Ken couldn't accept, and he proved just how much heart and determination he had when he resumed training only a few months after the accident.

Over the years, Bob and Ken had been through a lot together. At one point, the State had sent Ken back to his mother, who was then living in Napa, California. But, having found a home at the Shamrock Ranch, Ken returned of his own accord. Bob accepted the boy back with open arms, even though Ken was no longer being supported by the State. Along with becoming a leader for the other boys, Ken became the son Bob Shamrock never had. Shortly after Ken turned eighteen, Bob legally adopted him.

At nineteen, Ken Shamrock entered his first Toughman competition, in Redding, California. He weighed in at only 195 pounds, but, due to a shortage of fighters, he was bumped up to the heavyweight division. Although the first competitor he faced outweighed him by sixty pounds, it didn't stop Ken from knocking him out with a devastating body shot. The second brawler he took on weighed 245 pounds. Ken proceeded to knock him out, as well—along with several of the man's teeth. The competitor who was supposed to fight Ken in the finals wanted no part of "One Punch" Shamrock, so he claimed an injury to avoid winding up like the others.

It was evident that Ken had a natural ability for brawling, and this ability was exercised both inside and outside the ring. His reputation as a fighting machine grew as he worked as a bouncer in various nightclubs. But, on July 19, 1987, while working at the Premier Club in Reno, Nevada, Ken realized just how powerful his punches were.

Shamrock's victim was kicked out of the club for drunkenness and trying to start a fight with another patron. Feeling that he had been wrongfully ejected, the man pointed to Shamrock and declared that he wanted to fight him. The other bouncers tried to restrain him, but the determined drunk charged Ken. That's when Ken hit him; the drunk lay motionless on the floor. He was taken to the hospital, where surgeons removed an enormous blood clot from his brain.

Eventually, Ken realized that working the nightclub scene was a dead end. "I was just kind of floating around," says Ken, "bouncing in bars here and there." He began searching for other opportunities, and one day his father suggested that he go into professional wrestling. Bob was a huge fan, but at first Ken was not interested, considering it stupid and fake. However, after Ken realized just how much money a pro wrestler could make, he started taking to the idea.

Bob organized a tryout with the Buzz Sawyer Wrestling Academy in Sacramento, and Ken passed with flying colors. He enrolled in the classes, and, because of his wrestling background and natural athletic ability, he quickly excelled. Recognizing that his son had potential in the sport, Bob located a more prestigious wrestling school on the other side of the country. "I went down to Nelson Royal and Gene Anderson in Mooresville, North Carolina," says Ken. "I went through their tryout, and they saw some potential in me." Ken completed their program in four months; it usually took a student two years to finish. Both Ken and Bob made the move to North Carolina, where Ken exploded onto the scene. "After about three months, I started doing shows in the Mooresville, North Carolina area," remembers Ken, "and then I just kept doing bigger shows and bigger shows."

While touring and competing under the stage name "Vinnie Torrelli," Ken continued to enter Toughman competitions. In a two-day tournament held four miles outside of Charlotte in Statesville, Ken blew through his opponents, including a ringer brought in from Myrtle Beach. After winning another tournament in Hickory, he garnered a reputation as a dangerous competitor and was prevented from entering the bigger competitions in Charlotte because he was thought to be *too* good.

The wrestling wasn't paying much, however, and to make ends meet, Ken took odd jobs and even engaged in back-alley scraps for money. In one such event, he fought in a parking lot behind a bar surrounded by a ring of drunks. Ken ended the fight with just one punch and a suplex. Without even breaking a sweat, he walked away with $350 in his pocket. But this was not enough to satisfy his pugilistic tendencies, and he began searching for another outlet.

An opportunity soon presented itself. "Dean Malenko came up and did some tag team with me, and then we did some baby-face matches against each other," says Ken. "He showed me this tape that they were doing over in Japan, the UWF. I said, 'Damn, I want to do that!' He introduced me to Sammy Saranaka from Florida, and I went down and met with him. I went through a series of tests." After passing a brutal tryout in Florida, Ken was on a plane heading for Japan.

He made it through yet another grueling set of tryouts in the dojo of the Universal Wrestling Federation (UWF), just outside of Tokyo, but not without being humbled by submission masters Suzuki and Funaki. "I've always been able to pretty much handle myself in any situation," says Ken. "But when I went to Japan, the technique there was so much better that I was getting heel-hooked, arm barred, and choked. I was like, 'Oh, my God, this stuff is great.'"

Realizing his one "great punch" would not cut it at this level of competition, Ken stayed on in Japan, studying under the greats and learning countless ways to submit an opponent. Having found what he had been searching for, he quickly acquired the tools that made him a complete and feared competitor.

Ken spent a year competing in the UWF, and although most of the matches were worked, it was a cut above what he had experienced while wrestling in the States. But when the UWF began having problems, Ken began looking for an even more realistic medium through which he could test his skills and unleash his power in full-out combat. "There were a lot of internal problems with the UWF," explains Ken. "The company broke down and split up, and the fighters went to three different companies. There was Takada, there was Maeda, and there was Fujiwara. Of course, I slid off into Fujiwara, because Fujiwara and Sammy Saranaka were friends—and Sammy was the one who got me into it. Then, after that, it kind of broke apart with Funaki and Suzuki and all them. I had started training with Funaki, and I spent a lot of time with Funaki learning. And so when they broke off, Funaki asked me to go with him because they were going to start a new group called Pancrase. It was going to be a little more intense. I said, 'Well, okay, that sounds more like me.'" Ken went on to beat both Suzuki and Funaki, his teachers. And on December 19, 1994, he defeated Japanese competitor Manabu Yamada in front of 11,500 enthusiastic fans to be crowned the first King of Pancrase.

Ken became a superstar in Japan. His image was depicted in comic books and graced the covers of magazines; tens of thousands of spectators turned out monthly to watch him dominate his opponents.

Knowing he had a future in the sport, Ken returned to the United States and opened the now-world-renowned Lion's Den training facility in Lodi, California. His reason for doing this was twofold. First, it would be an official training facility for American Pancrase fighters before they headed for Japan. Second, it would provide Ken with partners to train with in the States. Pancrase embodied modern MMA competition, and at the time there weren't many potential training partners. Ken had to start them from the ground up, and over the years he would produce some of the most successful MMA competitors the sport has ever seen.

Then, in September of 1993, Shamrock came across an advertisement in *Black Belt* magazine seeking experts in the martial arts to compete in an event called the Ultimate Fighting Championship—a bare-knuckle event where there were no rules.

Both Bob and Ken were confident that Ken could win the tournament easily because of his fighting ability and his knowledge of submission. When Ken was younger, he'd competed in several karate competitions that were supposedly full contact. In one such tourney, in Reno, Ken kicked his opponent in the stomach, knocked the wind out of him, and then got disqualified because his kick was considered *too* full contact. In another event, in Redding, he knocked a competitor out by punching him in the head. This was also considered too full contact, and again Ken was disqualified.

From this, Bob and Ken got the idea that these guys running around in pajamas were not all that tough. The two didn't yet understand what jiu-jitsu fighters, like the Gracies, could do. Even while in Japan, Ken never got to see the jiu-jitsu practitioners in action. He figured that with his skills he would run right through the other UFC competitors, just as he had in his barroom brawls and Toughman competitions.

Although Bob was certain the event would take place, Ken had his doubts. "I thought it was just going to be another one of those deals that when you get there they go, 'Okay, this is how it works; this guy is going to win.' The only thing I've ever been a part of that involved any no-holds-barred, or anything like that where there were bare knuckles, the outcome was already pretty much determined. There were always stipulations—there was always something. So, when I got accepted into it, I was still fighting over in Pancrase. I had a fight three days before the fight over in Denver, and I wasn't going to cancel that fight, because I wasn't sure if this one was going to be the real deal." The first UFC, however, was bigger than anyone expected—especially Ken. When father and son arrived in Denver, everything was in place.

Shamrock and Gracie—The First Encounter

Art Davie and Rorion Gracie met Ken and Bob Shamrock at the airport, and father and son were taken to a luxurious hotel room. They were even fitted for tuxedos, courtesy of the UFC, for the after party. But fancy dress was the last thing on Ken's mind. After the long flight from Japan— where he'd defeated Takaku Fuke in the Pancrase bout—he was tired and jet-lagged and had only two days to become acclimatized to Denver's elevation.

Ken paid a visit to the gym to loosen up his muscles, and it was there that the other competitors got a first glimpse of his physique. Although on fight night each combatant would do whatever it took to come out on top, the competitors treated each other with respect. "There was a certain type of camaraderie between the fighters that you wouldn't find in boxing or professional wrestling," says Bob.

Ken's first bout was against Patrick Smith, and after defeating him with ease, it looked as if he was the man to run the gauntlet. But, still not fully adjusted to the altitude, Shamrock needed all the rest he could get after his quarterfinal bout. Unfortunately for Ken, that interval didn't prove to be very long. The next bout of the evening, between Gerard Gordeau and Kevin Rosier, lasted less than two minutes.

Gordeau was in bad shape going into the fight. His broken hand had swollen up, and he still had two of Telia Tuli's teeth embedded in his foot. Along with this disadvantage, Rosier outweighed him by almost a hundred pounds. But that didn't stop the Dutchman from chopping down the overweight behemoth in the first minute with jabs and leg kicks. Not letting up for a moment, he finished Rosier, who had squatted down submissively to shield his face, with a series of elbows to the skull and a foot stomp to the liver.

Without much rest, Ken was back on deck to face Royce Gracie in the semifinals. The bout started off quickly. Royce rushed forward and, faking with a front kick, went right for the takedown. Ken, an apt wrestler, managed to sprawl, and then using his strength flipped the Brazilian over onto his back. He went to mount him, but that was not where Royce wanted to be. The jiu-jitsu tactician managed to squirrel out from under Shamrock, bringing the fight back to the standing position. But Gracie wanted nothing to do with Ken's standup, either, and he wrapped his legs around his opponent, dragging him to the mat and securing him between his legs—a position known as "the guard."

Royce got to work chopping away at Ken's back with bothersome heel kicks. Shamrock, having just submitted Smith with a heel hook, wrapped his arm around Royce's ankle and dropped back, attempting the same submission. "I was sitting back for a heel hook," says Shamrock, "and I actually had the heel hook." But Royce was not such easy prey. "He had wrapped his gi around my arm," Shamrock continues. "So when I sat back, it basically pulled him up on top of me. Then I couldn't get my arm out of the gi to apply the heel hook and get my leg over. So I tried to turn on my side, and when I did he wrapped his gi and his hand around my throat. I didn't feel there was any danger there, because his other hand was tied up with mine. Then all of a sudden I felt this gi tighten around my neck. I was like, 'What the hell is that?' After being in Japan, I figured there was nobody that could handle me on the ground. He wouldn't have if I'd understood that the gi could be used as a weapon, and that it gave you three more inches on your grab. It was a learning experience for me." Knowing there was nothing more he could do, Shamrock tapped.

Royce let go of his hold, thinking the fight was over. But the referee yelled at them both to keep the action moving. Ken, realizing he had lost even though the referee didn't see him tap, admitted that the fight was over. The two fighters stood, and Royce's hand was lifted into the air. Although Shamrock was stunned, he handled his postfight interview with class. When asked if he was the number-two man in the tournament, he said, "No, I'm the third best," referring to the fact that he didn't make it into the finals.

The eight original combatants at the first Ultimate Fighting Championship were now down to two: Royce Gracie and Gerard Gordeau, a grappler versus a striker.

Although Royce had some trouble taking the wounded kickboxer down, Gordeau wasn't able to land a good strike. "The doctors told him I was injured," Gordeau says. "You can see it on the video. He blocked my good side, and so I had to fight with my injured side. But I don't deny that he was a good ground fighter. It was just easy to make it to the finals if you have the doctors with you, and the schedule makers with you."

Royce did take Gordeau down, and once they were on the mat he quickly turned Gordeau over onto his stomach. Struggling against Royce's submissions, the kickboxer decided to take advantage of the fact that there were no rules, and he bit into Royce's ear. Royce quickly wrested his ear from the mouth of his opponent and applied a choke. Gordeau tapped the mat, but Gracie held the hold for an extra few seconds to punish his opponent for the foul play.

When the two men were separated, Royce Gracie was declared the Ultimate Fighting Champion. Other than a small spot of blood on his ear where the hungry Gordeau had bitten him, he didn't have a scratch on him. He had torn effortlessly through the competition, and in the process he'd achieved his family's goal of introducing Brazilian jiu-jitsu to the world. Royce stood in the octagon, holding up a check for fifty thousand dollars, and his coronation as the first UFC champion signaled a new era in martial arts and in sports in general.

As Royce's brothers swept into the ring to hoist the young champion onto their shoulders, the pride in their father's eyes was evident. Helio's love and passion had been adopted by his sons and was now celebrated by the world. After the first UFC, it was never a question of Gracie fame, but rather of whether or not the Gracie family would be able to stay on top.

A Quest for Redemption

After Royce's victory, students flooded into Rorion's school in Torrance, California, to take lessons and buy videos and merchandise. While Rorion turned the family art into a multimillion dollar business, Ken Shamrock was sweating and bleeding in the gym, training tirelessly for a rematch with the Brazilian. "I knew, deep down, I could handle this guy," says Shamrock. "Just in the first meeting that we had, I felt I had a lot of opportunity to beat him, but because of the gi I had to learn a little more defense against it. The gi floats out there and can be wrapped around a lot of different parts of your body to help with grip, to turn or escape. So I had to learn that."

Ken returned to the Lion's Den armed with a new determination. He dressed his sparring partners up in gis. He learned everything he could about jiu-jitsu. He resolved to be more than prepared when he faced off against Royce Gracie in the next event. He even ignored the discouragement of Pancrase's promoters, who felt that if he lost in the UFC he would discredit their organization. Although he honored his agreement with them, fighting five days a month in Japan and defending his title as King of Pancrase, he would stop at nothing to meet Royce again in the octagon and earn back his pride. "I knew my ability was much higher than his," says Ken.

But then Shamrock met with disaster. While sparring with his student Vernon White just three weeks before he was to step once again into the octagon, he blocked a high kick and suffered an injury to his hand. At the hospital he learned that his hand was broken, and although he was still eager to compete, the doctors warned him that if he did he might never fight again.

Shamrock reluctantly dropped out of the event, and his redemption was put on hold. He did, however, make a guest appearance at UFC II to promote his much-anticipated return. While sitting on the sidelines, he witnessed some dramatic changes in the event.

UFC II—No Way Out/November 3, 1994
(Denver, Colorado)

After the UFC's debut, a host of excuses circulated in the martial arts world for why Royce had dominated the first show; they ranged from the inexperience of his competitors to the styles of martial arts involved.

Although his victories had been impressive, many martial artists were reluctant to jump onto the Gracie bandwagon. After spending years working for their black belts and breaking boards, after devouring martial arts flicks in which Bruce Lee and the like wowed the audience with showy kicks and lightning-fast punches, many still had hopes that their art was truly unbeatable. Many traditional martial artists refused to let go of the mysticism. Many were waiting for that elderly Eastern practitioner who would step into the octagon and lay waste to Royce Gracie with a single death-touch strike.

Rorion was determined to lay this mysticism to rest. Over two hundred fighter applications had been sent in for the second show, and fighters were chosen from an array of styles: karate, jiu-jitsu, Russian sambo, kung fu, tae kwon do, pencak silat, and muay Thai. This time, there would be sixteen competitors participating in the elimination tournament to determine an ultimate warrior. To draw a crowd, the promoters once again promised contusions, lacerations, hematomas, hyperextensions, torn ligaments, and blood. They boasted that victory could come by way of knockout, submission, or even death. The second Ultimate Fighting Championship boldly offered the martial arts world a chance to revenge itself on the 178-pound Brazilian.

But because of the way the show had been marketed—most notably as a blood sport in which victory could come in the form of death—it was already attracting unwanted attention. This included the scrutiny of Denver's mayor, who, at the last minute, threw a monkey wrench into the works by pulling the lease on the venue.

But SEG was not to be stopped, and they moved the show across town to a hole-in-the-wall auditorium called the Mammoth Gardens Event Center. The venue was much smaller than the original one—it only seated three thousand people—and the space available for the fighters to prepare themselves was inadequate. "They ended up getting a sleazy, stinking hotel across the street," remembers referee John McCarthy, who began his long career as the octagon's referee in the second show. "They were renting rooms out of that place. There were prostitutes in the hotel, and it was bad. Very bad."

There were also smaller changes made in the event. Because there was speculation that in the first UFC Rorion had given Royce the easiest quarterfinal opponent of the night, boxer Art Jimmerson, the fights for the second event were chosen by random draw. "A lot of people are going to say that things were set up for Royce," clarifies McCarthy. "In all honesty, I'd be the first one to tell if that was true. It's not true. In the

JOHN MCCARTHY

UFC referees "Big" John McCarthy (right) and Joe Hamilton (left) before UFC XX.

first one, there was no doubt that Rorion picked Royce to fight Jimmerson because he was a boxer. But in the second one it was a random draw. They used something like a bingo machine, and they would put a bunch of numbers in there. When they drew one out, that number would go with someone's name. They would end up fighting the next person drawn. There was no preferential treatment as to who Royce was going to fight. He got drawn the same way as everyone else."

Another controversy that was taken care of in the second show had to do with the referee. Many people thought the ref in the original show had stopped fights too soon. For the second show, SEG wanted to eliminate the referee all together. "They were thinking about putting someone on the outside with a red towel," remembers McCarthy. "If they threw in the towel the fighters had to stop. We talked about it, and I told them, 'You are absolutely psychotic if you think that's going to work.'"

John McCarthy, standing six-foot-four and weighing 260 pounds, seemed quite capable of controlling any volatile situation that might erupt in the octagon. But the decision to have him serve as a ref was not only due to his size. He was also a tactical officer for the Los Angeles Police Department and was responsible for training officers in hand-to-hand combat. "I needed a guy who was accustomed to seeing people get beat up," says Rorion Gracie. "He's a big guy. He knows jiu-jitsu, so he's not going to be lost if the fight goes to the ground. If you get a guy who is an experienced boxing referee, he has no idea what is happening on the ground. John seemed perfect. He's a cop, he's seen crime scenes, blood isn't going to distract or intimidate him, plus he knows ground fighting because he was a student of mine."

McCarthy had met Rorion Gracie at the Civilian Martial Arts Review Board. The two hit it off, and as they got to know one another they exchanged knowledge. McCarthy taught Rorion the tactics police officers use in the line of duty, and Rorion taught McCarthy his family art at his school in Torrance. McCarthy quickly became an apt student of Brazilian jiu-jitsu, and he even served as Royce's sparring partner for the first show.

After the first show, explains McCarthy, "Rorion came up and asked me if I would think about refereeing, because I knew what the fighters do. He understood that split-second decisions needed to be made in there, and he thought I would do well at it." McCarthy did it so well, in fact, that he was asked to return again and again. He began every fight the same way—by slashing his hand through the air and then shouting the four famous words, "Let's get it on!"

"Art Davie wanted me to do a hand signal and then say something to start the fight," says McCarthy. "I asked him what he wanted me to say, and he said I'd have to come up with it." While sitting around with some friends, McCarthy hit on what would become his signature intro: "Are you ready? Are you ready? Let's get it on!" Although he made the saying famous in mixed martial arts circles, he had not come up with it on his own. He had borrowed it from the well-known boxing referee Mills Lane, who would say the very same thing after reiterating the rules before a boxing match. When the saying became popular, McCarthy licensed it with Mills Lane. The understanding was that Mills could use it in boxing, and McCarthy could use it in MMA.

Although McCarthy became known for his quick thinking and his fairness, in the beginning there was a stipulation concerning his refereeing responsibilities. He wasn't allowed to stop the fights, even if a fighter was getting creamed. "Rorion wanted it that way," claims McCarthy. "He really didn't give a darn about anyone but his brother, and I can understand that. He felt that his brother would be fine, and he was right about that. But there were other guys out there that didn't have the skills that were necessary to handle themselves. I thought it might be a problem, and as I was in there it became a big problem."

Despite McCarthy's concerns, the sixteen-man elimination tournament produced some excellent match-ups, many coming in the first round, which was not aired on pay-per-view. One such bout was Jason DeLucia versus Scott Baker. DeLucia, a kung fu practitioner, had been working on his ground skills since his fight with Royce in the Gracie Challenge match long before the first UFC. Baker had been training with Pedro Sauer, a world-class grappler in Utah. It was a back-and-forth fight, with both fighters attempting triangle chokes on the other. It ended up with DeLucia getting Baker in a top-mounted triangle and raining down blows. DeLucia told Baker to tap out, that he didn't want to hit him any more. Baker tapped.

Gerard Gordeau returned to the second UFC. This time he wouldn't be fighting, however, but rather coaching his student Freek Hamaker. Hamaker had started training with Gordeau when he was a young boy suffering from cancer. "He told me he only wanted to do one big fight in his life," says Gordeau, "and I told him he could do the UFC." Hamaker shot in on his opponent and quickly defeated him via arm lock.

Although the preliminaries provoked the crowd to a frenzy, by no means was the aired tournament dull. The clashing of styles, and the limited ground skills of many of the combatants, gave the crowd the dramatic KOs they had been looking for. One classic beating came when UFC I veteran Patrick Smith took on ninjitsu practitioner Scott Morris.

After McCarthy slashed his hand through the air, Morris charged Smith with absolute confidence and attempted to take the kickboxer to the floor. But, in one swift move that landed Smith on top, Morris found himself pinned to the canvas, desperately clinging to his opponent's waist. Blow after crushing blow rained down on Morris's face, breaking his defensive hold. Smith followed with seven over-the-top elbow strikes to his opponent's skull and then more punches. Eleven of them, to be exact— thumping into the side of Morris's head and jaw. One landed on Morris's temple. His mouthpiece shot into the air, followed by a squirt of blood.

McCarthy's nightmare came true. He wanted to intervene, but he was not empowered to do so. All he could do was scream at Morris's coach, Robert Bussey, commanding him to throw in the towel. But upon witnessing McCarthy's demand, Bussey basically told him to kiss off and threw the towel into the crowd. "They took care of their fighter real well," McCarthy says sarcastically.

With Morris lying there abandoned, too discombobulated to tap out on his own, Smith dropped three crushing elbows that bounced Morris's skull off the canvas. Morris was gripped by temporary paralysis. His legs gave one last shudder and then straightened. Smith, who could clearly see his foe had been vanquished, dismounted. "Luckily Pat got off," recalls

McCarthy. "I would have *had* to stop it, because Morris would have gotten beat to death."

This fight did not sit well with McCarthy, and after the show he thanked Rorion for letting him ref, but he also said that he would never do it again. When Rorion asked him why, McCarthy replied, "Because you're going to get someone killed. I understand you really don't care about anyone but your brother, but someone's going to kill someone. You've got guys with fools in their corners that don't know what they're doing. Someone's got to be able to stop the fight if a fighter is injured."

Rorion subsequently agreed with McCarthy, and he granted him the power to stop a fight so long as he used that power with discretion. In other words, the fighter had to be getting beaten silly for him to intervene.

Another interesting bout of the evening, one that would go down in the UFC beat-down hall of fame, was between karate practitioner Fred Ettish and thirty-nine-year-old kickboxer Johnny Rhodes. Ettish, who appeared never to have competed in anything but point sparring matches, came out in a traditional karate stance. Rhodes quickly woke him up with a stern right hand, and then he delivered a flurry of punches that sent Ettish onto his back. Though Ettish displayed heart, he was no match for his opponent, who tore into his face with punches and knees.

The bout between grappler Remco Pardoel and Thai boxer Orlando Weit also produced a brutal knockout. Many people, including Pardoel, thought Weit was the one who would sweep the competition. Possessing deadly knees and elbows, and having annihilated his first opponent, he looked virtually unstoppable. But, once again, the superiority of ground fighting was proven.

In Pardoel's corner was Gerard Gordeau. Although Pardoel was a student of Gordeau, Gordeau hadn't known that he was coming to fight in the UFC. "He was alone there. He asked me to work his corner, but I was pissed off because he went there without telling me." But, after some convincing, Gordeau agreed to work Pardoel's corner. Knowing the abilities of a striker like Weit, Gordeau quickly worked out a game plan for his associate.

His strategy worked quite well. After quickly taking the Thai boxer to the ground, Pardoel wound up lying on his back on top of Weit's midsection. Having primarily competed in grappling tournaments, Pardoel was a little reluctant to strike. But once he saw the Thai boxer's head trapped under his armpit, he administered a series of devastating elbows that landed sharply on his opponent's skull, knocking him out cold. No one was more surprised than Pardoel.

Although the variation of styles gave rise to some exciting bouts, the lack of ground skills from the competitors led to easy victories for Royce. He first defeated karate practitioner Minoki Ichihara with an arm bar in just a few minutes. Then it was DeLucia. Although DeLucia's grappling capabilities had improved since their first meeting, he quickly tapped out when he found himself in an arm bar that threatened to break his bone. The only combatant who seemed to pose any threat to Royce was fellow grappler Remco Pardoel. Although Royce had some difficulty taking the Dutch jiu-jitsu expert down, once they were on the ground, Gracie used Pardoel's own gi to choke him out.

Sitting ringside, Ken Shamrock watched the birth of a legend as Royce Gracie took on Patrick Smith in the finals. They felt each other out for several moments, and then Smith threw a front kick that allowed Gracie to close the gap between them. Gracie tied up with his opponent, and, after a brief struggle, he swept the kickboxer's leg out from under him and brought him to the mat. Although Smith held on for dear life, this was Gracie's territory; he worked his magic and slowly slipped into the mount. Once there, he chopped away at Smith's ribs with punches, and then the face. Knowing he was now little more than a punching bag for his Brazilian opponent, Smith tapped the canvas before any real damage could be done.

Gracie was once again declared the Ultimate Fighting champion, and his victory would only feed Ken Shamrock's desire and determination. Although both of them would compete in UFC III, they would not confront each other in the octagon until UFC V, in the first-ever Superfight. Nonetheless, UFC III proved to be a memorable spectacle.

CHAPTER 4

The Spectacle

Out of the mist came a beautiful woman carrying a sign that read, "Jesus said, 'If anyone would come after me, he must deny himself and take up his cross and follow me.'" Behind this sign came Kimo Leopoldo, a warrior claiming to be in the service of the Lord, whose purpose in the octagon was to "ring the gospel of Jesus Christ throughout the whole world." Mounted on the back of the six-foot-two, 240-pound Hawaiian minister was a massive wooden cross that stretched out over the reaching fans on both sides of the aisle. With a black hood draped over his head, Kimo lumbered towards the cage with the weighty crucifix.

Kimo was a sight to behold. Almost as wide as he was tall, and sporting a menacing-looking goatee and ponytail, he appeared to be hungry. As the announcer made the introductions, he glared across the ring at his opponent, UFC champion Royce Gracie. After a tense few moments, referee John McCarthy stepped between the two and bawled, "Lets get it on!"

Kimo rushed across the ring and threw a massive uppercut, but Royce, not wanting to play standup with the muscle-bound street fighter, ducked the punch in an attempt to take him down. But Kimo's balance was keen, and once his hooks were on Gracie's gi, he manhandled his smaller opponent, shoving him to and fro and landing several uppercuts.

As the two struggled around the perimeter of the octagon, they crashed into the gate and it flew open. McCarthy stopped the fighters so the door could be closed, but he did not separate the two. The period of inactivity gave Royce a chance to snug his body even tighter against the minister's, eliminating Kimo's arsenal of strikes.

Softening up his opponent with knees and head butts, Royce hooked the big Hawaiian's leg and managed to take him down. But when they landed, Kimo came out on top, riding his 240 pounds on Royce's back. Guarding himself from a choke, Royce eventually rolled Kimo off him and took the mount. But he didn't stay there long. Kimo used his strength to reverse Gracie, and, bucking and thrashing, he wound up between Royce's legs.

Fighting from his back was Royce's forte, but while trying to get an arm lock on Kimo, he ate several bombs to the face. Kimo appeared to be pummeling the champ—until Royce grabbed hold of Kimo's dangling ponytail. As Kimo attempted to pull away, Royce held him in place by the hair and jabbed at his face with the knuckles of his free hand. Kimo, apparently feeling no pain, did everything he could to break away. But when his hair finally tore from his scalp, he was winded from the struggle. After one last, brief exchange on the ground, Royce sunk in an arm bar and the minister was forced to tap out.

The fight had been devastating for both fighters. Kimo rolled onto his back, gasping for breath. Royce couldn't stand on his own, and one of his brothers had to hold him up so McCarthy could raise his arm. With no energy left to celebrate his victory, Royce made his way out of the arena, his brothers supporting him by the belt so he wouldn't collapse.

*   *   *

UFC III—The American Dream/September 9, 1994
(Charlotte, North Carolina)

The gang banger turned preacher had done something no combatant had done before: he'd contested Royce Gracie's superiority in the octagon. Although Kimo didn't win the match, his brutality and ability to scrap had brought thousands of fans screaming to their feet, which was just what the show's promoters had been hoping for.

The original angle of the Ultimate Fighting Championship had been to pit fighters from various martial arts styles against each other to see how they fared in a full-contact competition. But after the first two shows, SEG had discovered that the majority of those buying the pay-per-views cared little about seeing martial artists square off; they just wanted to see two guys beating the tar out of each other in a cage.

Although the first two shows had been a tremendous success, and Rorion's dream of introducing Gracie jiu-jitsu to the world had been realized, the UFC was still a business. To meet the demand of the viewers, Art Davie rounded up several fighters for UFC III who not only had the bark, but also appeared to have the bite to back it up.

Kimo fell perfectly into that category. He wasn't a soft-spoken Zen master. He wasn't even a well-versed martial artist, despite his claim of being a third-degree black belt in tae kwon do. But, bearing a tattoo that read "Jesus" on his stomach, and another of a massive cross on his freakishly wide back, he looked as if he could scrap until the Second Coming of Christ. "Kimo was just a tough street kid who didn't have a lot of training," says John McCarthy. "But he gave Royce a heck of a go."

Although the fight between a street brawler and an experienced grappler hadn't been as one-sided as many had expected, not all of Art Davie's larger-than-life matchups ended the same way. "Art Davie was into the spectacle," McCarthy explains. "Anytime you put a good fighter with a bad fighter, you're probably going to end up with big-time highlight films with someone getting waylaid bad."

This is exactly what happened to Emmanuel Yarbrough, the six-foot-eight, 616-pound sumo wrestler who had been brought into UFC III simply because of his freakish appearance. Although at first Yarbrough wasn't keen on the idea of doing hand-to-hand battle in the octagon, he was eventually convinced and agreed to participate.

His opponent was kenpo karate stylist Keith Hackney. Unlike Kimo, Hackney was a well-versed martial artist; he had competed in wrestling, boxing, tae kwon do, tang su do, and kenpo karate for more than a decade. The UFC had intrigued him since he saw Royce sweep the first competition, and he wanted to see how his skills would fare against Gracie jiu-jitsu. He saw the ad in *Black Belt* magazine, sent in the application, and then immediately began training for the event without waiting for an answer. He halted his efforts, however, when he got a notice saying that the event was full. Taking some time off training, Hackney put his energy into managing his heating and air company, instead.

Less than a week before UFC III, Hackney received a call from Art Davie. Apparently, one of the competitors had pulled out at the last minute due to the fact that a 616-pound man had entered the tournament. Hackney was told that he would be allowed into the event, but only if he agreed to two stipulations. The first was that he wouldn't be in the random draw with the other fighters for the quarterfinals. For his first matchup, he would have to take on sumo giant Emmanuel Yarbrough. "I told Davie it really didn't matter who I had to fight," says Hackney, "because if I won, I had to fight everyone anyway."

The second stipulation was that Hackney had to come to Charlotte, North Carolina before the event and prove his skills in a little test. If Art Davie and Rorion Gracie liked what they saw, he would be allowed to compete. If they weren't impressed with his skills, then Hackney would be granted free front-row tickets to the show, free food, a free hotel room, and an invitation to the fight party afterwards. In response to the offer, Hackney said to Davie, "You know what, Art—no matter what happens, how can I turn that down?"

Two days later, Hackney flew to Charlotte, where he did a little demonstration in front of Rorion, Art Davie, and representatives from *Black Belt* magazine. They liked what they saw, and he was in the show.

Although the rest of the fighters' bouts were chosen by random draw, Hackney already knew who he'd be up against first. "Supposedly, they picked them out at random, but obviously I was one of the only guys who didn't [get picked that way]. A lot of people didn't know my fight had already been selected. I knew it was coming. I knew exactly what was coming."

Knowing that he'd soon be stepping into the cage with a man who was four feet wide and three feet thick, Hackney tried to relax backstage as he warmed up and talked strategy with his trainers. But once he stepped into the roar of the crowd, his competitive nature emerged. "I didn't care what happened," Hackney recalls. "I didn't care if he picked me up and slammed me, breaking my back or leg. I basically went out there to give Manny the fight of his life. Something he would never forget, and people would say 'Wow.' Whether I won or lost, it didn't really affect me. I went out there to give it all I had."

That's just what he did. After sizing up his mammoth opponent, Hackney stepped forward and swung an open hand up high. "It's the only way I could hit someone that tall," he explains. When the open palm landed flush to the side of Yarbrough's face, 616 pounds of sumo toppled to the mat. Seeing his immense foe downed, Hackney blindly rushed forward to put him away.

But Yarbrough still had some scrap left in him. Reaching his arms out like hooks, he drew the comparatively minuscule Hackney into his embrace. But instead of simply leaning his mass forward and crushing his opponent under his weight, Yarbrough chose to bat Hackney around between his mitts. Thrashing violently, Hackney escaped and quickly regained his footing. A flurry ensued, sending both fighters crashing through the octagon's gate.

After the two had briefly returned to their corners, Hackney began kicking his opponent's legs in an attempt to chop him down. Yarbrough, growing frustrated with the bothersome kicks, caught one just as it landed. But while Yarbrough used both of his hands to secure the leg, Hackney hopped on one foot and used the opportunity to rain punches into Yarbrough's unprotected face. He absorbed several firm strikes, and once again the Goliath was down.

This time, Hackney avoided getting caught by Yarbrough by coming around from the rear. He went to work, hammering his fists repeatedly into the massive face and head of his opponent. Taking unfamiliar abuse, the largest man ever to set foot in the octagon was forced to tap out. "Manny Yarbrough is a very nice man," says McCarthy. "A very big guy. But he's not a fighter, and he didn't belong in there. It's wrong to put somebody who doesn't have skills in that area in a position where he's just going to get beat on."

Although Hackney had won the bout, earning himself the title "Giant Killer"—which has stuck with him to this day—he had broken his hand on Yarbrough's head, and an alternate would take his place in the semifinals. But, having had a taste of true MMA competition, he would be back for the next UFC.

Despite the fact that the bout was more of a gladiatorial spectacle than a martial arts matchup, it was a tremendous success with the crowd. "Art was into the spectacle," reiterates McCarthy. "He was into the entertainment. He liked people who acted a certain way, said they were something. He wanted the guy that was grandiose. It seems to me that he really didn't care about the guys who were the good fighters. He wanted the guys who had the big mouths. I used to say that he put goldfish with sharks, meaning that all he was doing was feeding someone to another fighter."

Even though this type of matchmaking increased pay-per-view revenues, it caused its share of problems for McCarthy, who had to put a stop to many matches because they involved one-sided beatings. "I'm the bad guy who either lets something go too long or doesn't let it go long enough," McCarthy explains. "People say, 'He could have gone more,' when this guy doesn't have the skill to even be in the same ring with his opponent."

Another aspect that the UFC played up for its third show was the rematch between Royce Gracie and Ken Shamrock. This was something Shamrock had been waiting for since his defeat at the first event, and although SEG wanted to make it happen, both fighters were subjected to the random draw. As it turned out, Ken and Royce were on opposite sides of the quarterfinal brackets.

Shamrock, with Royce locked in his sights, finished off his first two opponents, including Keith Hackney's alternate, kung fu practitioner Felix Lee Mitchell. Now it was up to Royce to win his next match so the two could meet again.

This, unfortunately, did not happen. Royce, surrounded as usual by his entourage of brothers, made his way towards the ring. But once he entered the octagon, something went wrong. He turned to his corner and announced that he couldn't see anything. His vision had faded. His brothers, knowing they could not let Royce fight in this condition, were forced to throw in the towel before the match could even begin. His opponent, karate practitioner Harold Howard, was declared the victor without having to throw a single punch.

Word that Royce could not go on reached the backstage dressing room, and soon Kimo and his boisterous manager, Joe Son, emerged. They briefly took over the octagon to let the world know just who was responsible for the debilitated state of the UFC champ.

The finals were now set, with Harold Howard taking on Ken Shamrock. Strangely, this match did not happen, either. "Ken had a funny way of looking at things," explains Bob Shamrock. "He came into the event to fight Royce; he didn't care about anyone else. He didn't care about the purse. He could have beat Harold Howard with ease. The director came over and asked us if we were ready, and Ken said, 'No, I'm not going.' With Royce dropped out of the event, he had no reason to continue."

This led to conflict between Ken and his father/manager. "Ken wasn't thinking about his fans," Bob says, "he was thinking about Royce." Believing his son had given up the prize money and the title belt because of his own stubborn nature, Bob would no longer support him in a tournament-style event.

After the UFC, Art Davie contacted Bob about Ken coming and doing another tournament, but Bob, still disappointed that Ken had backed out with an easy victory ahead of him, explained his position to Davie. "But if you want to have a special fight between just Royce and Ken," Bob said to him, "that's fine." Robert Meyrowitz, the president of SEG, called Bob a few hours later, and the first Superfight was born. Royce Gracie and Ken Shamrock would finally meet again at UFC V.

For the finals of UFC III, alternate Steve Jennum, an Omaha, Nebraska police officer who studied ninjitsu, was dropped in to take on Harold Howard for the title. The match got started with Howard doing a comical front flip, attempting to drop his heel into Jennum's head. It failed miserably. After getting hit with a good right hand, Jennum rushed forward to take the wild striker to the ground. Although his art boasted complex takedowns, Howard was ready. As Jennum ducked low to seize the legs, Howard wrapped an arm around his head and applied a guillotine choke, holding it firmly as they hit the mat. The choke wasn't sunk, however, and Jennum was able to wrench himself free. Getting back to their feet, the two briefly exchanged blows, and Jennum landed a solid right that dropped Howard. Jennum quickly capitalized on the opportunity and mounted his fallen opponent, delivering downward blows until

Howard submitted. An alternate had won the third Ultimate Fighting Championship.

UFC III was both a success and a failure. It failed because Jennum couldn't accurately be called Ultimate Fighting champion, as he'd only fought one fight. It had succeeded because there had been knockouts and blood and a six-hundred-pound man. There had been upsets. It had become much like a pro-wrestling event, and for that it was even more adored.

Although many considered Art Davie's matchmaking to be one-sided, over the next several shows he did manage to find some of the best and most colorful champions MMA has ever produced. One such man made his debut at the next UFC.

CHAPTER 5

The Beast

Kickboxer Anthony "Mad Dog" Macias knew that his opponent, Dan Severn, outweighed him by sixty-five pounds. He knew Severn was a decorated amateur wrestler, and that it would be in his best interest to keep the fight standing. But what Mad Dog did not know as he stood in the octagon, staring the six-foot-two, 260-pound wrestler down, was that in just a few short seconds Severn was going to unleash the Beast and send him on the ride of his life.

That ride began when Severn timed Macias's kick and shot in, seizing both of his legs. Although Macias managed to work himself back onto his feet, he did not remain there long. Severn displayed flawless wrestling technique as he hoisted the kickboxer off the ground and dumped him on his head. Macias, still kicking, scrambled to his feet for the second time. Severn was attached to his backside, however, and again he suplexed Mad Dog over onto his skull. Macias, clearly stunned, shook his head and tried to regain his composure. He didn't try for his feet again. Instead, he attempted to get the wrestler off his back—but to no avail.

Severn, using his weight, simply smeared his opponent into the canvas and then began a somewhat lengthy quest to put him away. He tried cranking Mad Dog's face to the side. He tried smothering him. When nothing seemed to work, he went for the choke. With Severn's forearm sinking into his throat, Mad Dog pounded the canvas.

Dan Severn didn't have flashy kicks or punches; as a matter of fact, he had no strikes to speak of whatsoever. But in his first UFC match he had proven—just as Royce Gracie had proven—that strikes aren't necessary to finish off an opponent. Celebrating his triumph, Severn dramatically threw both arms into the air and screamed into the crowd.

* * *

Growing up in Michigan, Dan Severn started off his sports career with high school basketball. Not good enough to make the first string, he spent most of his time on the bench. When friends on the wrestling team

ANDY ANDERSON

Dan Severn getting ready to unleash "the Beast."

asked him to come to a wrestling tournament and fill in a weight class that would otherwise be forfeited, Dan was more than happy to do it. Although he got pinned twice in that tournament, he was hooked. He went back and occupied his spot on the bench for the remainder of the basketball season, and the following year he signed up for wrestling.

Contrary to what many might think, he did not excel in the sport immediately. "I eventually had a lot of success in wrestling," says Severn, "but only through the principles of hard work and application." His hard work paid off. While still a student at Hemmacle High School in Montrose, Michigan, he became two-time national champion and set eight national records. Afterwards, he attended Arizona State University, where he took wrestling to the next level. "I did a lot of things to enhance my wrestling ability," says Severn. "The judo coach there got a kick out of me. When my wrestling season came to an end, he asked me if I'd like to go watch a judo tournament sometime. So I went, and when I got there, he said, 'Now that you're here . . .'"

Luckily for Dan, they had a gi waiting for him. Although he didn't know all the formalities, he went out there and started executing combinations from freestyle wrestling. "The judges didn't even know how to judge it," recalls Severn. "I'm being penalized because I'm throwing cross faces. I was unorthodox, but I learned pretty quickly."

Interested in all of wrestling's hybrids, Severn went to watch the Sambo (a Russian form of grappling) National Championships a year later. "While I was sitting in the crowd, my coach asked me if I wanted to compete," he says. "To learn what I had to do, all I did was watch what the lightweights were doing, and then when it got time for the heavyweights, I went out there and mimicked what I had seen." That day Severn won the national title.

But it was wrestling Severn adored. During his time at Arizona State University, he had made such an impression with his wrestling abilities and competitive nature that when he graduated he was inducted into the school's Wrestling Hall of Fame.

While most wrestlers' careers come to an end after college, Dan's didn't. He pursued the sport, determined to become the best amateur wrestler in the world. From 1982 to 1994, he captured numerous titles around the globe and won thirteen national Amateur Athletic Union (AAU) wrestling championships.

But amateur wrestling was not paying the bills, and around the time Royce Gracie was cleaning house in the first UFC, Dan approached professional wrestling manager Phyllis Lee with the hope of breaking into the business with his wrestling skills. Phyllis told him that she would see what she could do, and a few days later she called him and asked if he would be interested in participating in the UFC. "He said," remembers Lee, "and this is an exact quote, 'What is the UFC?'" Because Coldwater, the small rural Michigan community where Severn was raised, didn't have pay-per-view, he had never seen the groundbreaking event. Phyllis quickly got him up to speed by giving him some tapes to view. "I looked at the tape and saw that this 175-pound Brazilian was doing pretty good with this grappling stuff," recalls Severn. "I thought, 'Well, I'm a pretty darn good wrestler, and this seems pretty similar.'"

With his sights set on competing in the event, Severn filled out the application from the *Black Belt* ad. To get him prepared for the event, Phyllis took him to the gym of WWF wrestler Al Snow for training. "Al Snow taught him a lot," says Lee. "He would have gotten his head taken off immediately in the first UFC if it hadn't been for Al Snow. Every time he dropped his hands, Al tagged him with his foot."

There was only one problem—due to the high volume of applications Art Davie was receiving on a daily basis, Severn was never contacted. Phyllis, who lived in Los Angeles at the time, repeatedly called Art Davie on Severn's behalf. "Art actually told me that the only reason he ever put Dan into the UFC was because he got sick of me calling him," she remembers.

But before Severn was added to the card, he needed to prove his skills. Art Davie came to watch Severn in action in a professional wrestling match with Al Snow. But, although the match was impressive, Severn was still not guaranteed a spot in the UFC. "I don't think Davie thought he had any real finishing qualities," says Lee. "I think [Davie] thought he was a good amateur wrestler, but as far as going all the way, he was a little skeptical. And it was probably his age, too."

Thinking that his chances of competing in the event were slim, Severn pursued his pro wrestling career. Then, shortly before UFC IV was to take place, he got a call. "I think someone who was supposed to be in it ended up getting hurt," says Severn. "By the time I was told I was in it, I only had about five days. What was against me was that submissions and striking were not my forte."

UFC IV—Revenge of the Warriors/December 16, 1994 (Tulsa, Oklahoma)

Dan Severn's lack of finishing moves did not prove to be a problem in his quarterfinal bout with Anthony "Mad Dog" Macias. As Severn tried to overcome his reluctance to strike another man in the octagon, he was rooted on by Jeff Blatnick, the newly appointed UFC color commentator, who happened to be a 1984 Olympic Greco-Roman gold medalist.

Although Blatnick had never even seen a tape of the Ultimate Fighting Championship before UFC IV, he knew the advantages a wrestler had over an opponent who wasn't versed in ground fighting. This was the very reason Blatnick had been brought into the show. "I was asked to come in and do commentary because of my wrestling background," says Blatnick, "and because of the fact that major names in the sport of wrestling were now entering the UFC, with Dan Severn being the first."

Blatnick's job was to do what many of the commentators had failed to do in the past: explain exactly what was going on in the octagon. But much of what he saw was new to him as well. "I had mixed emotions, to say the very least," confesses Blatnick. "I didn't even know exactly what to call the sport. It was a discipline versus discipline mentality, rather than an athlete versus athlete mentality."

This wasn't the only thing Blatnick had to get used to in this style of competition. During one of the more colorful matchups of the night, between "Giant Killer" Keith Hackney and Joe Son, he watched traditional sportsmanship go right out the window—when one man bested his opponent by striking him repeatedly in the groin.

Joe Son stood only five-foot-four, but he weighed in at a tremendous 230 pounds. Although he claimed to be proficient in tae kwon do, judo, and "Joe Son do" (his very own martial art), it wasn't his ability as a martial artist that got him into the event. He was the manager of Kimo, the street brawler who had gained tremendous popularity after damaging Royce Gracie in UFC III. Because Kimo had decided to take time off to improve on his ground fighting skills, Joe Son seemed the next best choice.

The tiny warrior made his way towards the octagon carrying a wooden cross, much like Kimo had, only this one had been downsized to fit his small frame. Just a few steps into the arena, he hunched over from the weight of the crucifix, and it looked like he might collapse before he made it to the ring. Even Jim Brown, one of the event's commentators, remarked, "The cross looks a little heavy for him."

After Joe Son screamed, "Jesus is my Lord" into the camera, the announcements were made and the cage was locked shut. Battle began slowly. Joe Son stood there with his arms down and his face out, taunting Hackney. After eating a leg kick and some punches, Joe Son shot in and took Hackney to the mat, securing a precarious guillotine choke. It wasn't sunk in, so Hackney was able to move to the side and drop several flush strikes to Joe Son's groin, using his testicles as a speed bag. "Every male in attendance," remembers Dan Severn, "every time they saw that shot to the old cup there, they were like, 'Ohhhh,' all hunching over protecting their own groins." Most people watching were unaware that Joe Son was wearing a cup, and they were astounded at the mental strength of the fighter.

When the groin strikes didn't work, Hackney latched onto Son's Adam's apple. Enduring this pressure for almost a minute, Son tapped out. Although this was a rather easy victory for Hackney, he would go on to the semifinals to face Royce Gracie, who had put his first opponent, fifty-one-year-old karate legend Ron Van Clief, away with a choke in just under four minutes. "When I went in to fight Royce," remembers Hackney, "I wanted to keep him on his feet, hit him, move around, and try to knock him out."

His strategy worked quite well in the beginning. After they had sized each other up, Gracie shot in and Hackney sprawled, taking the opportunity to deliver three powerful uppercuts to Gracie's face. Only a few seconds later, Gracie attempted to shoot in again, and this time Hackney sprawled and backed out. Hackney's time ran out, however, as Gracie backed him up against the fence. Closing the gap, Gracie leaned his weight in on the Giant Killer. But Hackney still had some fight left, and, managing to create some space between them, he gripped Gracie's gi with his left hand and rained down punches with his right.

Gracie again closed the gap, and this time he delivered a series of knees to Hackney's head. As Hackney went to deliver an uppercut, Gracie pulled him down into his guard and attempted to choke the kenpo fighter out. Hackney managed to break away and even land a punch in Gracie's face. But instead of backing out and forcing Gracie to his feet, Hackney decided to drop another bomb on his opponent's head. Gracie deflected the shot and pulled Hackney back down into his embrace. Gracie let loose with punches to the face, and, after roughing his opponent up, he secured an arm bar that forced Hackney to submit. "Beautiful, beautiful technique by Gracie," Blatnick commented.

Before Dan Severn could meet Royce in the finals, he had to put away karate expert Marcus Bossett. Although Severn took a round kick to the midsection only a few seconds into the match, he quickly brought the striker to the mat, folded Bossett's arm over his own throat, and then applied pressure, forcing his opponent to give in to the rudimentary choke.

Severn had defeated two opponents without throwing a single strike, but now he would be facing Gracie, a master grappler who would not fall victim to his crude submissions. Severn managed to take the jiu-jitsu expert to the mat quickly, but the Brazilian secured him in his guard. They would remain in this position for the next fifteen and a half minutes. Severn, not knowing submission or how to put his smaller opponent away, began hesitantly punching Gracie in the face.

Lying on top of Gracie, dominating the fight, Severn found himself in an awkward position. "I was struggling more with my conscience than I was with Royce," says Severn. He did not feel comfortable striking his opponent's throat to take him out. So Severn just lay there, working his wrestling skills. Meanwhile, the production crew from SEG was having its own problems on the sidelines. The cable companies had only allotted them a two-hour time slot for the event, and it was quickly elapsing. "They realized that time was running out," remembers Severn, "and that pretty soon they were going to go off the air. They were going to declare me the champion because I had dominated out there."

That didn't happen, however, and after fifteen minutes of continuous battle Gracie caught the break he was looking for. He managed to wrap his legs around Severn's head and apply a triangle choke. Severn tapped out to avoid losing consciousness. Severn seemed shocked, as did announcer Jeff Blatnick. "I just never thought there was a skill set out there that could take such advantage of what most people think is a very indefensible position, which is being put on your back," says Blatnick. "I had to go through a little bit of a learning curve."

Because SEG allowed the match to continue, they ended up paying a hefty price. The show had run three minutes over, and millions in revenue would have to be returned to viewers whose pay-per-view had cut off before the end of the bout.

Although Severn had been brought down by the two-time Ultimate Fighting Champion, he had proven that wrestling was a viable octagon discipline. He would go back to the drawing board and return to the next event, UFC V, to unleash his alter ego. With Royce Gracie out of the tournament picture—he would instead be facing Ken Shamrock in the first-ever Superfight—it looked as if Severn had the win in the bag.

UFC V—The Return of the Beast/July 4, 1995 (Charlotte, North Carolina)

When Dan Severn came to Charlotte, North Carolina to participate in UFC V on July 4, 1995, he was a changed man. In order to overcome his hesitation to strike another competitor, he had worked tirelessly on strikes in a training camp. In his opinion, the Gracie family didn't know what they were getting themselves into by allowing him to compete in their event. "Most people did not realize that the Gracie family owned half the show at that time," says Severn. "It was a business to win not just national, but also international exposure for the Gracie family and Gracie jiu-jitsu. It was a great marketing tool. They controlled the applicants. If an application came in, and they felt the guy was too much of a threat, they wouldn't put him in. It was nothing more than a business. When Art Davie interviewed me, I did not come across as a savage barbarian. They didn't do any kind of true background check. All they saw was a thirty-six-year old, out-of-shape, old wrestler."

Severn had proven that he was a worthy competitor at his debut in UFC IV—he'd done it so decisively that Jim Brown had aptly named him "the Beast." Severn says, "To have such an endorsement from one of the most punishing running backs in the history of the game, that's quite a feather in my hat. He called me a Dr. Jekyll and Mr. Hyde." With an

Dan Severn riling up the crowd.

array of strikes now in his arsenal, Severn planned to bring out Mr. Hyde at UFC V. "If Royce had to face me after my training camp," Severn said at the time, "it would have been tough. I'm not going to predict the outcome, but . . ."

Severn showed just how many obstacles he had overcome when he stepped into the octagon to face the six-foot-one, 260-pound Joe "the Ghetto Man" Charles for his quarterfinal bout. Quickly taking the Ghetto Man to the mat and pinning him against the octagon's fence, he unleashed knees to the face, elbow strikes, head butts, and punches. Charles, bleeding from his eye, attempted to get back to his feet. That's when Severn showed his diversity not only in strikes, but also in submissions. He wrapped his arm around his opponent's neck and choked him into submission at one minute and thirty-nine seconds into the bout.

But before he could claim the belt and the substantial purse, he would first have to get through the six-foot, 205-pound newcomer Oleg Taktarov in the semifinals. Despite the fact that Taktarov was a Russian grappling master, Severn wasted no time in taking him to the ground, where he dropped a solid knee to the face. Just as Royce had done, Taktarov got Severn in the guard, only this time the Beast had come prepared. He unleashed a flurry of strikes to the Russian's face and head. Taktarov kept amazingly cool, however, and as Severn scrambled on top of him, Taktarov got into position and snatched Severn's arm. But Severn was now versed in submission, and while Taktarov was working on his arm,

Severn dropped several knees into the Russian's face, opening a bad cut over Taktarov's eye. With Taktarov wounded, Severn went to work with more knees and head butts. When Taktarov showed no signs of submitting, McCarthy made a just call and intervened, bringing the abuse to an end.

Dan Severn moved on to the finals. But before this, there was the much-anticipated Superfight between Ken Shamrock and Royce Gracie. It had been hyped for months—the little man versus the big man. "They wanted to show the skinny guy beating the big guy," says Bob Shamrock. "But when Royce fought Ken the second time, Royce weighed 190 pounds, not 175 pounds, and Ken only weighed 205. They were trying to make it seem like there was a big weight difference—there wasn't."

Ken had waited almost a year and a half for this moment. But after the fight got under way, the minutes passed uneventfully, with Shamrock in Gracie's guard. It became evident that the fans were not going to get the knockout brawl they had hoped for. "I didn't want to go out and just beat Royce," says Ken Shamrock. "I wanted to shut down his whole bragging system, which was, 'We're in better condition, our skills are better, and we can beat anybody, anywhere, anytime.' My whole strategy going in was to wear him out, make him dog-assed tired to where he could hardly stand. I was going to beat him—beat on his ribs, slowly break him down, and then treat him like a baby. I mean, I really wanted to embarrass this guy. Unfortunately, two days before the fight I was brought into a room with myself, my dad, Rorion and Royce, and Art Davie, and told there was going to be a time limit put in place. I had trained for a two-hour fight. Like I said, I literally wanted to embarrass this guy. Obviously, with the half-hour time limit, I wasn't able to do what I wanted to do. I couldn't really change my game plan because I'd been training for it for so long that I had it down to a science. If you watch the fight, you'll see that everything I did was totally planned out, totally strategic—no big moves, but a lot of little stuff. Unfortunately, there was a time limit put in there, and I didn't change my strategy."

Despite Shamrock sticking to his game plan and slowly chopping away at Gracie, the crowd was not impressed. "Ken thought too much of Royce's abilities," says Bob Shamrock, who was cussing at his son from the corner to get busy. "I got frustrated in that fight because I felt Ken could have been more aggressive. That's one of the other things where Ken has his own way of looking at things. He wanted to beat Royce at his own game and show him he could outlast him. Sometimes proving one thing over another is stupid. You go out there and win the fight; you don't prove that kind of thing."

Nearing the end of the thirty-minute time limit, the announcers were informed that there would be a five-minute overtime. Because there were no judges, no way to determine a champion, the warriors were given extra time to see if one of them could come out on top.

When neither fighter changed his strategy and both remained lying inactive on the ground, John McCarthy stood them up. It was the break Shamrock had been waiting for. He delivered two powerful punches to Gracie's face—swelling up both eyes and opening a cut on his cheek— before the fight went back to the ground. "The reason why I was able to rock him was the fact that I was wearing him down," explains Ken Shamrock. "His legs weren't moving. I pounded him in the head several times. I bruised his ribs up pretty bad. I slowed him way down. I tried the same punch right in the beginning of the fight, but it didn't land. First time I missed it, but the second time he was worn out, a little bit slower, and I hit it." For the remaining minutes, Shamrock worked on Gracie's face with head butts, but it was not enough to put the jiu-jitsu expert away.

After thirty-five long minutes, the two fighters were brought back to their feet and the fight was pronounced a draw. Despite the booing from the crowd, in many ways the bout was a victory for Shamrock. He had done something no fighter had ever done before: he'd gone the distance with Royce Gracie. "Gracie is a mess," said commentator Bruce Beck. "Shamrock looks marvelous."

Shamrock would go on to compete in numerous events, but this would be the last public bout Royce Gracie would compete in for several years. Shortly after the show, Rorion Gracie and Art Davie would sell their stake in the production to Robert Meyrowitz. "Bob Meyrowitz was a strong-willed businessman. He wanted to do things his own way," says Rorion. "It got to a point where he just wanted to own the whole show. They started changing the rules of the show, adding time limits and the points and the gloves . . . 'You can't do this, you can't do that.' They were doing that to accommodate the political demands and the pay-per-view requests. They started changing things so the show could keep going. For them, it was a television show about fighting. For me, it was a fight that was being televised. I have always been much closer to keeping the integrity of the fight versus making it a television show. Meyrowitz doesn't mind changing the rules, putting on time limits and making rounds of five minutes. I think that messes up the whole thing. They wanted to change everything, and I said that wasn't going to work, it's going to kill the show. I decided to step out because it was no longer the vision I originally had. So I felt it was okay for me to move on, and I sold my interest in the company and stepped out. It was the right time to do it, because since I left, the show has never been the same." Although Art Davie also sold his stake in the show, he stayed on as the UFC matchmaker.

When Rorion withdrew from the Ultimate Fighting Championship, Royce withdrew as well. Many people thought that because his bout with Shamrock hadn't gone the way he'd wanted it to go, and because his opponents were getting more and more fierce, Royce was retiring. This was far from the case. When Royce went to fight for the UFC, he had signed a two-year contract that prevented him from competing in any other event.

Although his match with Ken Shamrock signaled the end of Royce's career in the octagon, Dan Severn was just getting geared up. After a thirty-five-minute Superfight that had only one highlight, it was up to the Beast to bring action to the octagon in his final match of the evening—with Canadian wrestler Dave Beneteau.

Beneteau stepped into the octagon with the intention of knocking the Beast out, but Severn quickly closed the distance and took the Canadian's punches away. Severn struggled with the power of his fellow wrestler and dropped several knees to wear him down. When Beneteau raised his leg to block the painful shots, Severn hooked Beneteau's leg and took him to the mat. Once there, it took less than a minute for Severn to secure an arm lock and force Beneteau to tap out. Severn had won the Ultimate Fighting Championship, and he walked away with a check for fifty thousand dollars.

In the following UFC, Severn would get promoted to the Superfight, where he would take on none other than submission expert Ken Shamrock. Another champion would take Severn's place on the main card at UFC VI, and he was called the Russian Bear.

CHAPTER 6

Tank and the Russian Bear

As if he wanted to exchange pleasantries rather than punches, David "Tank" Abbott casually walked across the octagon towards John Matua, a four-hundred-pound expert in the Hawaiian art of "bone breaking," with his arms hanging loosely at his side. It wasn't until the two hulking warriors were a few feet apart that Tank let his intentions be known by dropping a wild right that grazed Matua's shoulder and knocked him off balance.

Not hindered at all by his own jiggling belly, Tank chased Matua's head around the ring with his massive right hand. The first four swinging sledgehammers missed Matua's face by mere inches, but the fifth and sixth landed to Matua's cheek, turning his legs into rubber.

Matua's eyes went squirrelly, and Tank dropped yet another power bomb that not only knocked his bone-breaking opponent unconscious, but also caused every muscle in his body to spasm. Although Matua lay on the canvas with his arms and legs flexed involuntarily in the air, Tank ruthlessly went in for another piece. Dropping all of his 260 pounds down on top of the Hawaiian, he cracked Matua's jaw with a bashing forearm. When Tank showed no signs of discontinuing his dismantling of Matua, referee John McCarthy secured Abbott by the throat and pulled him off.

After thoroughly pummeling his opponent in just eighteen seconds, Tank made a victory lap around the octagon, throwing his hands into the air and doing a little "jitter dance" to mock his downed foe. He left the octagon without so much as a scratch on him, but the same could not be said for Matua. He slept in the cage for almost ten minutes before he was carried out with an oxygen mask strapped to his face.

*   *   *

This was Tank Abbott's debut in the octagon. His thick goatee, toothless grin, and heavy right hand instantly earned him the official position as

David "Tank" Abbott after delivering a beat-down in the octagon.

the UFC bad boy. He was loaded with sarcasm, he described himself as the "anti-martial artist," and beer-swilling fans across America fell in love.

Despite what his appearance and violent nature would lead one to believe, Abbott grew up in a middle-class family and graduated from the University of California Long Beach with a degree in history. "He's a lot more intelligent than what people think," comments Dan Severn, who would face Tank in Ultimate Ultimate '95. "The UFC had really not had a bad guy yet, and so Tank looked for his role. And he filled the bill, too. He made a lot of brash statements, and the man sold tickets. Whether you loved him or you hated him, the man sold tickets. A lot of people would buy a pay-per-view just based on Tank."

Although Tank's overflowing gut was not indicative of a proficient athlete, he had been wrestling since he was nine. At one point, he had dreamed of becoming a collegiate champion, but any hope of that happening ended after a long night of partying. The friend who was driving him home passed out behind the wheel and crashed into a pole. Abbott woke up to find his teeth knocked out and his leg nearly severed.

His vendetta against the world was not a response to a dream gone down the tubes, however. Brawling had been his favorite pastime for most of his youth. After taking up boxing and seeing what his sledgehammer fists could do, he vented his wrath in bars all over Huntington Beach. In 1997, Abbott allegedly flew into a car-kicking rage in the parking lot of the Majestic Beach Boulevard dance club before cold-cocking a fellow patron and then kicking him in the head.

This kind of behavior landed Tank behind bars on more than one occasion. Ironically, it was in lockup that he first heard about the Ultimate Fighting Championship. While serving a seven-month stint in the slammer for doing what he loved, Tank was told that Kimo, a fellow scrapper who also claimed to be from Huntington Beach, had fought in the show. Although Abbott's friends believed that the event—one that supposedly had no rules—was designed for a guy like him, Tank didn't get his hopes up. He told them if they could get him in, he would fight.

Dave Thomas, one of Abbott's friends, took him up on the offer and contacted Art Davie on his behalf. When asked to describe this badass street brawler, Thomas said that Abbott was like Tank Murdoch, the colorful, bare-fisted fighter in Clint Eastwood's *Every Which Way But Loose*. Davie liked what he heard, and he invited Abbott to UFC V as a spectator.

UFC VI—Clash of the Titans/July 14, 1995
(Casper, Wyoming)

While sitting in the stands at UFC V, Abbott made an impression on UFC matchmakers, and he was added on to the card of UFC VI, held in Casper, Wyoming on July 14, 1995. Abbott believed that the UFC promoters were planning on making an example of him, that they wanted to show what their martial artists could do to a street fighter. But Abbott planned on making a statement of his own—which he did quite well in his quarterfinal bout with John Matua.

While Tank made his way backstage after his first fight, corrections officer and tae kwon do practitioner Cal Worsham was on deck to take on Paul "the Polar Bear" Varelans, a street fighter claiming proficiency in the unknown style of "trap fighting." "I'm standing in the tunnel," remembers Worsham, "getting ready to go out because I'm the second fight. Tank and Matua start, I look up, and I watch Tank beat this guy into a seizure in eighteen seconds. Then I look behind me, and just a few yards away is Paul, standing there staring at my crew. I began thinking, 'What did I get into?' And then big old Tank walks by me and says, 'Kick that big pussy's ass!' I said, 'Sure thing, Mr. Tank, anything for you.'"

After Varelans defeated Worsham in one minute and four seconds, Tank got a chance to do what Worsham couldn't do when he took on the six-foot-eight, three-hundred-pound Polar Bear in the semifinals. Tank

*(From left to right) Patrick Smith, Oleg Taktarov, Paul Varelans, and
Cal Worsham—at a press conference before UFC VI.*

strolled towards his foe and then suddenly threw a huge right hand that
knocked Varelans back. Barreling in like a cannonball, Tank drove his
larger opponent back into the fence. Snatching one of Varelans's legs,
Tank took him to the ground and began to unleash punches.

Growing tired of bashing his opponent with body shots and hooks to
the face, Abbott changed his tactics. Placing a knee on Varelans's throat,
he grabbed hold of the chain-link fence to add even more downward
pressure. Doing what he loved to do the most—inflict pain—Abbott took
a moment to look up at the crowd and smirk before delivering four more
fists to the now gurgling Varelans. Referee John McCarthy, not wanting
the Polar Bear to end up like Matua, quickly jumped between.

As Abbott took his victory walk around the cage, Varelans jumped to
his feet with blood gushing from his mouth and nose. With McCarthy
holding him at bay, the Polar Bear acted like he wanted another shot at
the man who had just beaten him stupid. Tank simply smirked.

Even more entertaining than Tank's antics in the ring were the comments he made in his postfight interview: "Varelans said earlier in his
little preview thing that he likes to take people down and tickle them.
Well, I just wanted to tickle his brain a little bit." Jeff Blatnick, who was
conducting the interview, seemed a little stunned, and he went on to
show Tank the highlights of his fight. While watching himself beat on his
opponent, Tank said, "I'm starting to get sexually aroused—you better
get that off."

After delivering a beat-down in both the quarterfinals and the semifinals, Tank only had one more contender to whomp before he could win

the Ultimate Fighting Championship. However, the fighter who had been cleaning house on the other side of the bracket was not only a UFC veteran, but also a Russian sambo master.

The Russian Bear

Born on August 26, 1967, in Sarov, Russia, Oleg Taktarov had to overcome his share of obstacles to make it to the Ultimate Fighting Championship. His parents worked just outside of Sarov, in one of Russia's primary facilities for manufacturing weapons, and the environment Taktarov was raised in was not only heavily militarized, but also surrounded by an electrical fence. While many would consider this a stifling place to spend one's youth, Taktarov found it to be the opposite. In this fenced-off haven, Taktarov felt safe; and his family had access to supplies that were in short supply throughout the rest of the country. In addition, contained within the electrical fence were hundreds of acres of wilderness. Taktarov spent his early years exploring this terrain and camping in the wild.

But, at ten years of age, Taktarov discovered a new passion when his father took him to a local judo school. Realizing he had a thirst for competition, Taktarov began his training. He studied judo for six years before discovering sambo—a form of Russian wrestling that utilizes submission holds and locks. "Sambo is not just a style," says Taktarov, "but rather a combination of all the best techniques in any self-defense, martial art, and fighting style."

Taktarov began competing when he was only twelve, and his skills earned him many titles. He won six bare-knuckle tournaments. He was a four-time full-contact jiu-jitsu world champion, a two-time Russian sambo champion, and he was declared the champion of a European no-holds-barred tournament.

At eighteen years of age, Taktarov entered the Russian military to begin his mandatory two years of service. In the short time that Taktarov was in the military, he attained the rank of sergeant and traveled extensively in southern Russia and bordering countries. After his obligatory term, Taktarov stayed connected to the military as part of a special counter-terrorist unit, eventually specializing in training soldiers in hand-to-hand combat. He also worked with the Russian Special Forces unit Spetsnaz on military sambo, and he trained members of law-enforcement agencies ranging from the tax police to the federal security service.

After his time in the military, Taktarov began thinking about pursuing his lifelong dream of becoming a film actor. He visited the immigration office in 1994, and, thanks to a good-natured immigration chief, he obtained a visa to travel to the United States. But it wasn't so easy in the land of opportunity for a Russian who spoke little English and had little cash. Finding himself down and out, Taktarov made a call to the UFC, hoping his background in the fighting arts would get him into the event. Art Davie, realizing the potential of the Russian, shipped Taktarov off to Texas to be managed by Buddy Albin, who was doing local promotions for the UFC. But the arrangement was not the golden opportunity Taktarov had hoped it would be. "Buddy Albin was taking forty percent of his proceeds, plus expenses," says Bob Shamrock, who would later take the Russian under his wing. "He was just hogging all of Taktarov's money and telling him what to do."

On top of all this, Taktarov didn't have a place to train. "Albin basically dumped him off on me," says Guy Mezger, a Lion's Den fighter who had his own school in Texas. "I did what I could. He lived with me for a while, and then I got him an apartment." But with all the moving around, and a knee that caused him constant pain, Taktarov was in bad shape going into UFC V. Subsequently, he lost to Dan Severn in the semifinals.

This, however, was not the end of the Russian's UFC career. He made quite an impression at his debut and was invited back to compete in the next show. But, because his training was not going well in Texas, Taktarov decided to move back to California—this time to the northern part of the state, to train at the Lion's Den. "He lived in our fighter's house," says Bob Shamrock. "I tried to put him on a conditioning and diet program, but he just wouldn't follow it. One day I went to the store with him because he wanted to buy a turkey. I told him to buy the biggest turkey he could, so he could just slice strips off of it after it was cooked. We got him the turkey, and then I went away for several weeks. When I got back the whole kitchen was full of maggots. What he was doing was taking the turkey raw, cutting strips off of it, and cooking them in the microwave as he needed them. It was amazing he didn't die of salmonella. On top of this, he used to eat raw potatoes and onions. When he ate apples and got down to the core, he'd just throw them in the closet."

Despite his strange eating habits, Taktarov got the training he needed at the Lion's Den, including a wake-up call from Ken Shamrock. For their first sparring session, Ken and Oleg agreed not to go full force and not to punch. "They started rolling around," recalls Bob, "and Oleg punched Ken to the face. Ken took him down and just beat the shit out of him. Taktarov went into the bathroom and stayed there for forty-five

UFC Champion Oleg Taktarov showing his patriotism.

minutes because he was bleeding." Despite this exchange, there were no hard feelings and training resumed.

Coming off the loss to Dan Severn in UFC V, the Russian Bear planned on taking care of business at UFC VI. But so did his quarterfinal opponent, Dave Beneteau, who had also been bested by the Beast in the previous event. Action began quickly, as Beneteau rushed forward and took the Russian to the mat. After dragging Taktarov over to the fence, Beneteau unleashed with punches, allowing Taktarov to scramble back to his feet. Not wanting to give the Russian a chance to recuperate, Beneteau rained down another flurry of rights and lefts. Uncomfortable trading punches, Taktarov covered his head with his arms before dropping underneath the flurry and hooking a leg. Taking the wrestler to the mat, the Russian Bear secured a choke, and Beneteau tapped in submission just fifty-six seconds into the match.

Claiming stomach problems, Patrick Smith had backed out of the event after his first fight, and so Taktarov faced alternate Anthony Macias in the semifinals. As Macias entered the ring, he pointed to Taktarov and winked. Not only were the two fighters friends, but both were also being managed by Buddy Albin. Some have suggested that because Taktarov was the favorite to win the event, Macias was told to take it easy so that Taktarov could go out fresh for the finals. That was just speculation— either way, the bout ended quickly for Taktarov, who defeated Macias with a choke in twelve seconds. Jim Brown, a commentator at the event, summed up the match best by saying, "I wasn't really happy about the whole thing of friendship."

UFC VI Superfight—Ken Shamrock versus Dan Severn

Before Taktarov could face Tank in the finals, a Superfight between Ken Shamrock and Dan Severn still had to occur. Going into the bout, neither fighter cared much for the other. The tension between the two had arisen at a prefight press conference. Severn felt it was a poor setup to have both fighters talking about their game plans while in the same room; he wanted Shamrock to be able to talk freely with reporters. "So what I did," he explains, "was I quietly stood up and moved away from the table. As I got to the door, I saw one of the people with the production and said, 'I'm just going to sneak outside the door so Ken can answer his questions without him feeling weird with me sitting right here in the room.' Soon as I got out the door he wigged out and started cussing and saying, 'I'm going to kill him!' I'm thinking, the guy doesn't even know me. I don't even know the guy. Whatever time we shared, we weren't exactly exchanging pleasantries."

Ken, however, felt that he had been disrespected. "I was a little agitated because the odds were like seventy to thirty that he was going to beat me. And I was like, 'What are these people looking at?' This guy doesn't do anything—he's a wrestler. When we went into the press conference, it was myself, Oleg, and Dan. We all had our managers with us. Phyllis Lee was Dan's manager at the time. Dan had made some statement prior to the conference, which is cool because it's a fight game. But when we were in the conference, they started asking me questions first. They spent a little longer time with me, and I guess Dan felt they weren't asking him any questions, so he just got up and left. It was right in the middle of me talking about something, and I got pissed. I leaned over to Phyllis and said, 'I was just going to beat him, but now I'm going to hurt him.' Phyllis says, 'In your dreams.' I say, 'Well, my dreams have been pretty good lately.'"

On fight night, the talking was finished and it was time to determine who the better combatant was. Action got off to a quick start as Shamrock shot in for the legs of the Beast. When Severn sprawled, the two rose up into the clinch. Shamrock displayed his balance and wrestling ability as he countered the Beast's takedown attempts, and Severn proved his strength as he powered out of a choke hold. The fight looked as if it could go on for some time, but then Severn made a fatal mistake.

After driving Shamrock back into the fence, Severn dipped down to pull the submission fighter's legs out from under him, leaving his own neck exposed. Shamrock, who had learned countless chokes from Japanese

ANDY ANDERSON

Dan Severn and Ken Shamrock do battle from the clinch in UFC VI.

masters, spotted the submission instantly. Without thinking, he wrapped an arm around Severn's throat and tightened down. Severn, in one last effort to free himself, delivered a shot to Shamrock's groin, but it was not enough. Severn had no choice but to tap out. Even though harsh words had gone back and forth between the two before the fight, they shook hands and handled the outcome like true sportsmen.

UFC VI Finals—Oleg Taktarov versus David Abbott

Despite the camaraderie shown in the Superfight, the crowd had no illusions about the intentions of the next fighter who stepped into the octagon. Tank Abbott had come to do Oleg Taktarov damage in the finals, but Taktarov, wanting nothing to do with Tank's awesome punches, ran across the ring and attempted to take the pit bull to the ground. Using his weight to his advantage, Abbott effortlessly tossed the Russian onto his back and stood up.

Once Taktarov had risen, Tank went to work with crosses and hooks, batting his opponent around the ring. After taking some abuse, Taktarov finally managed to seize Abbott's head and bring the big man down into his expert guard. Abbott powered out of the choke, but the struggle to free his head came at a price. Too gassed out to throw heavy leather, he resorted to fishhooking Taktarov's mouth.

Although both fighters were relatively inactive on the ground, whenever the fight got back to standing position Abbott resumed with his screaming punches. After almost eighteen minutes, a bloodied Taktarov found the opportunity he was looking for when he turned Abbott onto his back. As the choke sank in, the one-man wrecking machine was forced to tap out.

Tank had lost in the finals, but it was not the last fight he would have that evening. Later on, in the Hilton, while Bob Shamrock and Art Davie were having a meeting in his room, Bob heard police sirens out front. "When we came down, Tank had cheap-shotted and beat Pat Smith," says Bob. "Pat had been partying with Andy Anderson, the competitor who fought John Hess in UFC V, in Anderson's suite. Later on, when Pat was coming out of the elevator by himself, Tank and a bunch of his cohorts just started whomping the daylights out of him. They really beat the snot out of him." When the police started swarming into the hotel, Tank and his accomplices fled the scene. "They even rented a car and went to another town to catch a plane," Bob remembers. "They took off from there because they were afraid they were going to get arrested."

Despite his speedy getaway, Tank would return two shows later to compete in the Ultimate Ultimate, as would Taktarov. But with both of them sitting out UFC VII, a new champion moved in to grace the octagon with his presence.

CHAPTER 7

The King of the Streets

UFC VII—The Brawl in Buffalo/August 9, 1995
(Buffalo, New York)

Marco Ruas was a virtual unknown in the United States when he entered the eight-man elimination tournament in UFC VII, held in Buffalo, New York on August 9, 1995. He was a different breed of fighter than any the competition had seen to that point. Not only could he kick and strike, but he could also take his opponents to the mat and submit them with his grappling skills. The name of his style, Ruas vale tudo, said it all. For Ruas, anything went.

Born in Rio de Janeiro, Brazil, Ruas began learning martial arts from his uncle at the age of thirteen. The training gave Ruas so much confidence that he decided to devote his life to the martial arts. In 1984, he entered his first MMA competition, taking on Pinduka, one of Brazil's most renowned jiu-jitsu practitioners. Although the match ended in a draw, Ruas had learned a valuable lesson. He now understood the importance of crosstraining, and he was determined to become a complete fighter. He studied a variety of styles, picking out what worked and throwing away what didn't.

His love for the fighting arts prompted Ruas to open a gym on the outskirts of a Rio slum. He did not discriminate—he taught everyone who wanted to learn, even those who didn't have money to pay for the classes. His giving nature soon earned him the title "King of the Streets."

One student who admired Ruas's diverse fighting style was a fifteen year old by the name of Pedro Rizzo. Rizzo came from an upper-class family, and his parents did not want him to become a fighter; but Ruas had made an impression on the boy, and every afternoon Rizzo snuck away and waited for Ruas to pick him up on the corner. At first, Rizzo, with a background in a Brazilian martial art known as capoeria, was more interested in learning kickboxing. That changed, however, after Ruas informed him that MMA was going to be the sport of the future. Together, the two trained and bled in the gym, and in no time at all they were like father and son.

But then, twelve years after Ruas's first MMA bout, he made a decision that would change his life forever. "I moved to California, because I felt that there were more opportunities for no-holds-barred athletes here," says Ruas. Although he had to leave his favorite student behind, Marco and Pedro would reunite in the future, and both would become superstars in the MMA world.

The land of opportunity proved to be just that for the muscle-bound Brazilian. Just months after moving to the States, Ruas got a call inviting him to compete in UFC VII, to be held in Buffalo, New York on August 8, 1995. Ruas accepted the invitation and gave the audience its first glimpse of his muay Thai strikes and grappling ability when he took on Larry Cureton in his quarterfinal bout and put him away with a heel hook in three minutes and twenty-three seconds. To win the entire tournament, however, Ruas still had to secure two more victories—and for his semifinal bout he would be taking on a UFC veteran, the expert grappler Remco Pardoel.

The two circled each other to get a feel for the contest, and then Pardoel came forward with a series of weak openhanded strikes. Ruas ducked them, but as he went for the takedown Pardoel wrapped an arm around his head and bulldozed him against the fence, looking to choke him out. Ruas remained calm. Guarding against foot sweeps and defending the choke, he began ruthlessly stomping his heel down on Pardoel's feet. Pardoel instantly began to play the hot-foot game, trying to keep the small bones in his feet from being broken.

Eventually, Pardoel managed to sweep a leg and take his opponent down. Still holding onto the choke, Pardoel went to mount his opponent, but Ruas defended brilliantly. Wedging his feet inside, he created the leverage he needed to roll Pardoel over onto his back, freeing himself from the choke in the process. Now on top, Ruas got to work. He attempted several submissions, including a heel hook, but when nothing worked he decided he would end it with strikes. Ruas craftily worked around his opponent and obtained the mount, but before he could land a single blow, the match came to an end. Pardoel, knowing there was little he could do with the Brazilian riding on top of him, tapped the canvas before enduring any abuse.

Ruas had made it to the finals, but before he could step into the octagon to battle for the tournament title, Oleg Taktarov faced former

Ken Shamrock (left), actor David Hasselhoff (middle), and Oleg Taktarov (right).

training partner Ken Shamrock in the Superfight. This matchup was not an easy one to make happen. Ken, who was still fighting for Pancrase, had been scheduled to compete in Japan during the same weekend UFC VII was to take place. Pancrase decided to strike a deal and granted Ken permission to fight in the UFC, but only if Oleg Taktarov would agree to come and fight in Pancrase at a later date. This posed another problem, because Taktarov had a three-contract deal to fight exclusively in the UFC. The UFC decided not to let Taktarov fight in Pancrase; so Pancrase withdrew permission for Ken to fight in the UFC. At this point, Bob Shamrock decided to step in and clear up the mess. He got on the phone to UFC attorney David Isaacs. "I was the one who negotiated the contract for Oleg to fight in Pancrase," says Bob. "We worked everything out in my office."

When the two former training partners finally stepped into the octagon together, in Buffalo, they brought plenty of politics with them. Taktarov, who had been bloodied by Ken in the gym, stated brashly that he would never tap. This did not sit well with the event's promoters, who were under mounting political pressure and wanted to keep the fights as clean as possible. In reaction to Taktarov's statement, Art Davie (who had stayed on as a matchmaker after selling his stake in the show) and Bob Meyrowitz pulled him aside and told him that if he was bleeding badly they would stop the bout for him.

Ken also knew that Taktarov would not tap. "I know Oleg," says Ken, "and I knew trying to leg lock him or arm bar him or get him in a choke would be a little difficult. I knew it would be difficult, and if I did get him in it, I would have to break it—and I like the guy, he's my friend. Not to say that I would have gotten him, but if I would have gotten the opportunity to do it, I would have had to break it because he wouldn't tap. So I thought my best thing to do was just knock him out, win the fight by grounding and pounding him and punching him." But Shamrock couldn't get the right punch, and the result was a thirty-five-minute stalemate that ended in a draw.

The crowd was growing restless when Ruas stepped back into the octagon to face yet another UFC veteran and one of the biggest competitors MMA had to offer: Paul "the Polar Bear" Varelans. Although victory didn't come to him as quickly as it had in his previous two bouts, Ruas played the game like a true tactician, keeping his distance and chopping Varelans down with leg kicks. After thirteen minutes, the Polar Bear finally fell.

Ruas had realized his dream: he had become the Ultimate Fighting champion. "UFC VII was a great opportunity for me because I was able to show my style as a complete fighter," says Ruas. "They treated me very well."

Although the show was a tremendous success for Ruas, from the standpoint of the promoters it was yet another nightmare. At one point there was a power outage, and the lights were off for twenty minutes, so the show went on much longer than expected. Many viewers never got to see Marco Ruas win his first-ever U.S. MMA event, and millions in revenue had to be returned to subscribers yet again.

Ruas did not remain inactive for long. At the very next event, he would see how his skills fared against the best of the best in the Ultimate Ultimate '95. Now was the time that legends could be made. Although MMA and the UFC were on top of the world and gearing up to be a very lucrative sports industry, a storm was brewing on the horizon.

CHAPTER 8

The Ultimate Showdown

Ultimate Ultimate '95/December 16, 1995
(Denver, Colorado)

Out of seven Ultimate Fighting Championships spread over two years, five different tournament champions had emerged: Royce Gracie, Steve Jennum, Dan Severn, Oleg Taktarov, and Marco Ruas. The sport was evolving, the fighters were becoming more qualified, and the world wanted to know who the ultimate champion was. What better way to decide this than to have four of the previous tournament champions, three of the toughest challengers who had made it to the semifinals, and Keith Hackney, the man responsible for dropping 616-pound Emmanuel Yarbrough, compete in one elimination tournament. There would be $250,000 in prize money, with $150,000 going to the last man standing. The card was like no other, despite the fact that Ken Shamrock would not be competing due to schedule conflicts with Pancrase.

Held in Mammoth Gardens in Denver, Colorado, the quarterfinal matches of Ultimate Ultimate '95 got off to a quick start. David "Tank" Abbott, a brawler known for his lawlessness, was pitted against police officer Steve Jennum. Despite Tank's reputation for throwing heavy leather, he hardly punched at all. Instead, he wasted no time in taking his smaller opponent to the mat and scooting him against the chain-link fence. Tank drove his skull into Jennum's chin, cranking his neck to the side. The Tulsa cop quickly tapped out.

Dan "the Beast" Severn dispensed of six-foot-eight, 300-pound Paul "the Polar Bear" Varelans just as quickly. Without throwing a punch, Severn took the Polar Bear to the ground, got into position, and laid on a choke that made him tap. Taktarov breezed through Dave Beneteau as well. As the two stood with their arms entangled in the center of the ring, Taktarov tucked and rolled beneath his larger opponent, seizing Beneteau's leg. After securing the wrestler's foot in his armpit, Taktarov cranked the heel, causing Beneteau to submit.

Although the last quarterfinal matchup between Keith "the Giant Killer" Hackney and Marco Ruas was short, it was action packed, and it gave the fans a taste of what they had come to see. Both fighters cautiously exchanged kicks to the legs. Then Ruas rushed in and took Hackney to the mat. Turning his opponent onto his stomach, Ruas mounted Hackney and softened him up with several authoritative punches to the back of the neck before sinking in the choke.

The original eight competitors had been whittled down to four: Dan Severn, Oleg Taktarov, Tank Abbott, and Marco Ruas. All of them had breezed through their quarterfinal matchups and still had plenty of strength to battle each other for the Ultimate Ultimate '95 title belt.

Ultimate Ultimate '95 Semifinal Bout—
Dan Severn versus David Abbott

It looked as if the tournament would be over well ahead of schedule when Tank stepped back into the octagon to take on Dan Severn. Unfortunately for Abbott, he was not able to land his six-hundred-pound sledgehammers before Severn ducked under and went for a takedown. Although Tank managed to sprawl, it was only a matter of time before Severn came out on top. For over fifteen minutes, the Beast administered a barrage of knees, elbows, and punches into the body and head of the pit fighter. Tank, who did little more than cover the back of his head, accepted the beating until he was finally able to get back onto his feet with only minutes remaining in the bout. Severn clung to the brawler's back, continuing to obstruct Tank's deadly striking advantage and working for a suplex. When the two were finally untangled, there were only seconds remaining.

The clock ticked down to zero, and, for the very first time, the outcome of a UFC bout was put into the hands of judges. Severn was given the unanimous decision. "He hit me three times in twenty minutes," says Severn. "I take a full knee to the head. I take a reverse head butt and a reverse elbow. Someone told me later that I had hit Tank Abbott with 276 elbow strikes alone. I had so many people call me up and thank me after that match. They were like, 'Thanks for shutting up that big mouth.' I had other people saying, 'Oh, Severn doesn't have any submission in his body, why didn't he finish him off?' I'm thinking I did probably the worst thing I could have ever done to Tank Abbott. In front of the live audience, and in front of all the people watching on pay-per-view, I simply manhandled him and beat him." Tank, rather than standing in the ring while Severn was declared the victor, climbed over the octagon's fence and worked his way down the aisles.

Despite his quick exit, Tank went on to fight in five more UFC events, including Ultimate Ultimate '96 and a Superfight against legendary kickboxer Maurice Smith. Although he lost as many times as he won, Abbott proved to be a crowd favorite, and, holding true to his nature, he remained the official UFC bad boy. But the methods Abbott employed to keep this title almost got him kicked out of the show for good.

Sitting in the audience at UFC VIII, which was held in Puerto Rico, Tank decided to settle an old score with jiu-jitsu practitioner Allan Goes. While training for his first UFC, Tank had gone down to Allan Goes's gym to see what jiu-jitsu was all about. Rolling with the jiu-jitsu master, Tank found himself caught in an arm lock. Goes took the sparring session as a victory, and the story spread that he was boasting about tapping out UFC competitor David "Tank" Abbott. Now Tank was looking for a little retribution.

"Tank drinks," says McCarthy. "He drinks like a goddamn racehorse. His girlfriend at the time was there, and Allan Goes was there. Allan Goes had said that he had tapped Tank out. My wife, who was sitting behind Tank, heard Tank's girlfriend telling him to go get him. So Tank finally gets up and hands his girlfriend his teeth and goes over to Allan Goes. He starts something, and I jump in there. I grab Allan Goes and Joe Hamilton (another referee) grabs Tank. We pull them apart. As we do that, my wife looks over at his girlfriend and says, 'Why did you tell him to go do that? You know we've had nothing but problems—it's not going to help.' About that time Tank is coming back, and his girlfriend starts saying, 'She's calling me a bitch!' As Tank walks by, he says, 'I'm going to fucking kill you,' or something like that to my wife. At the time, I was getting into the ring to do another fight. I didn't know anything had happened until after the show."

McCarthy's wife went to Bob Meyrowitz and told him that either Tank went, or she and her husband would be forced to leave the show. Tank was put on suspension, but when he returned to the octagon several shows later he was by no means apologetic. He went on to garner himself his share of enemies, including Ken Shamrock, who was upset with Tank for continually taunting Ken's student Jerry Bohlander. "Tank had a problem with everybody," explains Bohlander. "Tank started shit wherever he could. That was his MO. That was what he got paid for. It wasn't like there was anything more with us than with anybody else. He would talk shit about anybody, and it didn't matter if he got his ass kicked. He just spread the wealth."

Despite this, Shamrock's anger came to a head at Ultimate Ultimate '96. He told Bob Meyrowitz that he would fight Tank in the octagon for nothing. "He said that right in front of Dave Meyrowitz, Bob Meyrowitz's brother and an attorney for the UFC," remembers Bob Shamrock. "Dave Meyrowitz went and talked to Tank, and Tank said there was no way in hell he would fight Ken."

Along with bad-mouthing Jerry Bohlander at the Ultimate Ultimate '96, Tank was also proving just how dirty he could play. In his bout with Cal Worsham, Tank hoisted Worsham off his feet and tried to toss him over the top of the octagon fence and into the crowd. When the bout ended a few minutes later, Cal fumed to McCarthy about Tank's dirty fighting. "I was ticked that he hit me late," says Worsham, "and that he eye gouged me in my right eye with his thumb, which went in pretty deep." Because McCarthy hadn't seen the foul play, Tank was not disqualified and was declared the victor. But for Tank's crew the fight wasn't over. "A couple of his people tried to get funny with my brother and some others in my entourage," says Worsham, "and I told my guys no—I didn't want to go to that level."

Even Abbott's former training partner, Tito Ortiz, who went on to become a UFC champ and one of the most popular fighters the sport has known, had a falling out with the burly bar brawler. "He was not really a cool person," says Ortiz. "He was an asshole, to tell you the truth. Everything he did was against everything I believed in."

In 1998, three years after his UFC debut, Tank Abbott left MMA competition. Despite the flack he had given Ken Shamrock for joining the ranks of professional wrestlers just a few years earlier, Tank followed in his footsteps. Tank's defense was that Shamrock had left the MMA scene when there was still money for the fighters. Tank stated that he would have remained brawling in the octagon if not for the political oppression that kept the UFC from bringing in the kind of money necessary to pay their top fighters.

Although Tank was approached by both the World Wrestling Federation (now World Wrestling Entertainment) and World Championship Wrestling, he ended up choosing WCW partly because of his friendship with the infamous Steiner brothers—Rick and Scott. He made his WCW debut by aiding superstar "Macho Man" Randy Savage against rival Sting.

Although Tank's character wasn't used often, it was far from dull. He did everything from fight Sid Vicious in an attempt to gain control of the WCW World Heavyweight title to pulling a knife on an opponent while shouting, "I should fucking kill you right now!" Tank's pro-wrestling career came to an apparent end when WWF owner Vince McMahon bought the struggling WCW. Although Tank wasn't used by the new owners, he was still under contract and continued to collect his paychecks.

Ultimate Ultimate '95 Semifinal Bout— Oleg Taktarov versus Marco Ruas

After the Beast had bested Abbott, the second semifinal match of Ultimate Ultimate '95, between Oleg Taktarov and Marco Ruas, got off to an exciting start. While Taktarov attempted to take the Brazilian down, Ruas timed his kicks and punches. Taktarov, tired of chasing his opponent, attempted a front kick, but his knee popped out of its socket. He took a dangerous moment to put it back into place, and it was lucky for him that Ruas did not take advantage of the situation. Taktarov finally closed the distance and wrapped his arms around the Brazilian. Wasting no time, he once again tucked and rolled, seizing Ruas's leg. But Ruas was more aware of submissions than Beneteau, and he managed to get into Taktarov's guard and land several punches.

The two fighters worked their way back to their feet, but they didn't stay there long. Taktarov again closed the gap, wrapped his arm around Ruas's neck, and brought him to the mat. But the Russian was not able to sink his arm deep enough into the throat of the Brazilian—Ruas was said to have a neck of rubber—and the two remained entangled until the ref broke them apart so the doctor could look at a cut that had opened on Taktarov's face.

After getting clearance to continue, the two fighters met again in the center of the enclosure. This is when the bout grew stagnant. Taktarov continued to press the fight, and he made repeated attempts to take his opponent down, but Ruas, feeling he was ahead on points, tried to keep the fight standing. He landed several leg kicks and a few punches, but that wasn't enough to win over the judges. After fifteen minutes, Taktarov won by unanimous decision, and upon hearing the news he dropped to his knees in the center of the octagon, crying.

After the event, Marco Ruas fought and beat a former UFC champ, Steve Jennum, in the first World Vale Tudo Championship (WVC). In the second WVC, he would once again face Taktarov, and this time the fight would finish in a draw. He went on to face Patrick Smith in WVC 4, defeating the aggressive kickboxer with a heel hook. But Ruas was being courted by a new organization out of Japan called Pride, and on March 15, 1998, he traveled overseas to fight Gary Goodridge in the second Pride event in front of over forty thousand Japanese spectators.

Unfortunately for Ruas, while training for a Pride 4 bout with Alexander Otsuka, he seriously injured his knee. As if that weren't enough, he found out shortly thereafter that he had hepatitis. Sick and injured, Ruas entered the bout, but he was forced to throw in the towel between rounds.

Ruas had surgery on his knee, but upon returning to the octagon in UFC XXI, he met up with heavyweight Maurice Smith and was again defeated. He took some time off from competing, but he continued to train fighters and develop his team, aptly named after his style. One of his brightest stars, Pedro Rizzo, had been training with Ruas since the age of fifteen. "Ruas vale tudo is my style, my team, and my family," says Ruas. "I support my fighters in both situations—winning or losing. I see myself always being involved in martial arts, by teaching and going to my students' fights."

Ruas still trains twice a day. In the mornings he does a rigorous physical workout, and in the afternoons and evenings he works on the technical aspects of his game. "More or less, I am a calm person," he says. "I think in the ring you've got to be calm, to use your mind intelligently, with strategies; but you must also be aggressive. Hard training—easy fight. Easy training—hard fight."

Even though he's now forty years of age, Ruas continues to compete. He feels he's already accomplished a lot in his career, but he doesn't want to end it on a losing streak. He successfully reentered MMA competition, winning his bout in the Los Angeles-based promotion Ultimate Pankration in fifty-three seconds. "Fighting is a sport," insists Ruas, "and it does not affect my personal life. I am a family person and am very happy and blessed for what I've accomplished."

Ultimate Ultimate '95 Final Bout— Oleg Taktarov versus Dan Severn

Although Taktarov had only a few minutes' rest, all of which he spent being treated by the doctor, he stepped back into the octagon to fight Dan Severn for the Ultimate Ultimate '95 championship belt. After tak-

ANDY ANDERSON

Oleg Taktarov plays the villain in Robert De Niro's 15 minutes.

ing several slaps from the wrestler, Taktarov attempted the tuck and roll for the third time that evening. Once again, Taktarov secured the leg of his opponent, but just as Ruas had done, Severn, after a dangerous minute of scrambling, managed to get out and obtain the mount.

Severn then went to work with slaps and head butts (over three hundred of them), opening the cut on Taktarov's face still wider—it left a five-foot circular smear of blood on the canvas around them. The match was stopped twice due to Taktarov's bleeding, but the fighters were allowed to continue on both occasions. Despite Taktarov's attempts to mount a standing attack, Severn kept taking him down. Taktarov took the abuse, but he never tapped out. "You didn't see a mark on me," says Severn. "But after the fight, Taktarov had to be taken to the hospital for a CAT scan because his head had swollen up to the size of a pumpkin." After thirty-three grueling minutes for Taktarov, Dan Severn was unanimously declared the winner.

After this loss, Taktarov honored his contract to fight in Pancrase and went to Japan, but he didn't experience the kind of success he'd had in the United States. "Oleg got his ass handed to him on a platter, and they never called him back," recalls Bob Shamrock. "If he would have had a good showing, they would have given him a contract and brought him back."

Oleg Taktarov in the movie Rollerball.

Undaunted, Taktarov moved on to other martial arts events. After fighting Marco Ruas to a draw in the second World Vale Tudo Championships, he found himself losing to Renzo Gracie in a start-up promotion called Martial Arts Reality Superfights. Oleg Taktarov's last MMA fight was on October 11, 1997, at Pride, in Japan; he lost to the UFC veteran Gary "Big Daddy" Goodridge.

But Taktarov had other dreams, primarily the dream he'd held on to since childhood to act on America's silver screen. Between fights, he had acted in local theater and had appeared in a slew of low-budget independent films. Finally, all that hard work and never-say-die attitude resulted in a part as the villain in a Robert De Niro film called *15 Minutes*. This led to a lead role in director John McTiernon's remake of the classic *Rollerball*; Taktarov plays Denekin, the Kazakhstani miner turned hero.

Despite his growing film commitments, Taktarov has kept up his training, and maybe one day soon he will again grace the MMA arenas with his unique style and cool-headed toughness.

Ultimate Ultimate '95 Champion—Dan Severn

At the age of thirty-seven, Dan "the Beast" Severn became the Ultimate Ultimate champ and took home $150,000, the largest purse in the history of the martial arts. It was the greatest moment of his career. "Although my Ultimate Ultimate belt is the smallest, it is the one I cherish the most," says Severn. "The show was over two hours, and I fought three times. My matches represented roughly fifty percent of the show." But he didn't use this chunk of change to take a trip around the world or buy a Rolls Royce. Instead, the practical Severn put a new bathroom in his house.

The wrestler, who describes himself as a family man, returned to UFC IX, where he faced Ken Shamrock in their second Superfight. Although most people fell asleep during the match—which was referred to as "the thirty-five minute dance"—Severn feels that it was "the most well-thought-out, psychological match ever. When I walked out there, I was planning on eight or ten thousand people hating this match." His plan worked, and, before a crowd chanting "Redwings" and throwing garbage into the ring, Severn was awarded the victory. After this, he competed in UFC XII, where he battled fellow wrestler Mark "the Hammer" Coleman.

Ultimate Ultimate '95 represented the best of what the UFC had to offer. Due to an increasing pay-per-view audience, fighters like Dan Severn and Oleg Taktarov had become legendary. All around the world, hopeful fighters crosstrained in a variety of disciplines as they watched and learned from their heroes. But just as this new wave of athletes was preparing for battle in the octagon, a senator from Arizona named John McCain was preparing for a battle of his own, one that would knock the UFC out of the spotlight and drive MMA competition underground.

PART II

The Apocalypse

CHAPTER 9

The Battle Outside the Ring

About the time Dan Severn was battling Oleg Taktarov in UFC V, a tape of a previous Ultimate Fighting Championship mysteriously fell onto the desk of Republican Senator John McCain. The story goes that McCain viewed the tape, responded to MMA competition as a form of barbarism, and launched a campaign to stomp the growing sport out of existence in America. But, of course, there was more to the story than that.

The senator just happened to have both social and financial connections to Budweiser, one of boxing's largest sponsors. "His wife is heir to the Budweiser/Anheuser-Busch family legacy," says MMA promoter Paul Smith. "Budweiser is in real, real deep in boxing." At the time, pay-per-view was a very lucrative revenue stream for boxing, and with MMA competition claiming a large part of the pay-per-view market, the business of boxing was taking a direct hit. It was important for both the boxing world and its sponsors to get rid of this threat, and what better weapon could they use to accomplish this than a powerful and influential senator?

In addition to cutting into boxing's profit margins, MMA competition was also seriously challenging boxing as a comprehensive fighting discipline. With the almost comical defeat of top-ranked pro boxer Art Jimmerson in UFC I, and the decisive loss of pro boxer Melton Bowen in UFC IV, the sport of boxing was starting to appear drastically inferior to this new form of combative entertainment.

"It's not in boxing's interest to have a show like No Holds Barred growing up," says UFC founder Rorion Gracie. "In my eyes, I've always seen UFC to be way bigger than boxing. So, I think the boxing crowd got a taste of the fear that a show like that could take over boxing. So they get a guy like John McCain to go in and say, 'Look, this thing is too violent. There's no rules to this! It's crazy—let's stop this.'"

Because the UFC had been marketed as a spectacle and a blood sport to attract mainstream viewers—boasting that victory could come in the form of knockout, submission, or even death—MMA competition was a sitting duck for McCain and his conservative followers. The general public had been conditioned by generations of boxers and by the Marquis of Queensbury's rules—which, among other things, state that you cannot hit a man on the ground or below the waist—and McCain declared that any transgression of those rules was barbaric. He portrayed the MMA style of combat as savage. "I can believe that the critics who made these decisions were ignorant," says Greco-Roman gold medalist Jeff Blatnick. "They didn't understand ground fighting. They didn't understand submission. They couldn't believe in the concept of hitting a man on the ground. Whoever said it was safer to hit a man standing up? There's way more force behind your punch standing up than there ever could be from a mounted position, or even a kneeling position."

But in his attack on the sport, which was driven by personal interests, the senator elected to focus on the "apparent dangers" and chose to ignore the fact that MMA competition is actually much safer than boxing. "I think that boxing is the most damaging sport," says submission expert Frank Shamrock. "It's just repeated blows to the brain, and you can't tap out. The sport is specifically designed to get you knocked out. Every rule points towards that, looking for the knockout, and I think there are much gentler ways." Some of these gentler ways include submission holds such as arm locks, knee locks, and choke holds—none of which cause permanent damage, as opposed to the one hundred to five hundred shots a boxer takes to the head in an average bout. In addition, the MMA competitor can honorably tap out if he feels he is taking too much abuse.

None of this mattered to the senator, who had once attended a boxing match where a competitor was slain by his opponent. He kept up his derision, appearing on *Larry King Live* ten days prior to Ultimate Ultimate '95, allying himself with Marc Ratner, the Nevada State boxing commissioner, in expressing distaste for the sport. Bob Meyrowitz was there to defend the UFC, as well Ken Shamrock, who joined them all via live feed. Meyrowitz stated that he was in favor of regulating the sport, but this didn't appear to satisfy the senator. McCain even went so far as to state that MMA "appeals to the lowest common denominator in our society."

In addition to instigating this public "debate," McCain called for the support of the governors of all fifty states. He wrote a letter to Jim Geringer, the governor of Wyoming, concerning UFC VI. He also wrote to Governor George Pataki of New York, a fellow Republican, to say how distressed he was that Pataki had let UFC VII occur in Buffalo. All of this political fervor began to make Bob Meyrowitz extremely nervous about the future of his profitable new venture. He decided to fight politi-cal power with political influence, and he hired a lobbyist.

The lobbyist began by meeting with Senate Majority Leader Frank Bruno. Meyrowitz also met with Bruno and laid out his case for the continuance of the UFC and similar events. But Meyrowitz would soon learn that although Senator McCain didn't have the power to shut his event down, he certainly did have the influence to keep it from being seen.

Extreme Fighting/November 18, 1995

While the first Ultimate Fighting Championship was still on the drawing board, film producer Donald Zuckerman was toying with his own idea of starting a full-contact mixed martial arts tournament. "Richard Crudo, a director of photography here in Hollywood, showed me a tape of Brazilian fighting," recalls Zuckerman, "and I thought it was pretty wild. He thought it might be interesting for a movie idea, and I said, 'Actually, I think it would make a good pay-per-view television show.' So that's how I got interested in it, and I tried to set up an extreme fighting pay-per-view television show."

Zuckerman, a lawyer and former owner of the Ritz nightclub in New York, had cultivated numerous entertainment-industry connections, including some at Fox International. But when he began shopping the idea around, he didn't meet with much interest or even an understanding of his concept, so he decided to discontinue his efforts. "Then I saw that the UFC did their first show," says Zuckerman, "and it got a good review. It got a write-up in the *L.A. Times*, and it was a good write-up. I said, 'Shit, let me try again.' I didn't know if they were going to do other shows. I didn't know anything about them."

Zuckerman dusted off his proposal and brought it to the sports direc-tor at Caesar's Palace, who in turn referred him to Ron Semio of ESPN2. Semio was interested and wanted to do thirteen weekly shows. Zuckerman agreed, and the deal was made. Now he needed to raise the money to make the show happen.

He first approached an associate at Fox International, who agreed to buy the foreign rights to the show. Armed with the backing of ESPN and Fox, Zuckerman contacted a friend at Polygram named John Sher. He asked Sher if he would cover the deficit and become his partner in the endeavor. Sher agreed, and everything seemed set to go.

The first event, titled Extreme Fighting, was slated for production soon after Sher's current project, Woodstock 2, was completed. Unfortunately, Sher exceeded his budget for his rock and roll sequel by twenty-six million, and he was fired from Polygram. Zuckerman's deal with Polygram left with Sher, and Zuckerman found himself without funding for his event.

In a classic marriage of sex and violence, Zuckerman found his white knight: *Penthouse* mogul Bob Guccione. The idea of a weekly MMA television series was abandoned, and it was decided that the event would go on as a pay-per-view show. Zuckerman and Guccione formed a company called Battlecade to handle the production. With the financial backing of Guccione's company, General Media, everything started falling into place. The initial plan was to hold the first Extreme Fighting in Brooklyn's Park Slope Armory on November 18, 1995.

But there was still one important aspect of the event that needed to be taken care of—recruiting the fighters. Zuckerman was not a martial artist, or even a martial arts enthusiast; he was simply a businessman looking to make some money. While searching for someone who was capable of putting the fight card together, he was introduced to world-renowned judo expert Gene LeBell. Although LeBell wasn't interested in taking on the task himself, he introduced Zuckerman to his student John Perretti.

Perretti had been a martial artist since the early seventies, and while on a quest to determine which style was the best, he had studied everything from tae kwon do to tang su do. After competing in both local point sparring matches and full contact kickboxing tournaments, he was introduced to grappling. "I met Gene LeBell," says Perretti, "and I learned that I didn't know anything about fighting."

Learning the ground game, Perretti became one of LeBell's four black belts worldwide. With his universal knowledge of the martial arts, he seemed like the perfect matchmaker for Extreme Fighting. "And since he was good-looking, articulate, and knowledgeable," says Zuckerman, "I asked him if he wanted to be an on-the-air color commentator."

Perretti got on board with a vision of his own—he wanted Extreme Fighting to be a sport rather than a spectacle. He achieved this by introducing weight classes and rounds and by designing gloves. While he was making the adjustments and recruiting fighters, Zuckerman continued with the promotions.

Because, at first, MMA wasn't overwhelmingly popular, Zuckerman couldn't generate the publicity he so desperately desired for the initial show. He contacted an acquaintance, Dan Barry, a *New York Times* reporter, in an attempt to spark some hype. Barry contacted Senator Roy

Goodman of Manhattan, who had jumped on the McCain bandwagon along with New York Governor George Pataki and New York City's outspoken mayor, Rudolph Giuliani. "I was told by the *New York Times* guy," says Zuckerman, "that Roy Goodman was going to have a press conference on the steps of City Hall the next day. So I went to it. They didn't have any major press. They didn't have ABC, NBC, or CBS affiliates. They had all the small stations, and the *Daily News*, and some shitty little local papers."

Senator Goodman promptly proclaimed the "barbarism" of the sport. Goodman was ill-informed, however, and he erroneously told the press that Extreme Fighting would take place without a referee or a doctor in attendance. "When Goodman was done," recalls Zuckerman, "I raised my hand and said, 'Excuse me, I'm actually the promoter of the show, and I'd like to say something.'"

Zuckerman refuted the senator's claims and informed the press that there would indeed be a referee, and that an experienced fight doctor would also be on hand. When asked if there were any rules for the event, Zuckerman responded in classic promoter fashion by stating, "We have three rules: no biting, no eye gouging, and no mercy." The statement ignited a media frenzy. The Extreme Fighting story, a feature article, made page three of the *Daily News*. All of a sudden, Zuckerman's phone was ringing off the hook; local affiliates were clamoring for interviews. Senator Goodman, joined by Governor Pataki and Mayor Giuliani, insisted that the event would not take place in their state.

The Brooklyn Armory, the event's venue, happened to be owned by the State of New York. When the state revoked Zuckerman's lease, the promoter did not take it lying down. "We went to State Supreme Court in Brooklyn," says Zuckerman, "and we kicked their ass. The judge said, 'You [the state] have no right to do this, and I'm enjoining you from doing it. They have a valid lease, and a right to hold the show.'"

The state's agitated politicians didn't like the court's decision, and so they appealed. The Court of Appeals, in its infinite wisdom, decided that it didn't have time to hear the case that week and postponed the hearing until the Tuesday after Extreme Fighting was to take place—meaning that the event would have to be postponed as well. Things looked bleak, but it wasn't the end for Zuckerman. The state may have succeeded in taking away his venue, but the courts and the politicians couldn't stop the event from taking place.

Zuckerman did some maneuvering. "We kept saying we were doing the show in New York, but we really weren't, and I moved it down to

North Carolina to a soundstage," explains Zuckerman. "We all just got in buses and cars and planes and drove everything down there and did the show the next day." Despite having been moved hundreds of miles in just thirty-six hours, the first Extreme Fighting was a success. With legitimate warriors battling it out in a true sporting event, actor Mr. T on the mike, and a crew of *Penthouse* Pets shaking their tails, it had all the glitz, blood, and glam necessary to entertain the masses. Zuckerman had realized his vision—now all he needed was a venue that would hold a bigger audience and allow him to put on the show without hassles.

Extreme Fighting 2/April 26, 1996

For his second show, Zuckerman looked north to Quebec, Canada. Just across the river from Montreal—in Kahnawake, a Mohawk Indian reservation—he found a five-thousand-seat indoor hockey arena. Zuckerman contacted Victor Theriault—the brother of kickboxer Jean Yves Theriault —who introduced him to a member of the Mohawk Nation named Mike Thomas. Thomas had been promoting similar MMA events, such as the Iroquois Toughman Competition, and he had recently returned from Eastern Europe, where he had been involved with another MMA start-up promotion called the International Fighting Championship.

The Mohawks assured Zuckerman that the laws in Canada were similar to those in the United States, but that they were allowed to run their territory as they saw fit. Mike Thomas had, in fact, made sure of this before reporting to Zuckerman, but then things changed. "We had met with the Quebec Athletic Commission," says Mike Thomas, "and they said it wasn't their jurisdiction, and everything was going to be fine as long as we had a sanctioning body. We met with the Mohawk Council at Kahnawake, and they checked within the laws of the Indian Act, and they found that they had jurisdiction over any type of recreation or sporting event. So they formed a commission, and they had regulated the event, but I guess leading up to the show the government started saying no, it was their jurisdiction. And it became a big political battle."

Arriving in Montreal, Zuckerman and his crew found themselves caught in a firestorm of controversy. The Quebec government wanted to shut the event down, but the Indians stood firm in their intention to host the show. This same tribe had confronted the Quebec government once before. In the summer of 1990, armed Mohawk warriors barricaded a bridge used daily by seventy thousand suburban commuters to protest a planned golf course development that would have infringed on a native cemetery. The Quebec provincial police moved in, a police officer was killed, and a seventy-eight-day standoff ensued.

To keep another conflict from arising, the Quebec government attempted to intercept Zuckerman's fighters and production crew before they even reached their destination. They took a list of names of people to look out for from an Extreme Fighting video and turned back several members of the event's cast and crew at the border, including ring announcer Gary Dell'Abate of *The Howard Stern Show*. The fighters who had already made it into Canada were relocated to nearby Ottawa, Ontario to avoid arrest.

Even though Quebec government officials had promised to leave the Mohawks to conduct their own affairs, they were determined to do as much harm to the event as they could. The day of the show, they obtained an injunction that prevented Bell Canada from transmitting the signal from the uplink to the satellite. Thinking that they had stopped the event from being broadcast, the government officials informed the press that although the show would take place as planned, it would not be seen by greedy Americans on pay-per-view. But, unbeknownst to them, Zuckerman had gotten wind of their plot from his lawyers. He made a quick deal with AT&T, and an uplink truck was sent out to the event. "We had a TeleStar on standby, ready to go. And at 7:30 [P.M.] on April 26, it went off," laughs Mike Thomas.

The night after the show, embarrassed government officials sent police to arrest the fighters and crew members involved in the event. Mayhem erupted. Although some combatants hid in their closets to avoid capture and others made their escape, eight fighters were detained. Perretti had already returned to the U.S., but upon hearing of what happened, he quickly returned to Canada to support his fighters. He was also locked up. Battlecade fought the case on behalf of its employees, and eventually the charges were dismissed when Zuckerman, who had avoided arrest, signed a statement saying he would never again bring Extreme Fighting to Quebec.

Because of the near cancelation of Zuckerman's first two shows, the pay-per-view companies were growing wary; they would not going to do another show unless Extreme Fighting was sanctioned. Determined not to lose his only way to make the event profitable, Zuckerman went searching for a state that would sanction his event and allow the show to take place without harassment. After contacting dozens of athletic commissioners, he found a home for Extreme Fighting in Oklahoma. However, while the event went on as planned, he didn't receive the hype and controversy necessary to make the show a success.

His rival Meyrowitz, on the other hand, was gaining ground in New York. He had altered the UFC rules to make the sport more palatable. This, in conjunction with the efforts of SEG's hired lobbyist, had won the support of a large number of politicians for the regulation of MMA rather than its complete banishment. As a result, Senator Goodman retracted his initial call to ban the sport and asked instead that it be placed under the direct control of the New York State Athletic Commission. The bill passed, and Governor Pataki signed it into law in July of 1996. An overjoyed Bob Meyrowitz immediately made preparations for UFC XII to take place at the Niagara Falls Civic Center on February 7, 1997.

Not Without a Fight

Zuckerman, who was struggling in Oklahoma with his Extreme Fighting, decided to capitalize on Meyrowitz's efforts. "I knew Meyrowitz had been working on the State of New York to legalize MMA," says Zuckerman. "He hired a lobbyist—he was the main guy behind getting it legalized. And he succeeded. But he was also my competitor. I knew that he was going to do a show in the Nassau Coliseum, in Nassau County, which is a suburban area outside of New York, a month after my fourth show." To one-up Meyrowitz, Zuckerman decided to move his fourth show right into the heart of Manhattan, where everyone would see him.

To get the promotional ball rolling, Zuckerman again called up Dan Barry at the *New York Times*—Barry was the very journalist who had done everything he could to get MMA banned in the state. "I didn't know he was going to do this, but he ran a huge front-page article in the *New York Times*," says Zuckerman. "It was like three columns with a picture." Two days later, the *New York Times* ran yet another article, but this time the article called for a ban on the "blood sport."

The media machine was once again churning away, and Bob Meyrowitz, who had worked so hard to get the sport legalized, was not at all happy. "As soon as the atmosphere started to change in New York," says Zuckerman, "Meyrowitz called me up and basically said, 'Hey, you've got to pull your fight out of New York, and you've got to do this, and you've got to do that'—like telling me what do. And I said, 'Hey, Bob, you don't tell me what to do.' And he got pissy with me. And that was that."

Although Meyrowitz was upset with Zuckerman for rekindling the political fire, Zuckerman believes that Meyrowitz played his part. "When we got the *New York Times* article," says Zuckerman, "I also suggested to Dan Barry that he call Bob. Bob bragged to him that he hired the lobbyist, and that was a central part of the article. And that hurt us . . . he blamed me for destroying the sport, but frankly he was doing the same thing I was doing. His intentions were to come to the Nassau Coliseum; he would have gotten the same attention from the *New York Times*. Yet he told the *L.A. Times* he was only going to smaller markets and staying out of the spotlight. It's not true."

Whoever was responsible, the fire burned. The politicians who had passed a bill sanctioning a "blood sport" they had at first so vehemently opposed were made to look ridiculous in the mainstream media, and they began plotting their retaliation.

Due to all the upheaval in the Big Apple, Zuckerman picked up his show a day before it was scheduled to happen in Manhattan and pulled out of town. Although Extreme Fighting 4 took place in Iowa at a later date, it would be the promotion's last show. "McCain was leaning on us the whole time," says Zuckerman. "We just kept on losing distribution. Firstly, we were in one hundred percent of the pay-per-view hub markets, and then Cablevision stopped carrying it, and this company stopped, and that company stopped, and finally we lost Time Warner, and we were down to fifty percent. It just didn't pay to do it anymore."

Despite Zuckerman's withdrawal from New York, Meyrowitz decided to stick it out. But just a few days before UFC XII was to take place in upstate New York, Meyrowitz received a call from a *New York Times* journalist who claimed to have the new rule book for UFC XII, issued by the New York State Athletic Commission. The journalist sent the book to Meyrowitz, who was shocked to find that his action-packed brawl was to involve no head kicking, that headgear would be mandatory, and that the octagon would have to be expanded to a forty-foot diameter from its original thirty-foot diameter. Meyrowitz, along with competitor Dan Severn and referee John McCarthy, appeared before the commission to dispute the new rules. Their arguments were rejected. If the politicians couldn't ban the UFC, they were simply going to make it unmarketable.

Because of the heat brought on by the overzealous New York politicians and the manipulation of the rules by the State Athletic Commission, Meyrowitz believed the show would be compromised. In a move similar to Zuckerman's, Meyrowitz packed up UFC XII and moved the entire event to his alternate location in Dothan, Alabama in less than twenty-four hours. Although some of the fighters walked into the weigh-ins with little or no sleep, the crowd was treated to one of the most exciting UFCs to date.

Meyrowitz and Zuckerman were not the only promoters taking a bashing from the politicians. The UFC and Extreme Fighting had laid the groundwork for MMA competition in America, and promoters all across the nation were creating similar events in the hope of experiencing the same kind of success. Although most of these organizations failed to put on shows of any consequence and turned out to be flashes in the MMA pan, promoters like Monte Cox, who possessed marketing know-how and the ability to secure the talent necessary for a successful show, still didn't have it easy by any means. Just as Zuckerman and Meyrowitz had been blocked by the political establishment in New York, Cox found himself mired in red tape and controversy in his home state of Iowa.

From the Ground Up

Monte Cox was not a traditional martial artist; he was a boxer who had grown up on the Marquis of Queensbury's rules. After almost two-dozen professional boxing matches, he retired from the ring and began promoting the sport of boxing, working with networks such as ESPN and USA. In addition to this, Cox was the editor of several newspapers, including the *Quad City Times* of Davenport, Iowa. He knew little about MMA competition until a local athlete by the name of Pat Miletich spoke to him about an MMA event in which he was competing. "He was telling me what he was doing," remembers Cox, "and I thought it sounded crazy at the time. I went and watched him work out, and I liked what I saw. It was a lot more of a sport than I thought."

Although Miletich was new to the sport himself, he was a well-versed martial artist. When his wrestling career came to an end after college, he found himself bored and discontented, and he decided to learn how to fight. He started off with kickboxing, and once he stepped into the ring, his record grew to an amazing 12-0. But upon seeing Royce Gracie dominate the UFC with his jiu-jitsu skills, Miletich realized his fighting system was far from complete and began learning how to grapple. Just as he was polishing a system of fighting that meshed his striking and grappling abilities, he was approached by a friend named Tom Letulli, who was putting on an MMA competition called Battle of the Masters, to be held in neighboring Illinois. "I went with him to Chicago when he fought in the Battle of the Masters," says Cox. "It was an eight-man tournament, and he just destroyed everybody and won the money. When we came back, I did a story on him."

Miletich wasn't through impressing Cox, however. Several months later, when Miletich returned to Chicago to fight in the next Battle of the Masters, Cox was once again by his side. As was the case with the first tourney, there were no weight classes, but that didn't stop Miletich, who only weighed 170 pounds, from once again running through the competition. "After that one, Miletich tried talking me into doing an MMA show," remembers Cox, "but I wasn't actually interested in it at the time. Then, after a while, he talked me into doing it."

Cox shifted his promoting talents to MMA, and, with the help of Miletich, the first Quad City Ultimate was born. The event was held on January 20, 1996 in the Mark of the Quad Cities, a ten-thousand-seat venue. It was a tremendous success, and, in front of eight thousand spectators, Iowa's very own Pat Miletich won both his bouts of the evening.

From that night on, Cox was hooked on the sport, just as he had been hooked on boxing. The second Quad City Ultimate was equally successful, and it saw Pat Miletich in a classic knock-down, drag-out brawl with five-time Japanese bare-knuckle champion Yasunari Matsumoto. "I really didn't know what to expect," says Miletich, "He was a good judo guy and a good grappler too. I fought him and actually broke his elbow and put him in a joint lock about two or three minutes into the fight. He escaped from the move after I broke the capsule in his arm. He got back up to his feet and tried to guillotine me with the arm I had just broken; he had me in the guillotine for about three minutes before I took him back down and finally choked him out."

With the successes of his first two endeavors, Monte Cox grew determined to put on more events, despite the fact that he was entering the scene smack-dab in the middle of the mess created by political pressures. "We had a lot of problems," admits Cox. "We had letters written to the editors of papers to stop it. I had to go through athletic commissions and city councils. We had some wars."

Still, Cox didn't blame SEG's early UFC marketing strategies for erecting all those political barricades. "It's easy to jump on SEG and say they did a lot of the wrong things," says Cox. "SEG was faced with a product that nobody knew what it was. They opted to go for the sensationalism of calling it 'the most brutal sport' to get recognized. And it worked. They got up to 500,000 pay-per-view buys. It worked tremendously. But the same thing that caused their success ended up being their downfall. Pretty soon, word got out to politicians and such. They started believing the hype: the 'two men enter, one man leaves'; and that it was the most brutal sport. They started trying to stop the thing on that basis, on what SEG was saying. Without SEG, we would probably never have the sport, but by the way they went about it, it dropped the sport down. Now we're having to build it back up."

Cox wasn't battling it out alone, however. Miletich was right by his side, doing radio and television interviews and participating in various debates concerning the sport's legitimacy. He emphasized that MMA is a "thinking man's sport," and not just a crew of "punch-drunk boxers." He pointed out that a vast majority of MMA competitors were college educated, and that the sport itself demonstrated the highest levels of professional athleticism. "I tell all the young guys that are coming up that they've got it really easy," says Miletich, "because all they need to worry about is training for their fights. At the time I was training for fights, I didn't know if I was even training for anything because the sport was going downhill so fast."

Since the first Quad City Ultimate, Cox has successfully put on almost 140 MMA competitions, the most popular of which was the Extreme Challenge. "I've only been shut down once," says Cox. "That was a show in Michigan. After I'd already done three, they came up with a law from 1879 and shut one of the shows down. I moved it to Iowa and put it on anyway. I lost money pretty badly, but I've never canceled a show."

Through the efforts of promoters like Monte Cox and diehards like Pat Miletich, MMA was able to plant some very tenacious roots. Although the politics of the day were against the sport, the fact that promoters, fighters, and fans alike continued to breath life into MMA brought a ray of hope to the sport's ever-darkening future prospects.

CHAPTER 10

BRAWL
Ground and Pound

With Dan "the Beast" Severn working his corner, Don Frye stepped into the octagon for the first time on February 16, 1996 in San Juan, Puerto Rico. He would do battle with local street fighter Thomas Ramirez—a man who was twice Frye's weight and claimed to have two hundred back alley victories under his belt. It was the first bout of the night in the David versus Goliath tournament, and the atmosphere in the sweltering Ruben Rodriguez Coliseum was charged with anticipation. "My ex-wife used to get on my ass about having these wild-eyed get-rich-quick schemes," remembers Frye, "and that was the first thing I thought when I was standing there in the ring. I thought, 'Me and my wild-eyed get-rich-quick schemes!' I was also thinking, 'Man that guy is big.'"

Referee John McCarthy slashed his hand through the air, and UFC VIII got under way. Moving towards his mammoth opponent with his hands riding low, Frye suddenly got nailed with a jab. "He hit me, and I was like, 'Goddamn, he broke my nose,'" says Frye. "I thought, 'Wake up, Frye, you're in a fight!'"

Frye woke up all right. Ducking below his opponent's swinging fists, he lunged in with four hard jabs. Although the first three missed their mark, the fourth landed flush to the jaw of Ramirez. All 410 pounds of the Puerto Rican went limp as he fell to the canvas. Frye went in for the kill, hovering over his downed foe. He cracked Ramirez with a solid right before realizing he was already out cold. It seemed impossible: he had won in just ten seconds. Having worked out the cobwebs, Frye was charged with energy. "I don't want to say I was cocky, but I was confident that I was going to win the whole thing."

* * *

Don Frye was born the son of a lieutenant colonel in the U.S. Air Force, and his family was constantly on the move. "We shifted about every year and a half," says Frye. "About the time I wore out my welcome in the town, it was time to leave. It worked out perfectly." After having lived in almost a dozen states, Frye and his family moved west and started putting

DREAM STAGE ENTERTAINMENT

The Predator Don Frye at the Pride Fighting Championships.

down roots in Arizona when Don was in the ninth grade. With this newfound stability, Frye discovered wrestling. "As a freshman, I pinned everybody in the first round. Then they moved me up to varsity halfway through the season. Shit—I was just a big, strong, dumb cowboy. Once they moved me up to varsity, I started taking my lumps."

Frye continued to take those lumps on the wrestling mat at Arizona State University. But just as he was beginning to make an impact at the collegiate level, he suffered a shoulder injury that ended his season. While sitting on the sidelines, he watched Arizona State go on to win the 1988 national title. This made Frye determined to get back on the mat, and he began rehabilitating his shoulder.

He came back strong the next year. He won the Las Vegas Olympic qualifiers in both Greco-Roman and freestyle wrestling, and he placed fifth in the National Freestyle Competition. Having impressed many scouts with his victories, Frye was recruited by the prestigious Oklahoma State for his final year, and he competed internationally in both Greco-Roman and freestyle.

After college, Frye was looking for a change of pace, and he decided to try his hand at boxing. His trainers set up a one-year plan for him to go pro, but after only three short months of training he found himself competing in his first professional bout. "I was 5-2-1," explains Frye. "The thing is, I was good, but not great. And only great guys make it. But I was good enough to get out at the right time." Unfortunately, he didn't have all that much to look forward to when he got out. Entangled in a bad marriage and getting hell from the in-laws, he dropped out of athletics for four years and worked full time as a firefighter. Although he eventually began toying with judo, it was not enough to quell his competitive nature.

His future was looking bleak, but then Frye caught the break that he needed. "First, I end up getting a divorce, which is the best thing that ever happened to me. Then I saw Dan Severn win the UFC. Dan was the assistant wrestling coach when I was at Arizona State. After the divorce, I picked up the phone and said, 'Hey, Dan, remember me? Can you get me into this?' Dan was coming to Arizona to train, and he needed a training partner, so I was basically his main throwing dummy for the Ultimate Ultimate '95. He ended up winning, and he put in a good word for me with the UFC. The next thing I know, I get a phone call from them to compete in February."

So Frye began training in earnest with Severn. To get him ready for the event, Frye hooked him up with an underground fight in Atlanta. "It was supposed to be a high-dollar thing," says Frye, "but when I got there they said they couldn't pay me. I was there, so I thought I'd fight. My bout was against a guy who was a former Navy SEAL. A real nice guy. He came up to me and said, 'We're not getting paid for this shit. I won't hit you if you don't hit me.' I said, 'Yeah, sure.' He held true to his word, and I submitted him with a choke."

Frye returned to Arizona and continued his training with Severn. While the two were working on a fight strategy, UFC owner Bob Meyrowitz was working on a strategy of his own. Because of the mounting political attacks on MMA, Meyrowitz had moved the show to Puerto Rico. But Senator John McCain's influence extended even to the West Indian island. "We were in court for four days," says Big John McCarthy, "trying to make it so we wouldn't get shut down. There was a lot of pressure on everyone."

UFC VIII—David versus Goliath/February 16, 1996
(San Juan, Puerto Rico)

Frye felt none of the political pressure surrounding the UFC when he arrived in Puerto Rico. "Puerto Rico was great," he recalls. "I just loved it. For one thing, I was just a hillbilly happy to be on an island." Sporting a cowboy-like mustache and black trunks, he planned on unleashing his alter ego—"the Predator." Some thought he had earned the nickname by knocking opponents out in the boxing ring or slamming fellow wrestlers on the mat. Neither was correct. "I had an English bulldog," says Frye, "a great English bulldog. His name was Wizzer McGator. He weighed about 110 pounds, and he had the undershot jaw and good canine teeth. You'd pull his lips back and he looked like the Predator from the movie. I really loved that dog. He was my best friend, so I [took on the nickname] to honor him."

However he acquired the nickname, Frye displayed his predatory nature in the ring with Thomas Ramirez. After knocking his first opponent stupid in just ten seconds, he stepped back into the octagon to see if he could do the same to boxer Sam Adkins in the semifinals. Not wanting to trade punches with the boxer, Frye quickly shot in and took his bald-headed opponent to the mat. As if trying to beat his ten-second record, the Predator went wild with his right hand, splitting open Adkins's face. After the boxer had swallowed almost two dozen shots, referee John McCarthy intervened and put an end to the abuse.

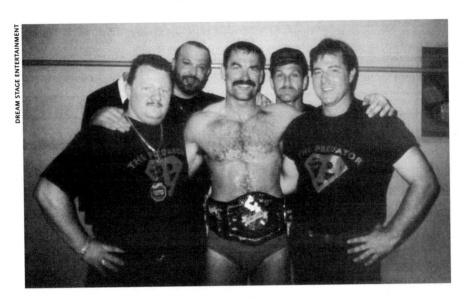

Don Frye and his crew.

Frye had hardly broken a sweat in his first two fights. But for the finals he would be taking on a much wilder opponent—258-pound Gary "Big Daddy" Goodridge, who had been making his own impression on the other side of the bracket.

Goodridge was a Canadian amateur boxing champion, and although he was not a well-versed martial artist, he was known for his wild fighting style. "Me and a couple of friends were sitting down watching a tape of UFC III," says Goodridge. "Before you know it, I saw Remco Pardoel smashing the hell out of Orlando with elbows to the head. My buddies were saying, 'You can do this!' In my mind I was thinking, 'Yeah, but I don't want to do this. Man, can this thing be legal? They can't allow this stuff to be going on.' There was a 1-800 number to call for UFC paraphernalia. Before you know it, I was talking to Art Davie on the phone. I thought I could do it just on my boxing abilities."

Goodridge's boxing skills and natural athleticism proved to be more than enough. He all but killed his quarterfinal opponent, Paul Herrera, one of Tank Abbott's cohorts. "Going into the match, I was thinking I could lose to anybody but this guy," says Goodridge. "My friends who helped me out with the fight told me how he was racist, and that he belonged to a racist group." Although Goodridge outweighed his opponent by seventy-three pounds, he wasn't taking the match lightly.

When Herrera charged for the takedown, Goodridge sprawled and quickly used his strength to his advantage. Securing one of Herrera's arms between his legs and grasping the other with his left hand (known in wrestling as a "crucifix"), he unleashed a series of bashing elbows to his opponent's face. The first one landed to Herrera's temple, knocking him out cold. But Big Daddy did not stop there. He dropped seven more elbows, as if he were trying to take Herrera's head off. It was a terrifying sight.

"I let the match go on too long," says referee John McCarthy. "That was definitely my fault. It should have been stopped sooner. I looked at Gary Goodridge, and I knew who Paul was. I really thought if Paul got Gary down, that would be the position he wanted to be in. He shot in on him right away and started to take him down. I moved a certain way, and by the time I realized what was happening, Gary was whaling the hell out of him in a crucifix."

Goodridge's next fight, against Lion's Den submission fighter Jerry Bohlander, would not be so one-sided. Outskilled by his smaller opponent, Big Daddy relied on his strength and punching power. Not able to finish Bohlander on the ground, Goodridge stood up and dropped a solid right cross that knocked Bohlander out, earning himself a spot in the finals.

"At that point, I just couldn't believe I was there," says Goodridge. "I had no strategy going into the fight with Frye. I was very, very exhausted from fighting five minutes prior to that fight. I didn't know cardio was necessary for the fighting game. I just thought I'd try my best."

Don Frye came into the finals having fought just over a minute in both his previous bouts combined. Despite the wrestling edge he had over his opponent, he chose to fight Goodridge standing up. He showed just how well-rounded a fighter he was when he landed a series of jabs to Goodridge's face.

Goodridge decided he would rather face his opponent on the mat. Clinging to Frye's back, eating several reverse elbows, Goodridge picked the Predator up and threw him through the air. As Frye was scrambling back to his feet, Big Daddy launched a kick that whistled past Frye's head. The good-natured cowboy simply grinned at Goodridge, as if to thank him for the wild ride.

The Predator got back to boxing. Driving Goodridge back into the fence, he landed six uppercuts to his adversary's jaw. This is not where Goodridge wanted to be, and again he tossed Frye through the air, this time mounting the wrestler's back as he landed. But Frye knew the ground game better than most, and he grabbed hold of Goodridge's ankles and scooted out between his legs. As he made this clever escape, he swept Big Daddy to the ground. Just as Frye was getting busy with punches, Goodridge tapped out.

"I knew I was going to win," says Frye. "Gary is obviously bigger and stronger, but I came in there with over five hundred competitive victories in wrestling. A lot of people choke because of the crowds and the atmosphere. I was used to it. I had wrestled in coliseums before—in Nebraska, Iowa, all that good stuff. I mean, shit, when I wrestled in Nebraska, we went out of bounds a couple times and they were kicking me and all that! It's just part of the business."

Don Frye, at 206 pounds, had won the David versus Goliath tournament. He ended the night by commenting on what the fans could expect of him. "This is going to be my career for several years. I will be on top of the game, and I will stay on top of the game."

Frye Up the Competition

After his tournament victory in UFC VIII, Don Frye returned to Arizona and began training for UFC IX, which was to be held in Detroit, Michigan, on May 17, 1996. But when he arrived at the event, he, along with the other fighters, was surprised to find that some dramatic changes had been instituted. First, the tournament-style competition had been replaced by single bouts. There were also some changes to the rules—and these hadn't been made by UFC officials, but by the courts. Once again, the show's promoters had found themselves involved in a legal war when the district attorney attempted to shut them down. The courtroom battle went right down to the wire. Finally, at 4:30 P.M. on the day of the show, the judge ruled that the bouts would be allowed to continue, but only under strict stipulations, the most damaging of which were no head butts and no closed-fist strikes to the head. Although the fighters were informed of these rules, it was hinted that there would be some leniency on the part of the referee.

The first bout of the night was between Cal Worsham and kickboxer Zane Frazier. Despite the new rules, this match produced one of the most serious injuries experienced in the octagon to date. Just a minute into the match, Worsham rushed in to take his opponent to the mat and ate a solid knee to the chest. He was pumped with adrenaline and had no idea how much damage he'd sustained. Thinking his breath had simply been knocked out of him, he shot in and took Frazier to the ground, attacking him with head butts, punches to the face, and elbows, until the kickboxer tapped out.

Sucking up his pain, Worsham made his victory lap around the octagon and then walked back down the aisle. But once he was out of sight of the crowd, he collapsed. He was rushed to the hospital, where it was discovered that he had a punctured lung. "I beat Zane," says Worsham, "but it almost cost me my life. Sometimes even when you win, you lose."

In Frye's only bout of the evening, he stepped into the octagon to take on a Carlson Gracie protégé, Amaury Bitetti. Despite the fact that the jiu-jitsu tactician was boasting an unbelievable record of 150-1, Frye elected to challenge himself by fighting Bitetti's game, and he kept much of the action on the ground. Dominating the entire match, Frye forced a referee stoppage after landing several stiff knees and a series of strong hooks to his opponent's face and head.

The champ was on the move, and he began preparing for his upcoming fights in UFC X, to be held in Birmingham, Alabama, on December 7, 1996. Frye studied his future opponents, and, judging by their backgrounds, he was pretty sure he would meet Mark "the Hammer" Coleman in the finals. Although Coleman was new to the sport, Frye understood the Hammer's background as a world-class wrestler and took him quite seriously, even though, in a prefight interview, he displayed typical Frye bravado by stating that he didn't feel there was anybody who could "handle" him.

Frye proved his point when he mounted his first UFC X opponent, Mark Hall, and, over the course of ten minutes, delivered dozens of shots to the body that blackened Hall's ribs. At one point, Frye begged Hall to tap out so he wouldn't have to hurt him anymore. When Hall refused, McCarthy intervened.

Frye's next fight, with kickboxer Brian Johnston, proved to be more difficult. Johnston stood toe to toe with the Predator, dominating the fight from his feet. But, not to be outdone, Frye shot in and took Johnston to the mat. The tide of battle quickly turned as Frye delivered a vicious elbow strike that opened a sinister-looking cut on Johnston's head. With blood flowing down his face, the kickboxer tapped out. To the spectators, and to Frye himself, it looked as if he was unstoppable. Then along came the Hammer . . .

The Hammer Comes Down

Growing up in a small town called Freemont, two hours north of
Columbus, Ohio, Mark Coleman set monumental goals for his future.
He excelled in baseball, but football and wrestling were his true loves, and
he became determined to play in the NFL or win an Olympic medal. But
after graduating from St. Joseph's High School, he didn't get recruited by
a Division One football school as he had hoped, and he found himself at
a crossroads. Setting aside his NFL dream for the time being, he opted
to accept a baseball scholarship from the University of Miami. While he
was at that institution, he pursued wrestling in an attempt to make at
least one of his dreams come true.

The University of Miami couldn't provide Coleman with adequate
wrestling partners or trainers, so he trained on his own; and after becoming two-time Mid-American champion and placing fourth in the National
Collegiate Athletic Association Division One finals as a junior, he earned
his ticket to the big leagues and was recruited by Ohio State. "I liked that
concept of winning or losing depending on me," claims Coleman. "I
didn't have to worry about teammates." With his future in his own hands,
Coleman became a man driven to the point of obsession. All his toil paid
off when he became a national champion as a Buckeye in his senior year.
Then, without even taking time to relish his victory, he set his sights on
the Olympics.

The year 1991 belonged to Coleman. In Cuba, he won a gold medal
in the Pan-American games. Then he won the United States National
Freestyle Championships before bringing home a silver medal from the
World Championships. Having remained undefeated for six entire tournaments, he stepped up to the plate in 1992 and made the Olympic team.
A month later, he traveled to Barcelona intent on achieving his goal of
bringing home an Olympic gold medal.

"I placed seventh in the Olympics," says Coleman. "A disappointing
seventh. I was probably seeded number two, and it was not a good day to
have a bad day. Both guys who beat me in the Olympics I had beaten six
months earlier. To say the least, I don't think I performed really well. No
excuses—I just got beat." Coleman spiraled into a depression, and his
training all but ceased. He had worked all his life for the chance to win
an Olympic medal, and when it didn't happen, his drive left him. Four
more years just seemed too long to wait.

"I lost the eye of the tiger and started partying," he admits. "I was
still acting like I was trying to be a world champion and that I was going

to try to make the '96 Olympic team, but when I look back at it, I realize I was just going through the motions." As Coleman slipped in his training, he also slipped in the U.S. rankings. In an attempt to regain his Olympic dream, Coleman trained for the 1995 Sunkist Open, beating the world champion, Kurt Angle (currently a professional wrestler with the WWF). But afterwards, he again fell into a personal slump. "I didn't pay my dues, and when '96 came around, I lost in the semifinals of the Olympic trials. It was sort of a blessing in disguise."

That blessing came in the form of a man named Richard Hamilton, who approached Coleman at the Olympic trials. Hamilton was scouting several wrestlers, including future MMA competitors Mark Kerr and Tom Erikson, for the upcoming UFC X. Although all three of them were up for the slot, Coleman persuaded Hamilton that he was the best choice for the show. "If I would have won the competition, I would have gone to the Olympics," said Coleman. "But since I lost, thirty days later I was in UFC X."

It was the opportunity of a lifetime. "All of a sudden," says Coleman, "I'm put in a position to make some money. In wrestling you don't make a dime. I put in thirty of the hardest days of my life getting ready for UFC X. Fighting is a little different than wrestling—when you lose a fight, you don't lose by points, you lose by punishment. For the first time since '92, I really, really trained seriously."

Part of that training involved research. He watched tapes of the previous UFCs, analyzing the various styles of his competition. But, most of all, realizing just how important conditioning was in such a tournament, he got into world-class shape. "I knew that was my belt," explains Coleman. "I really didn't feel in the beginning I had to learn a whole lot to be successful. With the head butt being legal, it was really kind of the truth. I really wasn't that nervous. I probably should have been. I was really confident I could beat the other guys. Nobody knew who I was, but I knew what I could do."

Coleman displayed that confidence in his first UFC X bout, with Israeli karate practitioner Moti Horenstein. Wasting no time in taking the Jean-Claude Van Damme look-alike down, Coleman mounted the kickboxer and began dropping rights and lefts, snapping Horenstein's head back and forth. When that didn't take his opponent out, Coleman moved to the side mount and dropped a knee into the kickboxer's head. Still Horenstein hung in there, all the while rapping bothersome knuckles into the back of Coleman's skull. The Hammer finally finished the fight with three large hooks to Horenstein's head. "It really wasn't as easy as I thought it would be," says Coleman. "I knew he was just a straight karate guy. I anticipated taking him down, and I didn't think it was going to last long at all. I found out real quick that these men have real big hearts, and they're not going to quit just because you're hitting them a few times. I found out these guys can take a hell of a punch."

In reaction to this new discovery, Coleman went backstage and told his manager that he was going to take off his gloves, hoping it would add power to his punches. Fortunately, his manager knew what damage a bare-fisted strike could do to a hand, and he convinced Coleman to keep the gloves on for his semifinal bout with powerful striker Gary "Big Daddy" Goodridge.

Not wanting to trade punches with the Canadian powerhouse, Coleman managed to take Goodridge to the ground before he could even throw a blow. Then the Hammer went to work with his secret weapon—head butts. But Goodridge outlasted the abuse, and, using his strength, he worked his way back to his feet. Coleman, not wanting to let his opponent unleash his strikes, clung to Goodridge's back, landing a series of uppercuts from behind. When the two broke apart several minutes later, Coleman was winded, and it looked as if the fight was in Goodridge's favor as he started to throw leather. But, in going for the knockout, Big Daddy left himself open for the takedown. Once on the mat, Coleman mounted Goodridge's back. Knowing there was nothing more he could do, Goodridge tapped out. "In all my wrestling years, I was normally the strongest guy on the mat," says Coleman. "In all my fights, it's been the same way as well. But Gary Goodridge . . . he's one man who I can say equaled me in strength."

However winded Coleman may have been after his semifinal bout, his stamina training paid off when he stepped into the octagon to face Don Frye. After bringing the Predator to the floor, he spent almost twelve minutes landing knees, elbows, punches, and head butts. But nothing he could deliver could put Frye away. "I was truly amazed that at the seven-minute mark Don Frye was still underneath me, and he was still going," says Coleman. "I was getting real worried. I was wondering why this guy wasn't stopping, and why the ref wouldn't stop it. And I was also getting very tired."

After seven grueling minutes, both of Frye's eyes were swollen shut and his face was covered with blood. And still he refused to give in. "I had a premonition about two weeks before that I was going to lose," recalls Frye. "I don't want to make excuses or anything, but I woke up that morning and I was sick. I had a fever and didn't have any energy. I was dehydrated going into the Coleman fight. The doctor came in and asked if I was okay. I looked at my guys and said, 'I'm done. I'm finished. But if you'll hang with me, let's go out there and do it.'"

Even with the fever and the abuse he was taking, Frye refused to give in to the pounding of the Hammer. "I don't get my thrills out of hurting people," says Coleman. "I don't want to hurt anybody. All I'm looking to do is perform well, put on a good show for the fans, and, most importantly, win the fight and get my hand raised." The bout didn't come to an end until Coleman dropped two elbows to Frye's face, causing referee McCarthy to do what Frye himself could not.

"I don't quit," Frye says humbly, "and that's the best thing about me. And God willing I never will. I got more respect from the Coleman fight than I did any other fight. When you fight, you either go to the party afterwards or you go to the hospital. It's pretty much fifty-fifty."

Unfortunately for Frye, that night he went to the hospital.

Coleman's Reign of Terror

Mark Coleman was the new UFC champion. "It was one of the greatest moments of my life," says Coleman. "Truly an overwhelming feeling of accomplishment at that point. I had been through some rough times leading up to that. I had never made a dime in my life, so at that moment I felt on top of the world."

Coleman's victory at UFC X signaled the dawn of a new era in MMA competition. His superlative wrestling and devastating head butts gave birth to a new fighting style that Coleman himself coined "ground and pound." Two months after his victory over Frye, Coleman returned to UFC XI, held in Augusta, Georgia, on September 20, 1996. He wanted to prove that the victory wasn't a fluke. After laying the smack-down on both Julian Travers and Brian Johnston, he was set to meet Scott Ferrozzo in the finals. But Ferrozzo dropped out after an exhausting bout with Tank Abbott, and his alternate claimed an injury. Having fought just two fights, Coleman was once again declared the champion and awarded $75,000. To give the fans more of the entertainment they had come to see, Coleman and his training partner, Kevin Randleman, staged a wrestling demonstration in the octagon as the crowd slowly filtered out.

Coleman was not only making a name for himself, but he was also becoming a wealthy man. He fired his manager, Richard Hamilton, because, Coleman explains, "We had a big falling out. He was basically a crook. He became my manager, and then a month later he tells me he's in a witness protection program." With his finances squared away, Coleman began training for the Ultimate Ultimate '96, but he was forced to pull out three weeks before the show for medical reasons. "I was diagnosed with thyroid problems and had to be put on Synthroid," he says. "I wasn't prepared to go."

Conquering his illness, he would come back strong for his most publicized matchup yet—in UFC XII, held on July 12, 1996, in Birmingham, Alabama. Coleman would be fighting fellow wrestler and former UFC champion Dan "the Beast" Severn for the first unified heavyweight title belt. "I had some mixed emotions going into that fight," says Coleman. "Back in the beginning, everyone had a lot of respect for people who [shared] their martial arts background. Wrestlers really stuck with wrestlers."

Amid the flashing lights and roaring crowd, the two wrestlers met in the center of the octagon, stalking each other for a brief moment before Severn shot in for a single-leg takedown. Coleman blocked it with a sprawl, taking the opportunity to slip his muscular arm around Severn's head and cinch down. Writhing and backing up like a dog with his head stuck in a bag, Severn broke free of the choke—but then he had the 240-pound Hammer storming at him, throwing a barrage of strikes. Severn got nailed with several shots before he ducked low and lunged in. Again Coleman sprawled, and after a brief scramble on the ground, Severn was forced into a crouch. Coleman rode on his back, and it would have looked like a classic wrestling match if it weren't for Coleman's pounding fists.

In a desperate attempt to save himself, Severn rolled onto his back, allowing Coleman to take the mount. The Hammer was in the prime position of destruction, but he did not deliver his trademark assault of elbows and head butts. "With Dan Severn, maybe I was thinking I didn't really want to hurt him," admits Coleman. "I just wanted to beat him." To accomplish this goal, Coleman slipped off the Beast and into the side mount, grabbing Severn in a headlock. He cranked Severn's chin to his chest, and although the Beast mounted his own feeble attack, slapping at Coleman's head, he eventually tapped. In just under three minutes, Mark Coleman tamed the Beast and was declared the first unified UFC Heavyweight Champion. "That was a supercool feeling," says Coleman, "because I felt that was for the first world title. It was great to beat him, because he has many accomplishments and is a hell of a fighter."

After this fight, Severn left the UFC, but by no means did he leave the sport of MMA. He went on to compete in more than two-dozen events, including the Extreme Challenge. "I think I'm the only UFC competitor who does all these small shows," says Severn. "I'm trying to help out the sport. There are a lot of fighters out there who only think about themselves. I'm trying to educate people about this sport."

Even though Severn remained active in MMA competition, he still had a family to feed. Following in the footsteps of Ken Shamrock, he joined the ranks of the WWF. His presence on weekly television did not last long, however. "They found out he couldn't do the WWF type wrestling," says Severn's former manager, Phyllis Lee. "And they let him ride his contract out."

Although Severn didn't achieve superstar statue, he enjoyed professional wrestling. "But then I also enjoy the full contact competition," he says. "My window of opportunity in the latter was very limited upon even starting. I started at thirty-six. I knew that I was going to squeak out a couple of years, and that was probably going to be about it. I'm surprised I'm still out there right now. I would like to have at least one last hurrah in the octagon, and I actually would prepare for it. I would like to finish it the same way I started."

A True Predator

Don Frye shared Severn's sentiment, and, despite having to spend a night in the hospital after his encounter with the Hammer, he continued on to compete in MMA undaunted. He returned to the UFC in Ultimate Ultimate '96, held in Birmingham, Alabama on July 7. In the quarterfinals, he defeated Gary Goodridge for the second time by wearing him down to exhaustion; and he beat Mark Hall for the third time in the semifinals via ankle lock. But stepping into the octagon for his final bout of the evening, Frye found himself up against the infamous Tank Abbott, who was having one of his better evenings after coming off a suspension for starting the brawl in the crowd at UFC VIII. After tossing Cal Worsham around the ring in the quarters, Abbott knocked out Steve Nelmark in the semifinals in classic Tank style.

The final bout of Ultimate Ultimate '96 proved to be the most exciting match of the evening. Right out of the gate, Tank landed a jab that knocked Frye on his back. As the Predator scrambled back to his feet, Abbott rushed forward, launching a series of missiles at the wrestler's face. Instead of trying for the takedown, Frye opted to go toe to toe with the experienced street fighter. Although he landed several good punches, Abbott got the

*Gilbert Yvel delivers a flying knee to Don Frye
at the Pride Fighting Championships.*

better of him. "I knew I could take my lumps," says Frye, "and I could take a beating and keep going. A lot of guys who are superior, when they get behind they falter."

After eating half a dozen shots to the head, Frye had wobbly legs, and his face was split open. It didn't look good for the Predator—until Tank tripped over his own feet and toppled to the canvas. A busted-up Frye quickly leapt on Abbott's back, sinking in a choke that forced the pit bull to tap out. Abbott was not pleased. Referee John McCarthy tried to keep him in the ring for the official announcements, but Abbott pushed him off and left the building with his crew.

"I really don't have a game plan," says Frye. "I'm not smart enough for a game plan. The thing is, I like to look the critter in the eye. I have a stupid streak . . . I like to beat the guys at their own game. That's why I fought Abbott standing up; that's why I fought Bitetti on the ground. Just to see if I could do it."

Although Frye was declared the victor, he sure didn't look like one. Along with the damage to his face, he had acquired a broken bone in his right hand that would require a temporary steel pin. This was the last MMA competition he would be involved in for some time. Shortly after Ultimate Ultimate '96, Frye left the UFC and headed east, making a move to New Japan Pro Wrestling, with its worked bouts. "They were looking for a UFC fighter," says Frye. "Originally they went for Ken Shamrock, for obvious reasons—because of all the titles that he won. He negotiated a deal, and they gave him a contract. Then he ran over to the WWF. So they were out a UFC fighter. Brad Regan, who was the American booker for New Japan, was friends with Jeff Blatnick. He called Jeff and asked whom he would recommend. Jeff, being a great guy, recommended me."

Frye hung in with New Japan for five years, but his past MMA defeats still haunted him—most notably his loss to Mark Coleman. "I just had the urge to go back and fight again. That Coleman thing still bothered me," chuckles Frye. "I'm just not mature enough to let it go after five years." Despite his urge to fight again, Frye was not thrilled about the transformation of the sport. "They ruined it. They watered it down. If they add any more rules, they're going to call it tennis."

Frye's return to MMA competition would happen in the Japanese organization Pride, where he'd face Dutch fighter Gilbert Yvel. It had been some time since the Predator had roamed the rings of MMA. "I used to think the tournament style was great," says Frye, "but now, at my age, I think the single fights are great. I think the tournament is better for the fans because it tells a story, and they can get involved in it. They see the guys come through, and it's a hell of a lot tougher. The thing is, anybody can win one or two fights in a night, but it takes a set of balls to fight a third fight. At that point you don't even warm up; it's just take off your shirt and go."

But before Frye could make his comeback, he would have to over-come several obstacles. While training for the fight, he received some devastating news. His New Japan Pro Wrestling companion and friend Brian Johnston had suffered a stroke. "So New Japan asked me if I would come back and take Brian's place, and I said sure, because they had been so good to me," says Frye. "So I ended up stepping up my training sched-ule, and I went with them for three weeks. Then, as Murphy's Law would have it, I got hurt in the last match, which was seven days before the Pride fight. I ended up pulling my abductor in my right thigh. So I took four days off, and when I went back to train again I tore it right away."

Frye couldn't train for the entire week before the bout with Yvel. All his coaches could do was give him acupuncture treatments and massages, tape him up, and shoot him full of lidocaine prior to the bout. The fight was nasty, and it ended with Yvel being disqualified for repeated foul play. "He gouged my eye out!" says Frye. "He stuck his fingers down to like his second knuckle. I figured I didn't do too bad for a one-legged blind man. All respect to Gilbert, though. He's one of the toughest guys around."

After making a successful comeback, Frye was still hungry for a rematch with the Hammer. "There are some great fighters out there. It's a great sport—probably the toughest sport out there," claims Frye. "I'm hoping I'll get the belt and then challenge Mark. I have all the respect in the world for Mark; I have to—he beat the shit out of me."

Frye had sustained plenty of injuries during his fighting career. While battling with Coleman, he suffered a broken occipital, and a year to the day after he fought Abbott, he rebroke his hand. This time, the damage was more serious, and a permanent steel plate had to be implanted. He had two shoulder operations to clean out the garbage that had built up in his joints. His nose was broken seven times; he suffered broken ankles, blown knees, sciatic nerve damage, a broken tailbone, and tendon damage; he had two herniated disks that required neck surgery. "It's all part of the business," Frye smiles. "It beats the hell out of working for a living."

So Frye's excitement about continuing his MMA career remained unabated. He locked his sights on two goals—the Pride championship title and a rematch with Mark "the Hammer" Coleman—and he never wavered.

CHAPTER 11

To Fight Another Day

While many MMA promoters were determined to mount their events in the United States, there were some who decided to break away from political restraints by putting on events overseas. This was the case with the International Fighting Championship (IFC). The first event was held on March 30, 1996, in Kiev, Ukraine, but although it played out thousands of miles from McCain and his followers, the event was far from hassle-free. Staging their show in the aftermath of the Soviet Union's breakup, the promoters found themselves up against a different type of politics—one ruled by mob organizations and machine guns. Although the IFC was eventually brought to North America to become one of the longest-running and most successful MMA promotions to date, the organization's initial promoters will forever remember its murky inception.

The IFC's story began when Buddy Albin—a former kickboxer who had managed Oleg Taktarov for a spell and frequently helped with on-site promotions for the UFC—was put in charge of prefight promotions for UFC VIII, which was to be held in Puerto Rico. SEG flew him to the island a month before the event, and he was soon joined by former UFC competitor Andy Anderson, who planned to party with Albin while he got things ready for the show. But Anderson began noticing that his friend was behaving strangely. "Buddy was, at the time, an excellent promoter," Anderson says, "but I think alcohol finally got to his mind, because he had delusions of grandeur, and he would forget conversations that he had." Although Anderson was prepared to tolerate Albin's forgetfulness, SEG was not. When UFC owner Bob Meyrowitz discovered that Albin was slacking considerably in his duties for the upcoming show, he fired him.

Albin may have been out of a job, but he was not out of the picture. In November of 1995, he was contacted by an organization calling itself the International Professional Kickboxing League. He spoke to a representative of the league named Yuri, a Ukrainian kickboxing promoter, who told him that they wanted him to put on an MMA event in the Ukraine. Albin jumped at the opportunity, and after calling upon his friend Andy Anderson to help out, he contacted an acquaintance named Howard Petschler.

Petschler, a former kickboxer and promoter for the Professional Karate Association, had produced kickboxing shows for Showtime and pay-per-view. He had met Buddy Albin while presenting a proposal to a financial investor for an MMA event that he wanted to put on in Tulsa, Oklahoma. Albin happened to be presenting his own proposal for an MMA event to the same investor, and he went so far as to claim that he owned a share of the UFC. Despite Albin's con-man tactics, Petschler's proposal was deemed superior. Although Petschler had secured backing for his event, his partner decided that he didn't want an outside investor after all. Frustrated, Petschler decided he would rather not be involved with the event and began exploring other opportunities.

"Albin calls me up," says Petschler, "and he's got a deal going in the Ukraine. Of course, he's told me that he owns the international rights to the UFC, and that he's not going to be working domestically with them anymore because he and Meyrowitz weren't seeing eye to eye with the way things were supposed to be done. So he was going to take the international rights and go on overseas." Albin also told Petschler that such superstars as Tank Abbott and Oleg Taktarov would be competing in the event. At this point, Petschler didn't know Albin's reputation as a con man. So, believing that Albin did in fact own international rights to the UFC, he agreed to partner with him for the event in the Ukraine.

Albin flew to the Ukraine well ahead of time, but Petschler didn't arrive until just a few weeks before the event. As soon as he set foot in the Kiev airport, Petschler knew something was amiss; the men sent to pick him up began shoving aside customs agents and demanding that Petschler's passport be stamped without question. Then Petschler was taken to see Albin, who had set up shop in a plush downtown apartment. "Initially," he recalls, "Buddy was working with a guy named Yuri over there who is a kickboxing promoter. To seal the deal, Yuri's sister is living with Buddy and taking care of him. I think she was actually the spy to keep an eye on him, but Buddy is in heaven, living in this grand old Kiev apartment." Albin assured Petschler that all was well before the two parted ways again.

Petschler was not, however, given a downtown apartment like Albin's. Instead, he was assigned quarters in the Ukrainian Olympic Training Center. The center, which had been converted into a small hotel, was protected by menacing-looking armed guards carrying machine guns, and the building was surrounded by a thick cement wall bristling with barbed wire. It was at about this time that Petschler realized his hosts were more than just promoters—they were a faction of the Ukrainian mob. When the Soviet Union had fallen, organized crime had not only taken over a number of industries, but it had also taken control of various sporting clubs. "We were living in kind of an armed camp," explains Petschler. "Every place we went, we had bodyguards with us. It was explained there was a potential for kidnapping, but actually there were rivalries between the different sporting organizations, and anything they could do to screw up the other ones, they would. They play hardball over there, especially at that time. It's kind of like the Wild West over there."

Despite it all, Petschler hung in there. Still under the dangerously false assumption that Albin owned the international rights to the UFC, he contacted two of his Canadian associates—Mike Thomas and Victor Theriault—and asked them to come and join the team. Thomas, a native of the Mohawk Nation and an ex-marine, had worked kickboxing promotions in Canada for some time, and Petschler was thinking that if the Kiev event went off well, the international rights that Albin had boasted could be used very profitably in Canada. Thomas agreed to come, but shortly after he arrived, Albin's scam began to unravel.

"The event was on a Saturday," says Petschler, "and on the Thursday night before the event, Buddy had got faxes and phone calls from the UFC saying, 'You can't use the word Ultimate,' which caused a lot of problems, of course, because that's what the Ukrainians had bought into. They thought they were doing the UFC Kiev." Kiev had been adorned with banners and posters proclaiming the event; comedian Eddie Murphy and boxing legend Muhammad Ali were scheduled to appear. The event was intended to celebrate an international presence in Kiev.

Albin somehow convinced his Ukrainian partners that it would be best to change the name of the production, later telling Petschler that Meyrowitz was planning to sue if the UFC name or logo was used. By simply changing one word, Petschler came up with a viable alternative: the International Fighting Championship.

The setup of the night was four single bouts followed by an eight-man elimination tournament. Five Americans made the trip to Eastern Europe to do battle: John Lober, Fred Floyd, Gerry Harris, Eric Hebestreit, John Dixson, and UFC veteran Paul "the Polar Bear" Varelans. "Varelans was kind of looked upon as the favorite going into the thing," says Petschler, "because he's such a monster."

When it came to accommodations, the American fighters didn't have it any easier than Petschler—they were also housed in the poorly heated Olympic Training Center. When Andy Anderson arrived at the center, he found the fighters in an uproar. Albin hadn't been seen for over a week, and the fighters' passports had been confiscated. Anderson was also asked to relinquish his passport to a member of the Ukrainian staff, but, knowing that something was very wrong, he refused.

Despite the uproar, all of the fighters stuck it out. On fight night, fourteen thousand spectators filled the National Sports Palace for the nearly sold-out event. Albin's promises of celebrity appearances never materialized, but the fans didn't seem to mind. They were there to see the Americans fight some of their own country's best. The Ukrainians "went out and banged," recalls Petschler. "They were some of the best-conditioned fighters you've ever seen. I don't remember any of them running out of stamina, but I remember them taking a lickin' and keeping on tickin'. They just kept going until they were either knocked out or forced to submit."

John Dixson kicked off the tournament by winning his fight over Alexander Mandrk with a guillotine choke in the first round. The quickest fight of the night, between Russian Igor Guerus and Gerry Harris, came next, with Guerus winning the bout in fifteen seconds with a one-punch KO. Paul Varelans brutalized his opponent, Valery Nikulin, until Nikulin's cornermen finally threw in the towel.

As the evening progressed, however, the pace of the show began to slow. Something between the locker room and the ring was holding up the Ukrainian fighters. "I had Mike Thomas and Vic Theriault helping me get the fighters out," says Petschler. "The rest of the help, of course, was Ukrainian, and I didn't speak the language. So I had them backstage, kind of helping at each dressing room. And so I kept on saying, 'What's going on? We need to get these fighters going!' We're used to having one fight on after the other. And so finally [Thomas and Theriault] got on in the locker room . . . and as it turned out the holdup was that one Ukrainian fighter had to go back, get undressed, take off his jock, and give it to the other Ukrainian fighter, who then had to put it on before he could come out. They only had one cup between them." Petschler didn't find out about this until the event was almost over.

The last quarterfinal bout of the night was between the biggest man in the tournament, 340-pound Fred Floyd, and the exciting Ukrainian striker Igor Vovchanchyn. Although Vovchanchyn gave up more than 130 pounds to Floyd, he dominated the bout, literally pounding Floyd

ANDY ANDERSON

Paul "the Polar Bear" Varelans before the first IFC in Russia.

into submission. After thirteen minutes and forty seconds of bombard-ment, Floyd tapped on his own arm to end the fight.

Vovchanchyn then went on to destroy the 330-pound Varelans. "I will always remember the American fighter whose fighting name was the Polar Bear," says Vovchanchyn. "He was extremely tough, and I was very proud that I won." After this victory, Vovchanchyn met John Dixson in the finals. "He pretty much broke Dixson's face," says Andy Anderson, who was refereeing the bouts. "He hit him so hard, John was like, 'Stop!' You could just instantly hear the bones snap." Dixson verbally submitted at 6:18 into the bout. "Vovchanchyn beat the shit out of everybody," recalls Anderson. "Igor just went through them like a hot knife through butter."

Later that night, the fighters partied as hard as they had fought. The most memorable antics were courtesy of Dutch kickboxer Bas Rutten, who had been brought in as commentator for the event. Bas's night of mayhem began with a friendly scuffle with Varelans. "Paul was drunk; I was drunk," remembers Rutten. "He's a very nice guy, but he attacked me

ANDY ANDERSON

The fun-loving Bas Rutten.

from the back. I tried to apply an arm bar on him, and I had the arm. But he started biting my back, and he actually bit a hole in my back! So I told him to let go, and he didn't let go, so I threw him through a window."

The chaos didn't end there. Later on, at one of Kiev's many strip joints, Bas took it upon himself once again to provide a little fun. "Bas jumped on the main stage with some of the entertainers, and then one of the security guards walks over to Bas," recounts Anderson. "The security guard happened to have a gun—a machine gun—and Bas reaches down and bitch slaps him. I grab Bas, throw him over my shoulder, and carry him out the door. On the way back to the hotel, he proceeds to stand up in the backseat and piss on the driver. And the driver stops, gets out, cusses, hollers, and screams. Then Bas does it *again*!"

Although the night may have been a bit crazy, the good-natured fun of a bunch of drunken fighters was nothing to be concerned about when compared to what lay ahead. The following day, one of Yuri's thugs approached Anderson to tell him that because the show had gone so well, his superiors had decided that the whole IFC crew should stay and do another event. Anderson informed the mobster that they could do what-ever they wanted, but the IFC group was leaving. The hoodlum informed him that he had misunderstood: it wasn't a request; they were not going to be allowed to leave. Anderson protested, but, "Everyone had a machine gun but us."

The following day, Anderson and three others, now under constant guard, managed to bribe one of their captors to take them to the airport, and from there they escaped to Paris. Mike Thomas and Victor Theriault made it to the airport on their own, and at one point, they were compelled to hide in a bathroom. When their flight was called, they made a break for the gate. "We jumped on the plane and never looked back!" says Thomas.

In the meantime, Howard Petschler was running into his own problems. He had elected to stay in the Ukraine a little while longer to transfer the formats of the video production into something he could work with more easily upon his return to the States. Randy Kamay, who had worked with Petschler during his PKA days, stayed behind to help him with those transfers.

The day after the show, at around three in the afternoon, an attorney for Yuri and one of his assistants marched into the editing room where Petschler and Kamay were working. "We're rushing to get the rough edit done so we can pull out the next day or the day after," says Petschler. "And [the attorney] said they needed to go get preclearance at customs, so they needed all the tapes. And I said, 'Well, I can't do that.' Just the way they were fidgeting and dancing around made me a little nervous."

Petschler walked out of the room and made his way to the central office where one of the building's few telephones was located. He knew that some bad blood had arisen between Yuri and Buddy Albin concerning the reconciliation of the money owed to the American group, and he wanted to see if Albin knew anything about the attorney's demands for the tapes. While he was gone, the Ukrainians, brandishing guns, shoved Kamay aside, took the tapes—which contained hours of interviews and fight footage—and left. The only tape they didn't steal recorded the bout between Vovchanchyn and Dixson—it happened to be still in the transfer machine.

Fortunately, Petschler had had the presence of mind to store the backup tapes of the event in his hotel room. He and Kamay raced from the facility, flagged down a car, and paid the driver to take them to the hotel. While there, Petschler received a call from Buddy Albin, who told him to pack up and get out of the hotel. A car, sent by Albin, arrived to pick up Petschler and Kamay and take them to an apartment that Albin had secured.

While Albin was booking flights out of the country for themselves and the crew, Petschler learned that the Ukrainian mob was bent on preventing the backup tapes from leaving Kiev. On the way to the airport, Petschler, remembering the mob's relationship with airport customs officers, decided that the only way to get the tapes to the United States was to drop them off at a Federal Express office. They did so and then headed straight to the airport, where they were promptly searched by customs officers. "Apparently, customs had been told that we were some sort of American network film crew here in disguise, taking photos of Chernobyl," says Petschler.

They finally boarded the plane and returned safely to America. A few weeks later, the Fed Ex package with the videotapes still hadn't arrived. The bulk of Petschler's profits resided in those tapes, so he was faced with a tough decision: either write the whole thing off as a loss, or go back to the Ukraine and get his tapes. He chose to go back.

Upon arriving in Kiev, Petschler was met by Gene Fabercaun, a Ukrainian wrestling coach who had originally helped the IFC group navigate the politics of the Ukrainian mob. Fabercaun had been working with one of the mob-run sporting clubs, a rival of the one that Petschler had dealt with. The club Fabercaun was involved in had provided one of the fighters for the event, but he'd never been paid. Petschler promised to pay the fighter if the tapes were recovered, and the gangsters behind Fabercaun's club agreed to help.

After stealthily weaving their way through Kiev, Petschler and his allies ended up in the apartment of a high-ranking female mobster. Finally allowed some breathing room, they got down to planning their move on Fed Ex, scheduled for the following morning.

"Off we go to Fed Ex," recalls Petschler. "There're two cars going to Fed Ex. I'm in a car with this woman and two other guys, and there are four other people following us in a car behind. As we turn to go down the hill to the Fed Ex station, I notice the other car is no longer with us— with Gene in it! My lifeline!"

Petschler's car arrived at the Fed Ex office, and his group entered and rousted the sleepy-eyed customs agent, who didn't seem particularly concerned about the situation. After some time wrangling, he handed the tapes over to Petschler. Assuming that by this time phone calls were being made to alert the mob faction that had tried to hold on to the tapes, the group made a speedy getaway. "Word spreads pretty quickly," says Petschler.

Petschler met up with Fabercaun again and the two were taken to the enormous Kiev train station and delivered into the protective custody of a group of armed guards whose duty it was to ensure the safe operation of the depot. After a few drinks and a couple of rounds of poker, Petschler and Fabercaun were escorted to the train by a heavily armed contingent and concealed in a compartment on an overnight train to Odessa.

After a nervous night, they arrived in Odessa and were met by a police captain, who took them to the home of the woman who ran the Odessa Film Studios. That night, the woman held a cocktail party in celebration of Petschler and Fabercaun's escape, and among the guests was a Moldavian army general, a longtime friend of the hostess. The general offered to take the tapes to Romania and ship them from there to Petschler's address in the United States. Petschler agreed. Leaving the country the following night, he was once again searched and questioned as to the whereabouts of the tapes. This time, the airline personnel helped him through the ordeal and he was finally able to leave the Ukraine.

Petschler did receive the tapes, but the one containing the final bout, between Vovchanchyn and Dixson, was missing. "When the mob had grabbed the tapes from Randy Kamay, the tape that we had in the machine at the time turned out to be the Vovchanchyn/Dixson fight. They did not have that fight. So we had two reels of that fight that we packed into the Fed Ex box. What the mob did is they somehow got to Fed Ex and swapped tapes. They put other tapes that looked just the same in the same cases and put them back in the box. So I didn't realize I didn't have that fight until I got back."

Eventually, the taped show resurfaced in its entirety; it was sold by Marco Ruas's former manager, Frederico Lapenda. Lapenda, who had originally been introduced to Yuri by Buddy Albin, had stayed in contact with the Ukrainians, and he cut a deal with Yuri to sell the event under the title *Night of Diamonds*, in reference to the shape of the fighting cage.

A Crook Is Unmasked

With no intention of throwing in the IFC towel after such an ordeal, Petschler, Albin, Theriault, and Thomas decided to put on a second show, only this time it would be held in the U.S. "I really believed in the sport," says Thomas, who provided backing for the second event. "I wanted to see it be viewed as a sport, and not just a spectacle. It was important for me and it was important for Howard [Petschler]. I think that's why we had so much success at getting the sport legalized."

First, they had to locate a state willing to host an MMA event. Albin remembered from his days as a kickboxer that the state of Mississippi had been fairly open-minded, so the crew got the ball rolling there. Petschler began revamping a set of rules he had been working on for an earlier MMA idea, and he soon formalized a draft. They presented it to Billy Lyons of the Mississippi State Athletic Commission. This set of rules, along with footage from Kiev, won them the sanctioning of MMA in Mississippi. It was the first time such a victory had been won in North America.

To help promote the event, the local ABC affiliate ran the Kiev show in two one-hour segments; it would be the first time MMA was broadcast on television in America. Petschler and Thomas traveled to Mississippi for the show. When they got to their hotel, they were informed that they would be sharing a room. Albin, however, was living it up in a plush two-bedroom penthouse, and he had plenty of cash to throw around because he had withdrawn most of the money generated from advance ticket sales.

The show, held at the Gulf Coliseum, went off without a hitch and was cheered on by nearly 7,500 fans. Although the gate receipts indicated that the show had made a tidy profit, when Thomas and Petschler went to collect, Albin claimed that the endeavor had actually lost money. With IFC 3 slated to go forward in Mobile, Alabama and no funds to produce the show, Thomas once again had to put up the money. "I said, 'Look, I'm going to give this one more try, and if it doesn't work we're going to discuss what we're going to do.'"

Thomas and Petschler were growing wary of Albin. In a meeting prior to IFC 3, they informed him that this would be his last chance to prove that he could work as part of the IFC team. Albin, knowing that his jig was almost up, quickly and quietly bled the show of every dime he could.

Mike Thomas first uncovered Albin's thievery while distributing the paychecks to the fighters after the third event. Albin had only written checks for half of what was owed and taken the rest. Andy Anderson discovered that he'd also been on the hit list when he checked his credit card statement. Albin had charged a good deal of the fighters' expenses from IFC II (in excess of twenty thousand dollars) to Anderson's credit card and pocketed the money that Thomas had given him for these expenses. Neither of these issues could be resolved, however, because by the time all of this was discovered Albin had skipped town.

Convinced that Buddy Albin and his dirty dealings were finally behind them, Thomas and Petschler were stunned to learn, after the third show, that Albin had sold the rights to the Mississippi and Kiev shows to a video outlet in Atlanta for a measly five thousand dollars. They contacted the outlet, explained the situation, and were eventually able to buy back the rights. The last Petschler had to do with the crooked promoter was when he sent Albin a cease and desist order for an event Albin was putting on in Louisiana using the IFC logo.

Despite Albin's corruption, the first several IFCs drew crowds. Knowing the event could make money if it was done right, Thomas incorporated the IFC and located its headquarters in Canada. Soon after, he began consulting with longtime martial artist and budding promoter Paul Smith concerning locations for upcoming IFC events, as well as ways to make the shows safer for the fighters. Smith was asked to join the IFC team, and a year later he was named commissioner of the organization.

A New Beginning

Before becoming a part of the IFC team, Paul Smith had been dealing with athletic commissions concerning MMA events for some time. He had first approached the California State Athletic Commission in '96, while trying to help Ken Shamrock get an event off the ground. But in 1997, when he started working for the IFC, he went after that athletic commission more aggressively. He did some investigating and found a loophole in California's regulations: a law stating that if a tournament was school sponsored, school run, and the participants were school members, then the school did not fall under the jurisdiction of the athletic commission. Armed with this knowledge, Smith set up his first IFC-related event, called the Warrior's Challenge, backed by his own school, the Warrior's Lodge. The event was held in Jackson, a small town in Northern California.

"The athletic commission called the chief of police and tried to shut it down," says Smith. "I went before the city council in Jackson and showed them in the commission's own rules that it was all legal and they had no jurisdiction. The City of Jackson issued us our permit, and told us to go ahead, and told this chief of police to keep his nose out of it."

The members of the California State Athletic Commission were not, however, the only ones trying to shut down the Warrior's Challenge. According to Smith, promoters Steve Fossum and Kevin Smith, from an organization called the International Kickboxing Federation (a sanctioning committee), began demanding that the commission make itself the sanctioning body for MMA. "They didn't know anything about the sport," maintains Paul Smith. "Kevin Smith had approached me about doing a show, and what he was talking about doing was with tag teams. He showed me these videos, and I had to tell him, 'You knucklehead— this isn't real. This is shoot-wrestling from Japan.' I mean guys bouncing off the ropes!"

When the pair from the IKF learned that the Warrior's Challenge had been issued a permit, they turned their destructive efforts on an event being put on by MMA competitor John Lober. To ensure that Lober's event was shut down, the dynamic duo of Fossum and Smith informed the commission as to where it would be taking place. "It was going to be proper Pancrase-type rules," explains Paul Smith. "It would have been a pretty decent event. Lober had about sixteen grand in it, and they came with the police and shut it down. He lost the sixteen grand, and then Lober and the whole Metal Militia went looking for Steve Fossum. I think they're still waiting to see him show up in southern California."

Although Smith had been issued a permit for his Warrior's Challenge, an investigator from the State Athletic Commission was still sent out to videotape the event and comment on Smith's adherence to state laws. The event proved to be one of the best-run shows the investigator had seen, and he congratulated Smith in a report to the commission. After holding another successful event, Smith was asked by the commission to become the martial arts advisor to the State Martial Arts Advisory Committee.

Smith was on the warpath, determined to make the sport legal in as many states as possible. Backed by the IFC, he began fighting against MMA's political opponents in a state-by-state battle for sanctioning. Howard Petschler's efforts had garnered sanctioning in Mississippi and Alabama, but Smith still thought the rules needed to be reworked, so he drafted a new rule book.

Louisiana reviewed the IFC's requests for sanctioning and agreed to Smith's rules. Mike Thomas took the new rule book home with him to Canada—to Montreal, Quebec, where Donald Zuckerman's Extreme Fighting 2 had caused such a stir. Due to Thomas's continuing efforts, there had been a complete turnaround in the Quebec government's stance towards MMA. "Now it's thriving again in Quebec," says Smith. "They have everybody's pay-per-views. For a year and a half, we ran a syndicated TV series—an hour one night a week. When it ended up beating everybody out of the sports ratings, including hockey, they ended up running it three times a week."

But California hadn't fully accepted the IFC rules, and Smith was going to have to do some political sparring. "The very first time that I stepped into the California Athletic Commission's office," remembers Smith, "I sat down in [Commissioner] Rob Lynch's office, and there is a lounge area in the front, and, coming in, the walls are covered in pictures of boxers covered in blood. He went about telling me how this sport [MMA] was no better than human cockfighting and it was no better than having pit bull fights. I looked around those walls and said, 'I guarantee you it'll take you years and years and years to find this amount of blood in a Mixed Martial Arts event.' And I just started pulverizing him with the facts."

Another athletic commissioner, Al Ducheny, was also bent on preventing MMA from being sanctioned in California. He used the carotid artery choke (a common technique used to secure victory in MMA competition) as the basis of his argument. At one particular meeting, a doctor appeared to testify to Ducheny's contention that chokes are extremely dangerous. "Ducheny set us up at a meeting," says Smith. "He had this doctor appear. He still claims he had nothing to do with it, but we know that it was him—the whole thing was set up. They had this doctor appear at the last minute to stand up and say that, as a professional medical doctor, he could not condone the chokes of any type because they could cause death or serious injury."

Smith and the UFC's Jeff Blatnik, who were both at the commission meeting, quickly refuted the doctor's testimony. The hearing was put on hold, and the commission kicked the issue back to the Martial Arts Advisory Committee, of which Smith was a member. Smith brought in testimonials of his own and began to stir the pot by contacting the International Olympic Committee, as well as the U.S. judo team. Judo happens to be an Olympic sport, and the executive director of United States Judo Incorporated, William Rosenberg, wrote a letter to the California State Athletic Commission in which he stated that the banning of such standard chokes (which are common in judo, as well) would cripple the Los Angeles and San Francisco bids to host the 2012 Olympic Games.

Ducheny, the primary opponent of MMA in California, changed his position as soon as he was warned of the political and economic ramifications of his stubbornness. He backed away from his anti-choke stance at a commission meeting held on April 28, 1999, and mixed martial arts was sanctioned in California. But this sanctioning meant that appropriate personnel would be required to handle the new regulatory responsibilities, and the approval for an MMA hiring budget was stalled, pending approval by Governor Gray Davis. "When the commission asked for an increase in their budget for mixed martial arts," says Smith, "and they showed how it was going to create a positive cash flow from their taxes on the sport, the governor would not sign on anything that increased or changed budgets, laws, licensing, or fees. It was presented to him twice, and he shut it down both times."

But the California State Athletic Commission had sanctioned MMA, and this piqued the interest of other states. On April 29, 1999, the day after the California victory, Larry Hazaard of the New Jersey Athletic Commission called Smith and told him that New Jersey would pass similar regulations if the IFC would hold an MMA event there first. The IFC agreed, and New Jersey was on board.

The efforts of Paul Smith and the IFC to sanction MMA in as many states as possible was a key part of the IFC's strategy. Another was to collect as much videotape footage as possible as material for a syndicated weekly television series (this also explains why there aren't many MMA videotapes floating around). "That's how pro wrestling took off," says Smith. "People watched one or two nights a week and started following certain wrestlers, and then they started buying those big pay-per-views every month." To initiate this effort, Paul Smith and Howard Petschler hammered out a deal in January of 2002 with the Microsoft-owned broadband network METV for an all-MMA channel, bringing MMA one step closer to the mainstream.

Because organizations like the IFC resisted the political oppression of Senator John McCain and his supporters, MMA did not disappear from the United States. Instead, it struggled on in obscurity. But as it did so, the true character of the fighters, promoters, and die-hard fans began to surface. The sport was down, but it wasn't out, and between 1997 and 2002 MMA developed professional levels of competition.

PART III

Out of the Ashes

CHAPTER 12

Never Say Die

Senator John McCain's tireless quest to crush the sport of MMA finally gained some serious ground in 1997 when he was appointed chair of the Commerce Committee, the governing body that oversees America's cable television industry. McCain's stance on MMA competition was no secret, and soon after he was appointed, the president of the National Cable Television Association sent out a general warning to all providers, informing them that any support of MMA events could weaken the cable industry's influence in Washington. Letting go of the UFC and MMA competitions seemed a small sacrifice to make for the continued ability to air larger draws, such as pro wrestling and programs with heavy sexual content.

Despite SEG's efforts to make its event more acceptable to the mainstream—those efforts included the introduction of mandatory six-ounce gloves and the prohibition of head butts and groin strikes—MMA competition in America was becoming a losing proposition. Shortly after Robert Meyrowitz awarded Mark Coleman the first unified heavyweight title belt, at UFC XII, Leo Hindery Jr.—the newly appointed president of the cable giant TCI and a friend of Senator McCain—dropped all MMA events from his roster. Although TCI claimed that its primary reason was to shield children from violent television content, the company was still willing to air professional wrestling, violent films, and, of course, one of McCain's favorites: boxing.

Along with TCI went Time Warner, Request, Cablevision Systems, and Viewer's Choice (which would later become On Demand). The smaller cable companies quickly followed suit, and as the events stopped reaching the viewers, promoters like Donald Zuckerman began closing up shop. The few promoters who stuck it out could barely afford to pay their fighters, and soon even the superstars of the sport were earning next to nothing.

While some fighters, such as David "Tank" Abbott and Dan Severn, made the transition to the lucrative world of American professional wrestling, and others were courted by Japanese organizations, such as Pancrase and RINGS, to fight in front of thousands of eager spectators, most of the fighters stuck it out in the U.S. The overzealous politicians who had charged so blindly into their crusade had forgotten one crucial thing: they were pitting themselves against fighters, and fighters, by nature, don't give up.

Even Cal Worsham, after suffering a punctured lung (the worst injury ever in American MMA competition), displayed his dedication to the sport. Working full time as a corrections officer, he still managed to coach his team of fighters and pursue his MMA passion. "It's tough," Worsham has admitted. "Sometimes I come to the gym with no sleep and hardly have time to get my students trained. Every six months I have to rotate, which means I go from days, to graveyard, to release, and somehow I've got to train. I've been a corrections officer for about five years, and it's been a tough five years. Unfortunately, we can't all be Don Fryes, or Tito Ortizes, or Frank Shamrocks even—but we've got to be the guys in there trying. There are people who would if they could, but they can't, and those are the people we've got to do it for."

Not only did fighters like Worsham keep the events alive by stepping into the ring and laying it on the line for little or no money, but they also turned the spectacle into a sport. Seeing beyond MMA competition's bleak prospects, they grouped together to share knowledge and improve their game. These groups became rigorous interdisciplinary training camps and eventually made the one-dimensional fighter a thing of the past. Teams such as Ken Shamrock's Lion's Den and RAW (Real American Wrestlers, an organization representing several Olympic wrestlers) produced new and more skillful competitors whose determination and talent began to win back the devotion of their fans and renew recognition for the sport in the mainstream media.

"I'm hoping that MMA is successful," says Worsham, "and that it's still going strong when I'm an old man so I can have a little bragging rights. There can be serious injury, but there's that in boxing. There are no kicks and elbows in boxing, and there are still deaths. There's paralysis and deaths in football. Or you never know when you're going to get anthrax in a letter. Every day is a risk. MMA is geared towards being a sport, and it's something I take pride in being associated with."

CHAPTER 13

A Family of Fighters

Before the Ultimate Fighting Championship was formed, Ken Shamrock dominated the Japanese pro wrestling scene, drawing spectators by the tens of thousands with his charisma and natural athletic ability. But the bouts he fought in were worked, and he missed the days of the Toughman competitions and real fighting. So when two of his teachers, Funaki and Suzuki, broke off from pro wrestling to found Pancrase, Shamrock joined them. It didn't matter to him that if the organization failed his career in Japan would be over. Professional combat was what he had been looking for all along, so he returned to the gym and began training for his first match.

Once again, he dominated his opponents, this time in full-out combat. He brought the new organization into the fight world's spotlight, and soon his Adonis-like physique was being depicted in Japanese comic books and gracing the covers of magazines. Shamrock was sitting on top of the world—a place he planned to remain.

To prepare for the five days a month he fought in Japan, he opened his first gym, near his home in Lodi, a town of sixty thousand inhabitants located in California's Central Valley. It was called the Lion's Den, and it was not your typical martial arts studio, to say the least. The walls were not decorated with posters of Bruce Lee, shelves of trophies, or mirrors. There were no showers or even a water fountain. Situated in a warehouse in Lodi's industrial district, the gym had cement walls and floors; it was furnished with grappling mats, a boxing ring for sparring, state of the art weight-lifting equipment, and plenty of towels for wiping up blood and sweat. Those who trained there were being groomed to fight the toughest MMA competitors in the world.

"Ken just took the cream of the crop," says Bob Shamrock. "Nobody skated through." To weed out the weak, Ken created a grueling tryout that only those who possessed heart in abundance could pass. "The test was not made for you to pass," he explains. "It was made for you to want

ANDY ANDERSON

Ken Shamrock preparing for battle in the octagon.

to quit. So by making you want to quit, it shows me the intensity or the will that you have to succeed." In some tryouts, as many as twenty hopefuls would turn up, and on rare occasions one might make it to the end of the day. Most days, everyone had already quit by noon.

But, over time, Shamrock collected a small team of fighters capable of surviving the unthinkable. Without so much as a pat on the back, their heads were shaven and they were moved into the Lion's Den Fighter House. In exchange for room, board, and initiation into the secrets of submission fighting, they were expected to cater to the seasoned fighters, mop the gym floors every night, and endure the pain Shamrock inflicted upon them. If they proved themselves by enduring for at least half a year, they were shipped off to the Pancrase Kanagawa Ku dojo in Japan for more training before entering Pancrase's professional fighting circuit. Needless to say, few made it that far. But one of them happened to be Ken's own adopted brother, Frank Shamrock.

On April 4, 1994, Frank traveled to Lodi to try out for the team. He was twenty-two years old and had no martial arts training to speak of. He had been forewarned of the monumental task before him, but he had climbed mountains before. At twelve, he had entered the California justice system, surviving many turbulent years in group homes, juvenile halls, and foster homes before finding his way to Bob Shamrock's home for boys, the Shamrock Ranch. He knew what it was like to suffer and sacrifice; and he had already made the decision never to give up.

Frank's tryout was more brutal than most. Bob Shamrock had told him to respect Ken as his coach and trainer, "and not just think of him as being your brother." And Bob told Ken, "You'll have to hurt him so he'll respect you."

On a warm spring morning, Frank began his tryout with the requisite 500 squats, 500 sit-ups, 250 push-ups, and 500 leg lifts. After running bleachers and performing a series of other exhausting cardiovascular tests, he was brought back to the gym for a sparring session with Ken. "Frank got two of his ribs broken, his nose broken, and his medial meniscus was torn out of his knee," says Bob. "After Ken had mauled him a little bit, and I could see that Frank was hurt, I told Ken he could back off. But it was tough. Ken was a tough teacher. He wasn't one to explain a lot of stuff, because he'd learned himself by experience."

After eight hours of abuse, Frank became an official "Young Boy." His determination had paid off. Taking little time to recover from his injuries, he began training with only one goal in mind—to survive. He learned countless ways to submit his opponent through holds such as chokes, ankle locks, and arm bars. He studied submission in his dreams. For seven months, he did nothing but train, eat, and sleep—and then it was off to Kanagawa Ku. For six more intensive weeks, he studied under the Japanese masters, acclimating to the Pancrase style of fighting and the Japanese culture. Then, only eight months after having stepped onto the mat for the first time, he made his MMA debut in Pancrase. Although Ken would be fighting in the same event, Frank knew that once he stepped into the ring he would be on his own. And his opponent was no patsy—Frank was to fight none other than the Dutch kickboxing legend Bas Rutten.

"Fear and survival was my motivation," says Frank. "I excelled at the athletic portion of it, and in the mental and muscular conditioning, but in actual combat I had no experience whatsoever." That inexperience showed when Rutten broke Frank's nose with a front kick. Frank, who had only trained submission, defended himself in the only way he knew— by taking the kickboxer to the mat. "It was very strange to me," recalls Frank. "The bell rang, there was lots of moving around, and then the bell rang again. To me it seemed like it was two minutes long!" Because of his aggressiveness and his ability to dominate his opponent on the mat, Frank won by unanimous decision. As his hand was raised in the air, a new Lion's Den fighter was born.

FRANK SHAMROCK

Frank Shamrock and his King of Pancrase Title Belt.

For the next few years, Frank climbed the ranks of the Japanese fighting circuit. He learned from his losses and gained confidence with every win, finding his own fighting style. Of all his Pancrase fights, however, one stood out more clearly than the rest: his bout with Allan Goes in the tournament Eyes of the Beast 4. "I had been fighting Japanese fighters, so I understood their mentality and what they do and how they trained," says Frank. "They told me I was going to fight this Brazilian guy. In my mind I thought, 'Nobody is as tough, nobody is as structured, nobody is as technical as the Japanese fighters are, so fighting anybody else will be a walk in the park.' So I didn't really train for it. I was hanging out, drinking wine with my friends. They said, 'You're fighting a foreigner.' So I thought, 'Great—I have a month off!'"

This fight turned out to be one of Frank's most difficult. At that time, the rules of Pancrase stated that a standing fighter could only strike his opponent in the face with an open hand, and there was also a gentleman's rule that you did not strike your opponent while he was on the ground. "Soon as we went to the ground, *whack*, he hits me upside the head," says Frank. "Then it just went downhill from there—we just started slugging each other. At one point, I break his leg! You can hear it audibly breaking, and he doesn't care! I heel hooked him, and he didn't tap. So I turned it a little more, and he didn't tap. I turned it a little more . . . he didn't tap! So I turned it again and it just started popping. It popped a good four or five times. The first couple of pops were ligaments, I could tell, popping over each other. Then the last one was a good solid *pop*! I felt it! Then he rolled into the ropes and we had to break."

Goes continued to fight, despite his broken leg. At one point, he got Shamrock's back and attempted a choke. When Shamrock defended the choke, Goes fishhooked Shamrock's eye to pull up his head. "So the match ends," says Frank. "I've got a swollen eyeball, he has a broken leg . . . and the match is declared a draw. I was amazed he was still standing there."

While Frank worked his way up the Pancrase ladder, Ken was garnering his share of victories at the top. The two brothers seemed unstoppable. That never seemed truer than when Ken defeated kickboxing great Maurice Smith in December of 1994.

Smith had been recruited by Pancrase after being undefeated in the kickboxing world for almost a decade. But competing in MMA competition was different from what Smith was used to, and he had to make some dramatic adjustments to his fighting style. "I learned that I needed to know how to grapple," says Smith, "and that I needed to be a complete fighter. To fight the people in this business, it's not so much how long before I submit them, but how long before they submit me. First I had to learn to sprawl, and second I had to learn how to work from the bottom a little bit."

To acquire these skills, Maurice Smith turned to Ken Shamrock, the very man who had submitted him in the first round of their Pancrase bout. While Ken and Smith were swapping knowledge, Frank jumped into the mix. "I was a terrible striker, and Maurice was a so-so grappler," says Frank. "We developed a friendship through all our training together. That friendship kept growing and growing."

As Ken and Frank continued to excel as fighters, their skill and their victories caught the eye of hopefuls all over the world, and soon they were inundated with young athletes looking to break into this new and challenging sport.

Building the Team

An experienced kickboxer by the name of Guy Mezger, who stood six-foot-one and weighed 180 pounds, grew enamored of the accomplishments and fighting ability of Ken Shamrock. "It was funny, because when I saw Ken walk out in UFC I," says Mezger, "I had this feeling that I would train with that guy one day."

Less than a year after Mezger saw Ken battle it out with Royce Gracie, he received a call from the UFC asking if he wanted to compete in the event. "They wanted a kickboxer to fight in the tournament," says Mezger. "That was back when they were doing that gimmick of style versus style." Mezger was flown out to UFC III to check out the show and see if he was interested in competing. It was there that he first met Ken, Frank, and their father, Bob. "When it came time to fight, I asked Ken if he could assess my skills," Mezger remembers. "I had never fought no-holds-barred, and back then there were no rules, no gloves, and you couldn't be disqualified. The last thing I needed was to have my ass kicked in front of the whole world. So I asked him to assess my skills. I was a good wrestler, a pretty good kickboxer, and I was the Texas judo champion. Ken invited me out to the Lion's Den, and when I got there he asked me if I was interested in trying out."

After securing victories in the octagon in UFC IV and UFC V, Mezger tried out for the team and became an official Lion's Den fighter. Although he didn't move to Lodi like the rest of the Young Boys—he already had a gym in Dallas—he did travel there on a regular basis for lessons. Ken

Lion's Den fighters taking a break.

prepared him to fight in Pancrase, and when Mezger was ready, he moved to Japan to train, just like Frank. Although he lost his first bout, with Masakatsu Funaki on September 1, 1995, he eventually went on to become the King of Pancrase.

Despite the fact that the Lion's Den was filling up with some serious fighters, there were still more on their way. Jerry Bohlander had seen the first several UFC shows with his childhood friend Pete Williams. "We used to have parties and watch the UFCs," says Bohlander. "When I saw Ken Shamrock fight Royce Gracie for the second time, I decided that I was going to find out where he was and go train with him."

Doing some investigating, Bohlander discovered that the Lion's Den was only an hour away from his home in Livermore. He drove there and was invited to roll around with one of Ken's top students. Not only did Bohlander—who was five-foot-eleven and weighed 180 pounds—hold his own, but he also managed to choke out his opponent. Ken was impressed, and after class he asked Bohlander if he would like to fight professionally. Bohlander felt honored, but his family was not well off, and he was responsible for taking care of his mother and younger sisters. He returned home, but the notion of becoming a professional fighter kept growing in the back of his mind, and after several months he could no longer ignore the call. "I worked, saved up some money, and took out some loans to take care of my family while I couldn't," says Bohlander. "Then I went and tried out."

Bohlander's initiation consisted of several hundred squats, push-ups, and leg lifts; then he did bleacher runs, camel runs (where the runner carries another person on his shoulders), an eighty-yard wheelbarrow walk, a duckwalk up and down a steep hill, some kickboxing, some wrestling, and, finally, a series of pull-ups. All of this in 110-degree central California heat.

Bohlander passed as the top initiate among six other hopefuls. He moved into the Fighter House at Lodi and began his training the very next day. At the time, Ken was preparing for his Superfight in UFC VII with Oleg Taktarov, and because of Bohlander's wrestling background, Ken chose the new recruit to work with him on sprawling techniques. "I had to be the guy shooting on him as he was punching and stopping my takedowns," explains Bohlander. "But I took him down twice. I shot in, lifted him up off the ground, and slammed him down. He was like, 'What the fuck! This little 180-pound kid!' He couldn't believe it. Then I shot in again, and I did it again. Then after that he just smashed me."

Bohlander had impressed Ken Shamrock with his takedown abilities, and two weeks later, when Ken left to fight Taktarov in Buffalo, he brought Bohlander with him. Although Bohlander didn't know it yet, Ken was planning to gear him for the UFC. "It's not that Jerry was a great wrestler," says Bob Shamrock. "He was just a mediocre wrestler in high school, but he had the right attitude. He was trying really hard, and he was learning and moving—all the while supporting his family in Livermore."

Upon returning from Buffalo, Bohlander settled on a routine at the Lion's Den. He trained three times a day, five days a week. He lifted weights in the mornings, trained submissions and kickboxing in the afternoons, and spent his evenings rigorously developing his conditioning. To earn his keep at the Lion's Den, Bohlander taught classes in the afternoons. He was eating, sleeping, and breathing as a fighter. Thrilled by what he was learning from his experienced teammates, he decided to give his old friend Pete Williams a call. "I brought him down, and he dug it," says Bohlander. "He came and tried out a month and a half after I did."

With UFC VIII approaching, Shamrock told Bohlander and Williams that one of them was going to be competing in the octagon, but in order for him to decide which, he'd have to see them fight for it. Although Williams, standing six-foot-three and weighing 225 pounds, was much larger than Bohlander, the two went at it. "I had the benefit of not wearing shoes at the time," recalls Bohlander, "and he was wearing shoes. After a long, hard fight, where we were both beat to hell, I finally got him in a heel hook. Since he was wearing shoes, I had the grip."

JOHN MCCARTHY

A victorious Jerry Bohlander.

Conditioning was the name of the game for Bohlander's pre-UFC training. He worked takedowns, submissions, and even kickboxing with Japanese pro wrestling legend Funaki. To supplement this, says Bohlander, "Ken brought in a big guy, Dan Freeman, and he's like five-foot-ten and 280. Ken would make me work my takedowns while Dan was trying to squeeze my damn head off!"

Just after his twenty-first birthday, on February 16, 1996, Bohlander made his UFC debut in San Juan, Puerto Rico. The tournament was dubbed "David and Goliath," and that would be the theme of the night for Bohlander, whose first opponent was the 330-pound giant Scott Ferrozzo.

"He's big! That's what was going through my mind," says Bohlander. "But I wasn't nervous, strangely enough, and if you ask the people around me they'll tell you I don't get nervous very often. I wish I did—maybe I'd get pumped up more often. I saw Ferrozzo and thought, 'Boy, he's awful big . . . make him get tired. Let him get himself tired on me.'"

Bohlander's game plan worked perfectly. Ferrozzo burned himself out as he squished Bohlander up against the fence for the first eight minutes, and when the overweight warrior went for a double-leg takedown, Bohlander sunk in a guillotine choke at the nine-minute mark, causing Ferrozzo to tap out. But beating one giant wasn't enough to bring home the belt. In the semifinals, Bohlander faced the 260-pound Gary "Big Daddy" Goodridge. Although Bohlander controlled his larger opponent for most of the fight, he got caught with a right hand and lost by technical knockout.

With this impressive debut under his belt, Bohlander went on to fight in the Hawaiian MMA competition, Superbrawl. Even though the tournament wasn't as well organized as the UFC, it divided fighters into weight classes, and Bohlander secured the overall victory by defeating Alan Schaible and Chris Charnos. He continued this winning streak in UFC XI, when he won a decision over Fabio Gurgel. Although all these matches were impressive, Bohlander's biggest victory came in UFC XII, held in Dothan, Alabama on February 8, 1997.

With his teacher and mentor Ken Shamrock sitting ringside in the commentator's booth, Bohlander made his way through the throng of screaming Alabaman fans and onto the battleground. Waiting for him was Rainy Martinez, a wrestler with a strong amateur kickboxing background.

After exchanging a few low kicks, Bohlander shot in and grabbed a leg, driving Martinez across the enclosure and up against the fence. Bohlander worked from the top as Martinez scrambled to avoid a submission hold. At one point, Martinez was able to roll Bohlander off him, but the relentless

Bohlander came right back at him, once again plowing Martinez onto his back and into the fence. When Martinez turned his back, Bohlander capitalized on the opportunity in an instant and applied a rear naked choke, submitting his opponent and winning the first round in the four-man lightweight tournament.

In Bohlander's final match, alternate Nick Sanzo approached him cautiously, his arms outstretched. Bohlander remained confident and poised, and when Sanzo grabbed a single leg, he defended and went for a front choke; but he couldn't secure it. After throwing a couple of knee strikes, Bohlander dumped Sanzo onto his back, sinking a double underhook that pushed Sanzo's chin to his chest—a crucifix. Sanzo tapped thirty-five seconds into the match. Bohlander had won the first-ever Lightweight Tournament title.

The newly crowned Lightweight Tournament Champion of the UFC didn't stop there, however. Just a few months later, he traveled to Brazil to face Murilo Bustamante, a 210-pound Brazilian with powerful, spider-like legs, in the Pentagon Combat Championships. But upon arriving in Brazil, Bohlander discovered that not every promotion was as professional as the UFC.

Because of an injured toe, Bohlander planned to wear shoes during the fight. His game plan had been to take Bustamante to the mat, stand up, and then knock out his fallen opponent with a kick. A day before the event, however, the promoters told him that they had changed the rules, and that he would not be allowed to kick a downed competitor. "The promoters were pretty snaky to begin with," says Bohlander, "but I was going to get a pretty good check if I won that fight. They went and changed the rules the day before, and that was bad, but I thought, 'Ya know what? I can handle not kicking him when he's on the ground.' Then, ten minutes before the fight, they change the rules again and tell me I can't kick with shoes at all. I was already in the arena, and the crowd was going crazy. I couldn't take off my shoes because I had torn a tendon in my toe. I was like, 'Aw, fuck! If I leave now, I'm going to get killed.' I had to fight."

Bohlander landed punches throughout the fight, but, he explains, "What I didn't take into account was just how long Bustamante's legs were and how flexible he was. I was in his guard and he pushes me away. I thought I was far enough away that he couldn't kick me in the face or that he couldn't get his foot in that position. Well, he was very flexible, and he got his foot in a funky position and then he launched that long-ass leg right into my jaw and knocked me the fuck out."

Bohlander took the loss gracefully and returned to California to continue his training. Meanwhile, Pete Williams was doing his share to keep the Lion's Den on the map. Like Frank Shamrock and Guy Mezger, Williams had started off in Pancrase, winning two of his first three fights before moving on to less restrictive MMA competition. In the Hawaiian Superbrawl 2, he submitted UFC veteran and judo superstar Joe Charles with a knee bar before returning—in Superbrawl 3, held a few months later—to defeat John Renfro via arm bar.

The Lion's Den was becoming known and respected around the world. But the Lion's Den team would not be complete without a true lightweight. This slot was filled by Mikey Burnett, "the East Side Assassin." Born and raised in East Tulsa, Oklahoma, the five-foot-six, 170-pound Burnett was a power lifter who was dabbling in boxing when he got his sights locked on the UFC. Knowing he wasn't going to jump to the big time right away, he entered a local MMA competition called Oklahoma Free Fighting, just to see where he stood. Even with minimal preparation, he took second place in the three-man tourney. He accepted what he called "the loss," and continued to fight locally around Tulsa.

Then he heard that Donald Zuckerman's Extreme Fight was coming to town. Burnett had a promoter who promised to get him into the preshow fight, but the promoter didn't make good on his word and ended up securing the spot for another fighter. Fed up but not discouraged, Burnett decided to make things happen on his own. He was confident in his natural abilities and believed that with the proper training he could excel. "I said, 'You know what? Something's got to give.' And I began looking on the Internet. I had never met any of the Lion's Den fighters. I had never met Ken or Frank. I didn't know what Frank even looked like. I just went out to San Francisco. I hung out for a couple of days and then went up [to Lodi] and tried out."

Burnett made the team, but before he could follow his teammates into the UFC, he had to learn the tricks of the trade as a Young Boy. As he was being schooled in submission, waiting for his day in the octagon (which would come in UFC XVI, held on March 3, 1998), his teammates continued to dominate.

Stepping Up

On January 17, 1997, Frank Shamrock made what he considered to be the transition from Pancrase competitor to fighter when he took on the determined John Lober in Superbrawl 3. "What I found out from the fight was that some people you just couldn't finesse holds out of," says Frank. "For some people, the art wasn't enough, because they didn't care if you broke their limbs—they'd just keep going. At that point, I wasn't ready to break anyone's arms or leg, and Lober was, so I took a lot of punishment."

The fight continued for thirty minutes, nonstop, and although Frank managed to knock out Lober's front teeth, the bout ended in a split decision, Lober being awarded the victory. "In my opinion, any fight that goes to a decision I deserve to lose, because I didn't finish it," asserts Frank. "I look at every fight as a war, and someone has to win the war, or the war should just keep going on. Any fight where I lose the decision, I've lost it anyway."

After that fight, Frank found himself at a crossroads. He told himself that he would either quit the sport that very day, or devote one hundred percent of his energy to it and never lose again. He chose the latter option, and, to ensure that he would never again walk away from a bout in defeat, he changed his entire approach to MMA. He reexamined his views on violence and competition, as well as his training and mental conditioning. "When I first started fighting, I disliked it completely, because I have a hard time hurting people," says Frank. "I knew in the back of my mind that what I was doing was causing this guy pain. I felt that doing that was wrong. When I started fighting, I didn't want to hurt people; I would just make them tired and then get them in holds. I would outwrestle them, outwork them, outcondition them. I would take advantage of that with a submission and give them the decision whether they wanted to give up or not. That's how I viewed this martial art. I thought it was supposed to be that way. Then, when I fought Lober, I found a guy who wasn't going to get tired. He wasn't going to give up. And he didn't care if I broke something, so I had to condition myself not to care. I had to tell myself, 'It's okay if he gets hurt, if he's trying to hurt me.' And once I made that decision I never looked back. I changed how I viewed the art."

Frank brought his new outlook into his next bout. It was against Enson Inoue, the reigning shooto champion, in the 1997 Japan Vale Tudo tournament. Inoue, who was initially supposed to make 202 pounds, came in at 218. Frank weighed in at his usual 199. To this day, Frank considers this fight to be the toughest of his life. At the beginning of the second round, he and Inoue clinched up. Inoue folded Frank to his back and took the mount, unleashing with elbow strikes and heavy punches.

"At that point," recalls Frank, "it finally dawned on me that there was

Frank Shamrock and Enson Inoue do battle.

a possibility that I could lose this fight, and that was a big scare to myself. But I decided not to, and I got out, and we went wild. It was a Rocky fight, where everybody's throwing blows, and you know someone's going to drop. We were clinching; I got in with some good knees, got some distance, caught him with a left hook, a right hand, and a knee right to the chin that knocked him completely out. As he's falling down, I'm looking to improve my position on top of him. And then his brother, Egan, jumps in the ring, runs all the way across because he was worried for his brother, and just tackles me and slams me into the corner. The whole ring just fills with people. Maurice [Smith] was in my corner. Everyone was just about to start throwing punches, but then they all settled down."

Frank had defeated the World Heavyweight Shooto Champion. With this victory, his experience in Pancrase, and his fights in Superbrawl and Vale Tudo, Frank felt more than ready to enter the UFC. But before he could make this jump, he had to coach his teammate Guy Mezger through his UFC XIII bouts. Mezger was fighting for the Lightweight Tournament title (then 199 pounds and below), and after being awarded a judges' decision over judo expert Christophe Leininger in his first match of the evening, he stepped into the finals to take on Tito Ortiz.

UFC XIII—Ultimate Force/May 30, 1997
(Birmingham, Alabama)

Lightweight Tournament Title—Guy Mezger versus Tito Ortiz

Born in Huntington Beach, California on January 23, 1975, Jacob Ortiz (who was given the nickname Tito at two years of age) grew up in a broken home and within a gang environment. He found salvation in sports, and he began wrestling during his sophomore year at Huntington Beach High School, going on to become a two-time state champion at Golden West Junior College. Ortiz possessed toughness, heart, and drive, so when local UFC competitor David "Tank" Abbott needed sparring partners for his upcoming UFC event, Ortiz was a perfect candidate.

Ortiz jumped at the chance, both for the experience and in the hope of one day competing in the event. After proving himself with Tank on the mat, he was introduced to the UFC matchmakers. The six-foot-two, 205-pound Ortiz, with his bleached hair and rippled physique, made a strong impression. He was given a shot at a qualifying bout to be an alternate at UFC XIII, in Birmingham, Alabama. To make sure he had what it took to handle such a job, Ortiz entered a smaller MMA event just a week before the big show. "I took the guy out in eight minutes," he remembers.

Feeling confident, Ortiz flew to Birmingham. Before the main event of the evening, he stepped into the octagon to face Wes Albritton for a spot as an alternate. The bleached-blond bomber came out swinging, annihilating his opponent in twenty seconds. Thinking that he was finished for the night, Ortiz went backstage to relax. Then he got word that Enson Inoue had dropped out of the tournament due to injury; next thing he knew, he was in the finals facing Lion's Den veteran Guy Mezger.

"You take yourself to him," Frank Shamrock advised Mezger just before the fight. "Use your weapons, and make him react. This is your time, and I'm here to help you." Ortiz came out throwing heavy leather, and Mezger wasted no time in trying to take him down. But when Ortiz sprawled, Mezger found himself trapped in an inside cradle under his larger opponent, who began dropping knees into his skull. When Mezger showed no sign of giving in, Ortiz applied a guillotine choke.

"Pull your arm out and don't let him sink the choke in," Frank shouted from the corner. Mezger took his advice and powered out, but it opened him up for more knees to the face. As he tried to block the devastating shots, his hand grazed the canvas. "It's a tap out," shouted commentator Bruce Beck. But referee John McCarthy, who was hovering over the fighters, knew it was not a tap and did not end the bout. He did, however, separate the fighters so the doctors could examine the cut that had opened on Mezger's face.

"Follow up with your hands and then your kicks," Frank instructed as Mezger was being checked. Once again, Mezger took his advice, and he came out with a hard right that collided with Ortiz's cheek. Not wanting to tangle with the kickboxer's hands and feet, Ortiz tried to take Mezger down. As he did so, Mezger locked Ortiz in a guillotine, forcing the Tank Abbott protégé to submit.

The entire Lion's Den camp rushed into the octagon to lift their teammate off the ground. Then Mezger went over to Ortiz to show his respect, but the Huntington Beach Bad Boy was still fuming about the loss.

In a postfight interview, Mezger was asked how he felt, and he responded by saying, "On top of the world!" This summed up the status of the Lion's Den itself. Frank Shamrock had gone from being a Pancrase competitor to being a full-contact fighter. Jerry Bohlander was the Lightweight Tournament Champion of UFC XII. Pete Williams was making waves in MMA competitions overseas, and Mikey Burnett was poised to rock the newly devised 170-pound-and-under division. They were indeed a family sitting on top of the world, and Ken Shamrock was right there with them. "Being a fighter is one thing," he says, "but being able to teach the skills that you have learned is another. I think I've done real well being able to pass on some of the things that I've learned."

"I'll never forget what was done for me out there," insists Burnett. "It was like a bunch of brothers living together. Ken is a great deal like my older brother; they're both [Ken and Frank] hard people to please, and for some reason you want to please them. Pete, Jerry, and Frank—I lived with those guys, and there's nothing that can ever change how that happened. It's a year of training, eating, sleeping . . . you bled with these guys and sweated with them. We had a lot of good times, and we had a lot of hard times."

Those hard times began in the spring of 1997, when the leader of the Lion's Den, Ken Shamrock, left MMA competition to try his hand at professional wrestling.

CHAPTER 14

A New Direction

After suffering a controversial loss to Dan Severn in UFC IX, Ken Sham-rock returned to Ultimate Ultimate '96 for redemption. The beating he delivered to Brian Johnston in his quarterfinal bout was one of the most severe the octagon had ever seen. But in the course of it, Shamrock injured his hand—the same one he had broken while training for UFC II. Since he was unable to proceed to the semifinals, pay-per-view program-mer SEG wanted to lower his pay for the next event, and for a month Bob Shamrock argued with the people at SEG, telling them that Ken was one of the UFC's biggest stars, and that he should be paid accordingly. In addition to being involved in this dispute, the UFC was in the process of being dropped by the cable companies due to McCain's anti-MMA campaign.

The future of MMA competition in America did not look bright. But Ken still had a family to support, along with a houseful of fighters. "At the time, the UFC was really having problems," he recalls. "It was hard to get it sanctioned anywhere. Pay-per-view was closing down on them. I just felt it was time to move on to something else because I wasn't going to be able to pay my bills if things kept going the way they were. I had dabbled a little bit in pro wrestling prior to the fighting game. I figured I did pretty well at that, and that maybe I could use the reputation to move over into the big-time world of the WWF."

"I called the WWF and talked to Bret Hart," remembers Bob Sham-rock. "Bret came down in February and we met at the Black Angus. Bret told Ken that he had a five-year contract with the WWF, and that he was going to be retiring. Bret told Ken, 'I want you to take my place because you have a real natural ability for it.' The following week, Ken flew back to Connecticut to meet with Vince McMahon." Shortly after this, the WCW called Bob, as they were also interested in Ken, but the WWF came through with the right price. "And so we said, 'Okay, we'll go with the WWF.' That Sunday night, we were on a plane headed for New York for Monday Night RAW."

While Ken was living up to his title as "the World's Most Dangerous Man" on weekly television, the Lion's Den was left without a leader. "I turned the Lion's Den over to Frank," says Ken. "That's when Frank and I started having our problems. It was a little difficult for all the boys to accept the fact that I was moving on to something else, and that it wasn't real, and that people were saying things like, 'Shamrock is a traitor.' It was really difficult; a lot of them had a hard time understanding why I was leaving them—I had to move on in order to support the gym, the lifestyle I'd put myself into, and them. I had a fighters' house, and I had a gym I had to run."

While Ken was on the road, Bob Shamrock did the best he could to keep things going and to manage the careers of the fighters. "Ken had turned the training over to Frank and Jerry to run," explains Bob. "But they were just two kids. Eventually, I just backed out of the Lion's Den altogether, and it went downhill from there, because they didn't have any business sense."

Frank and Maurice

While Ken was on the road, Frank grew closer to kickboxer Maurice Smith, and they began to form a partnership. The two had trained together to get Smith ready for his debut in Extreme Fight 3 against Marcus "Conan" Silveira. Using his newly acquired grappling skills, Smith had taken on the muscle-bound Brazilian and won the heavyweight title. But after he'd defended that title in Extreme Fight 4, the promotion shut down due to the financial pressure created by the cable ban. Without a venue in which to test his skills, Smith turned his attention to the UFC. His debut bout would be against Mark "the Hammer" Coleman in UFC XIV, held in Birmingham, Alabama on July 27, 1997. For this fight, he would need Frank's assistance.

The two trained tirelessly, working on Smith's guard. By the time fight night arrived, Smith felt confident that he could beat the "ground and pound" wrestler. He was so confident, in fact, that in a prefight interview he went so far as to say that Coleman punched "like a girl."

The Hammer took Smith's comments personally, and all the prefight hype came to a head when the two stepped into the octagon. Less than half a minute into the match, Coleman did what he did best—he shot in, taking Smith to the mat. Although Smith trapped the wrestler in his guard, it did little to stop the furious Coleman from raining head butts and punches onto Smith's face and head. Smith weathered the storm, however, and then he showed just how versatile he had become as he launched his own attack with punches and elbows from his back.

After being trapped under Coleman for nine grueling minutes, Smith slipped out the back door and rose to his feet. The Hammer was exhausted. "Frank and I figured that he'd be strong for about five, ten minutes," says Smith. "As it happened, he got tired, just as we figured."

Things looked grim for Coleman. Standing up against the octagon fence, he became little more than a punching bag for his opponent. But when Smith got greedy and went for a kick to the head, Coleman found one last ounce of energy and ducked under for the takedown. Once they hit the mat, however, it was Smith who dominated, landing elbows and punches from his back before reversing Coleman and getting to his feet again. With only thirty seconds to go in regulation time, Smith was unable to muster the strikes necessary to knock his opponent out.

When the two fighters were separated, Coleman clung to the octagon fence for support. The brief rest did little to replenish his energy. When Smith came forward in the first three-minute overtime, Coleman was still too exhausted to execute an effective takedown, and he became a sitting duck for the kickboxer's combinations to the legs and head. But Coleman proved his heart as he weathered the beating through six minutes of overtime, placing the decision in the hands of the judges. Smith was declared the new UFC Heavyweight Champion.

"My fight with Maurice was probably one of the biggest lessons in life I have ever learned," admits Coleman. "A very important lesson. He taught me you have to have respect for everybody, because you don't know what kind of work they're doing. You never know how much they have improved. My problem with Maurice was I watched tapes of him from two years earlier, and I totally convinced myself that it was going to be one of my easier fights to date. I trained like it. I did not put in any of the time to fight him. He had a great game plan, and he stuck to it. He tired me out, and that was it. It was a horrible, horrible feeling. That was the most tired I had ever been in my entire life. I was tired at the two-minute mark, and it ended up going twenty-one minutes. It took me over an hour to get my heart rate down after the fight was over. I also took a hell of a beating on my leg. I didn't quit, and I kept fighting. I paid the price for not paying my dues. I was out having some fun, being lazy, and Maurice

Smith kicked me right in the ass. But for me that was a much-needed ass-kicking."

After winning the title at UFC XIV, Maurice Smith was king. But being on top meant that others were hungry to knock him down. One such competitor, who got a shot at it during UFC XV, held in St. Louis, Missouri on October 17, 1997, was barroom brawler David "Tank" Abbott. But Smith fought intelligently, beginning the fight by sticking and moving. Tank eventually grew frustrated with Smith's quickness, and he managed to bulldog him up against the fence and land a hook that knocked Smith to his back. "I was worried about Tank punching me," says Smith. "I wasn't worried about him beating me up. I knew he had the potential to punch me hard and could knock me out. And he almost did it."

Abbott went in for the kill, but, just as he'd done with Coleman, Smith not only showed good defense on the ground but also mounted his own offense, delivering relentless elbow strikes to the back of Tank's head. Both attempted to submit the other with key locks, but to no avail. Tank continued to drop power punches, and in doing so he played right into Smith's hands and tired himself out.

When the two fighters were brought to the standing position due to inactivity at seven and a half minutes, Abbott was exhausted. As Abbott rested, hands on knees, Smith dropped two devastating leg kicks. When the third one landed, Tank indicated to McCarthy that he'd had enough.

Smith had successfully defended his title as UFC Heavyweight Champion. He would go to UFC Japan for his second title defense, and there he would meet yet another wrestler—only this one had hands like lightning.

Out of the Lion's Shadow

Frank Shamrock had trained Maurice Smith for his two title fights, just as he had trained all the other Lion's Den members for their fights. "I was at UFC II, and I had been to all of them," says Frank. "I had always been the observer. I had always been the trainer, and I never stepped into the light. And I never said, 'I trained so and so. I did this, and I did that.' I was there to help other people. I was there to support and help those people. So when the opportunity came along for me to step into the light and show people who I was, I took it." Unfortunately, his decision to fight in the next UFC, which would take place in Japan, would lead to Frank's dismissal from the Lion's Den.

According to Bob Shamrock, the problem wasn't Frank's decision to fight, but rather how he went about landing the fight. Bob, acting on behalf of the Lion's Den, helped set the deal up with the UFC. "We started negotiating the terms and stuff," he says, "and then after about a week, none of the contracts had come in. They're pretty good about sending them out, and I was always good about getting them back right away. So I called Art Davie and asked why he hadn't sent the contracts. He said, 'Well, Frank called us and told us to send them directly to him.'" Bob relayed this news to Ken, and when Frank's big brother came home from the WWF, all hell broke loose. When the dust settled, Frank left the Lion's Den for good.

"Probably the hardest thing I've ever done in my life," admits Frank. "Those people were my family. Everybody there—I've trained everybody from the bottom up. I was in all their corners. I was the trainer. As soon as Ken realized I could fight, I was the trainer. I didn't have a life. I lived with all those people, and all I did every day was train and focus and help them in their careers. And then when I thought it was my time, Ken said, 'It's not . . . no, it's not your time.' And I thought it was. I put in my time, I trained everybody, I did my work, I did what I was supposed to do, and I wanted it to be my time. And Ken didn't want that. He said, 'You can go, [but] you take nothing with you, you never use the name, and you're no longer part of this family.' And I went. And I never use the name, and I've never trained with those people again, and I have no relation whatsoever to them. They don't associate with me. I left with the clothes in my car and a pair of blue boxing gloves. That was a little while ago."

The future of the Lion's Den was now uncertain, and only time would tell if the crew that had made such an impressive impact on the world of MMA competition would remain on top.

CHAPTER 15

Joining Forces

UFC Japan/December 21, 1997
(Yokohama, Japan)

For the first time, the UFC would be staged overseas. The infamous octagon was shipped by boat to Japan and set up in the Shin Yokohama Arena, where the competition would take place on December 21, 1997 before thousands of quiet, yet intense Japanese fans. The heavyweight title fight between Randy Couture, a six-foot-one, 220-pound world-class wrestler, and Maurice Smith was eagerly anticipated, but several other crucial battles would also be waged, making this first international UFC one of the more monumental. For Frank Shamrock, it was an opportunity to shine. It was his first UFC, and he had to pull out the win.

But Frank's task was not an easy one. To get his hands on the middleweight championship belt, he first had to beat the five-foot-ten, 199-pound Kevin Jackson. Not only did Jackson have an astounding MMA record, but he'd also brought home the 1992 Olympic gold medal in wrestling. "Because he was so specialized in one art, it was hard to combat it," explains Frank. "I didn't really know what to do—so I went to the Stanford wrestling team. I hooked up with Eric Duce, who is a phenomenal wrestler. I told him I was going to fight Kevin Jackson. He said, 'He's going to kill you!' I told him to hold on and wrestle with me a little bit, then let me know. From that day forward, he believed in me, and we became training partners. When I saw the things I could do to him, I knew I was going to win."

In addition to training with the Stanford University wrestling team, Frank continued to train with Maurice Smith to improve upon his striking skills. "At that point, Maurice and I formed a partnership," says Frank, "and now I consider him my brother. Shortly after he fought Conan, I fought [Tsuyoshi] Kohsaka in RINGS. It was another thirty-minute fight. Kohsaka weighted 240, and I weighed 190. It was thirty

FRANK SHAMROCK

Frank Shamrock submits Kevin Jackson via arm bar in UFC Japan.

minutes of complete agony. But after the fight, Maurice invited Kohsaka to come down and train, and we all began training together. At that point, we all sat down and said, 'We've got a good thing going here, and we're strong as a threesome. We should search out other styles to make our style stronger, and we should build an alliance with those.' Someone said, 'Hey, that's a great word.' We became the Alliance from that day forward. It was just a bunch of guys at a good point in their careers looking to help each other out. And that's why I felt like it became successful." The Alliance was a community of equals, and it was different from the Lion's Den because it had no leader.

With all the knowledge and experience of his new teammates in his corner, Frank felt more than ready to dominate the UFC. As he stretched out in his corner, a pumped-up Kevin Jackson made his way towards the octagon to the thumping bass of rap music. For the first time since the UFC's inception, the crowd was hushed as legendary ring announcer Bruce Buffer made the announcements.

After the two had briefly sized each other up, Jackson rushed in. He drove Frank backward, slammed him hard into the chain-link fence, and then brought him to the mat. Although Jackson landed on top, Frank was by no means in trouble. Remaining composed, he clutched Jackson's right arm tightly to his chest. Then he quickly raised his legs, wrapping them around Jackson's head. Now, with the wrestler's arm locked between his thighs, Frank arched his body like a cat. The result was instantaneous—bone-breaking pressure on Jackson's elbow. The surprised wrestler had just been introduced to submission. He had no choice but to tap out.

In just twenty-two seconds, Frank Shamrock had won the first middle-weight title. "I knew I was going to win," he claims. "I knew exactly how I was going to win, and I was just waiting to make the celebration. That fight distinguished me from being Ken's brother, or 'their' trainer, or being a Lion's Den fighter. That fight made me Frank Shamrock. Through all my preparation, I just knew it, and I couldn't wait to show everybody. That was my coming-out party."

Without taking time to celebrate his victory, Frank made his way back to the octagon for the second time that night—only now he was working as a cornerman for Maurice Smith, who was to defend his heavy-weight title against world-class wrestler Randy "the Natural" Couture.

The Natural

Like Jackson, Couture had already enjoyed a long and illustrious wrestling career. After winning the Washington State Championships in high school, he enlisted in the army and rapidly made the All-Army Wrestling Team. "That is where I really got my first taste of competitive wrestling and what it takes to compete at that level," he says. "Basically, all I did was wrestle for the service—I hardly ever wore a uniform. My last three years in the military, I was assigned to the sports department, and wrestling was basically my job. I just wrestled and trained. I went to all the national training camps and national tournaments; it was a great place to compete. I got some national recognition that I didn't have coming out of high school that allowed me to go to college for four years."

Although Couture was primarily a wrestler, by the time he got out of the army he had also acquired some boxing skills. While he was in advanced training at Fort Rutgers, Alabama, a series of amateur boxing matches was scheduled between the air traffic controllers, the aircraft mechanics, and the helicopter pilots. Couture trained for it for three weeks with a boxing coach, but at the competition he was not paired up with an opponent and never fought a match. He ceased training, not knowing that those three short weeks of boxing would one day come in handy.

After getting out of the military, Couture was accepted to Oklahoma State and began wrestling at the Division One powerhouse. In 1991, he won the Big 8 Championship and went on to become a three-time National Collegiate Athletic Association All-American and a two-time NCAA finalist. But it wasn't until after college that Couture realized some of his bigger accomplishments, including winning the gold medal in the 1991 Pan-American Games in Cuba.

Couture was always on the lookout for new ways to test his skills. Then one day he saw his old wrestling friend Don Frye compete in the UFC. Couture was instantly intrigued—he knew he possessed the skills to enter such a competition. "As far as a fighting style, I think Greco-Roman is a little better style for mixed martial arts," says Couture, "because so many of the fights end up in the clinch. A lot of the guys are learning to stop open takedowns and sprawl, and defend the open shoots a lot better. If you have the ability to tie a guy up and clinch, and take him down from the clinch, which is what Greco-Roman is all about, I think it's an advantage."

Couture sent an application to SEG, but because the event's quota of wrestlers was already filled, he heard nothing back. A few months later, Couture was approached by some old wrestling acquaintances who had started Real American Wrestlers, or team RAW. "They had this brainstorm to get a bunch of world-class wrestlers, both in freestyle and Greco, and form a fighting stable," explains Couture. "Having been friends of theirs through wrestling, I was one of the athletes they approached about being a member of the RAW team. At one time there, they had several of the top fighters." The team was originally comprised of Couture, Frank Trigg, and Tom Erikson.

Couture's chance to step into the octagon came just a few weeks before UFC XIII. He was in Puerto Rico at the time, competing in the Pan-American Games, when SEG contacted him and asked if he would like to participate. Another competitor had suffered a hand injury, and SEG couldn't find anybody who would take the fight on such short notice. With only two weeks to go before the event, Couture began preparing for his first MMA competition. He flew from Puerto Rico to Atlanta, where he trained for the five remaining days before the tournament.

Despite his lack of preparation, Couture proceeded to choke out his first opponent, Tony Halme, and he won the tournament by delivering a technical knockout to Steve Graham with a barrage of unanswered strikes. Just as he had been hooked on wrestling, he was now hooked on MMA.

Couture returned in UFC XV to fight Brazilian phenom Vitor Belfort in the Superfight. "I was a serious underdog," says Couture, "and nobody had really lasted more than about two minutes with Vitor up to that

ANDY ANDERSON

The Brazilian phenomenon, Vitor Belfort.

point." Despite this, Couture had accepted the fight. Belfort had never been tested on the ground, and he hadn't had to fight for any extended length of time. Couture thought that Belfort's conditioning was suspect, and he believed that if he could outlast the Brazilian, the fight would be his. Couture's strategy was to tie him up, make him work hard, and then bring him to the ground.

Belfort came out swinging, and Couture did what he said he was going to do in his prefight interview—take the Brazilian to the mat. But Belfort proved to be a worthy wrestler as well, and Couture was forced to stand up and trade blows, eating several punches in the process. Couture finally found the opportunity he was looking for when Belfort extended himself with a jab. Couture ducked, seized the Brazilian's legs, and took him to the floor. Although Couture didn't manage to land any devastating blows to his opponent while they were down, he did manage to tire Belfort out. When the fighters got back on their feet at six minutes and forty-five seconds into the bout, Couture made use of his boxing skills. Clinching with Belfort, he landed almost thirty uppercuts, sending his opponent back to the mat. Couture came down on top of him and continued to pound away at the Brazilian's face until John McCarthy intervened.

"It was pretty much what I expected, but it wasn't what anybody else expected," recalls Couture. "When we really sat back and analyzed Belfort's fights, we realized he had quick, accurate hands, but as a technical boxer he

*Maurice Smith (left) and Bas Rutten (right), two of the most powerful strikers
in the sport, being playful backstage at the UFC.*

Frank Shamrock giving Patrick Smith some advice.

wasn't all that great as long as you didn't stand right in front of him. He didn't make a lot of adjustments. He didn't throw a lot of combinations; they were real straight punches. So, as long as you didn't just stand there and be a target for him, you had a good chance." Couture's strategy worked, and he shocked the MMA world. Shortly after this bout, he was given the apt nickname "the Natural."

UFC Japan/Heavyweight Title Bout— Maurice Smith versus Randy Couture

With the Belfort bout, Randy Couture had earned himself a shot at the heavyweight title. That opportunity came in Japan, against Maurice Smith. His basic game plan was to stay out of Smith's striking range and concentrate on taking him down. But Smith, a member of the Alliance, had been working on submissions and promised to be a tough customer.

Right out of the gate, Smith made use of his striking skills and landed two hard leg kicks. When Couture tried to advance on him, he was met with a jab to the face. Smith circled, keeping the grappler at bay. But time ran out for Smith when Couture cornered him up against the fence and took him down with a double leg.

Once on the ground, Couture played it safe and managed to keep his opponent down for the entire fifteen minutes of regulation time, despite some crafty escape attempts by Smith. Only twenty seconds into the first overtime, Smith threw a leg kick that again allowed Couture to take him to the mat. "Every time he kicked me," says Couture, "I wanted to put him on the ground, make him pay for kicking me."

In the second overtime, Smith moved more swiftly and landed several punches to Couture's face before getting taken down yet again. With only two minutes left in the fight, Couture got more active on the ground, landing knees and punches. When the bout came to an end, neither fighter looked confident that he had won.

One judge called it a draw, and the two others called it for Couture. For the first time in seventeen years, Maurice Smith had lost a title fight. "Fortunately, I think the format—the straight fifteen minutes with two three-minute overtimes—made it so I only had to take him down three times," says Couture. "And I don't think he'd done a whole lot of cross training as far as defending takedowns up to that point. He'd never really learned how to stop the takedowns, or to keep the fight on its feet."

Randy "the Natural" Couture was the new UFC Heavyweight

Champion. Still, despite his impressive showing, he would not retain his title for long. "I had a major contract problem with SEG," explains Couture. "They had signed me to a three-fight deal, with a certain amount of money to show and a certain amount of money to win each of the three fights. I was supposed to fight against Bas Rutten in UFC Brazil. They came back and said, 'Well, we're not going to pay you what the contract says.' They offered me a little over a quarter of what the contract said they were supposed to pay me and basically said take it or leave it. I said, 'I'm prepared to fight, I want to fight, but if you're not going to honor the contract, I'm not going to fight.'" Couture took a leave of absence from the UFC, and SEG put his heavyweight title belt up for grabs. But when Couture returned a year and a half later, it would be with a bang.

Maurice Smith, in his postfight interview, promised the fans that he would be back. He made good on his word at UFC XIX, but he was defeated by another world-class wrestler, Kevin Randleman. Smith did not remain in his slump for long, however. He returned for redemption in UFC XXI, defeating Marco Ruas before traveling to Japan to beat Branco Civitic in Pride 7, held on September 12, 1999. After securing several more victories in MMA competition, however, Smith returned to his kickboxing roots. Although he was competing as a kickboxer, he didn't leave the MMA world behind him, by any means: he continued to train many of MMA's top competitors, such as Randy Couture, working on their strikes and improving their overall stand-up game. Maurice Smith is one of the most revered competitors in the sport and a true champion on all fronts.

CHAPTER 16

Running the Gauntlet

UFC XVI—The Battle in the Bayou/March 13, 1998
(New Orleans, Louisiana)

After Frank Shamrock triumphed over Kevin Jackson, he wasted no time in getting back into the octagon. He went to the swamplands of Louisiana to challenge Extreme Fighting veteran Igor Zinoviev in UFC XVI: The Battle in the Bayou, held on March 13, 1998 in New Orleans. Frank had studied Zinoviev as closely as he had studied Jackson, and he realized that every time someone would shoot in on the Russian, he would simply sit back and try to sink in a guillotine choke. Frank planned to capitalize on that. He'd shoot in, let Zinoviev go for the choke, and then pick him up and slam him. He was so sure that his strategy would work, that he meticulously practiced this shoot-and-slam every day for thirty-six days in a row.

The fight was extraordinarily fast, and visually stunning. After Frank dropped two kicks to the Russian's legs, Zinoviev threw a huge right hand. Frank ducked the punch, and when Zinoviev went for the anticipated guillotine, Frank hoisted him off his feet and slammed him to the mat. "Everything was perfect," Frank recalls. "He felt as if he weighed three pounds. All I could hear was my corner giving instructions and his bones breaking when he hit the mat."

Zinoviev was out cold, and UFC officials and medics hovered over him. In the twenty-four seconds it took him to lose the match, he suffered a broken collarbone, a fractured vertebra in his neck, and a dislocated shoulder. "I felt terrible after the fight," admits Frank. "I thought I had killed him. I thought my worst fear had come true—that I hurt somebody forever."

Frank visited the wounded Zinoviev several times in the hospital, apologizing for the outcome of the bout. Igor was matter-of-fact, and he

Frank Shamrock lands a Thai kick to the leg of Igor Zinoviev in UFC XVI.

told Frank not to worry, that they were both fighters and it was the name
of the game. The whole experience moved Frank Shamrock deeply. Igor
Zinoviev hasn't fought since.

UFC XVI—Mikey Burnett versus Eugenio Tadeau

Frank was not the only one making a huge impact at UFC XVI. Two of
his old teammates, Mikey Burnett and Jerry Bohlander, were also competing. It would be Mikey's UFC debut, and he was to face the dangerous
Brazilian fighter Eugenio Tadeau.

"I knew I was good, but I had just been to Brazil five months earlier
and seen Eugenio actually beat Renzo Gracie," says Burnett. "My fight
that night got changed around a couple of times. First I was supposed to
fight Townsend Saunders, the wrestler—I was okay with that—and then
I was supposed to fight Pat Miletich. It got changed back and forth, and
finally they said I was going to fight Eugenio. My mindset going into it
was, 'All right, I'm going to try to knock him out, or he's going to knock
me out.'"

Burnett considered Eugenio's style to be similar to his own, and he was admittedly a little intimidated upon hearing the confirmation of his match. He knew that if nothing else, it was going to be a knock-down, drag-out brawl.

Eugenio Tadeau stepped quickly to the center of the octagon to meet the stark-white Mikey Burnett. Burnett glared ferociously at the Brazilian, who was advancing on him with a wide-eyed, soulless stare. Both took boxing stances and stutter-stepped for a moment. Each threw some exploratory punches. Then Burnett threw a quick right that didn't connect, and Tadeau shot under. Burnett sprawled, and, bouncing to his feet, he slammed Tadeau into the fence, landing a heavy knee. After the two fighters had exchanged punches, Burnett managed to sink in a standing choke. Tadeau struggled to pry himself free, and they both fell to the mat. When Tadeau finally squirmed his head out of the lock, he found himself riding the Lion's Den fighter.

The fight stayed on the ground for six minutes, with several reversals. Burnett stayed very active, constantly trying to pass Tadeau's guard and delivering short, hard punches to Tadeau's body and head. At about the eight-minute mark, referee Joe Hamilton stood them back up. Tadeau was winded and a bit shaken by Burnett's hard punching.

There was a flurry of punches, during which Tadeau took a couple of rights and a solid uppercut from Burnett. Afterwards, they clung to each other in the center of the octagon for almost a minute, exhausted. Burnett's superior conditioning paid off, however; he separated himself from Tadeau and went wild in one last flurry, landing a severe uppercut to Tadeau's chin that lifted the Brazilian off his feet. Hamilton stepped in and stopped the fight at nine minutes and forty-four seconds. A dazed Eugenio Tadeau was escorted from the ring, his head lolling as he stumbled away from the octagon.

Although Burnett broke his hand during the bout and was unable to continue on into the finals, he believed that the injury was well worth it: he had dethroned the fighter whom he considered to be the best 170-pound competitor on the scene.

UFC XVI—Jerry Bohlander versus Kevin Jackson

The Lion's Den wasn't through claiming victory that night, however. Jerry Bohlander was up next, taking on none other than Frank's former victim, the adept wrestler Kevin Jackson. "A couple of months before the fight, SEG called and said, 'Hey, you want to fight Kevin Jackson?'" says Bohlander. "And I was like, 'Hell, yeah!' So I started training, and I was training Pete Williams at the time to fight Dan Severn in the IFC, and I was training Mikey Burnett for the UFC. So everything was going good. Then they called me like a week later and said, 'You know what? We really want to have a Brazilian fight a wrestler, so we're going to skip over you and use Fabio Gurgel.' I had already beaten Fabio, and that pissed me off."

Bohlander felt fed up with the whole situation and decided he was just going to enjoy himself—so he let loose a bit. He started partying with his friends and relaxing; then, a month before the scheduled fight, he got a call from Bob Shamrock. "Jerry, I've got something really important to tell you," said Bob. Jerry didn't know what was going on; he thought something horrible must have happened to a friend or family member. Then Bob continued, "You're in the fight."

"I was like, 'Holy shit!'" says Bohlander. "And I was right in the middle of training those other guys, so we went right into it." Focusing on conditioning, Bohlander stepped up his training. He practiced explosive movement techniques and running sprints; he worked on wrestling drills and takedowns, and on improving his striking. With only three weeks left until UFC XVI, the three Lion's Den competitors trained around the clock.

Jackson dominated the majority of the fight, forcing Bohlander to hold him off in his guard. But then, at ten minutes and twenty-five seconds into the bout, just as things were looking hopeless for Bohlander, he exploded, rolling Jackson and seizing his arm. In seconds, Jackson was tapping the canvas, a painful reminder of his loss to Frank Shamrock just a few months earlier in Japan.

Although the Lion's Den crew had made the statement that they were still on top of their game, the spotlight shone on Frank Shamrock that night. He had defended his title spectacularly. In the last two events, he had won both of his fights in under thirty seconds, firmly establishing himself as the man to beat. However, his next opponent, at UFC XVII, would not go down so easily.

UFC XVII—Redemption/May 15, 1998
(Mobile, Alabama)

"You know what happened?" says Frank. "This is why I stopped doing business with SEG. They called me last minute, three weeks out. They said, 'Frank, we've got a show coming up, and we can't afford to throw a full show. We want you to fight on this card, and then we want you to commentate, and we're willing to give you a chump fighter. We're not going to pay you very much because this guy is not good at all, but we are still willing to do it. You can fight him the first of the night and then commentate the rest of the night, and we'll show it on a later show.' The guy shows up and he's Jeremy Horn. And then I'm on my back and it's like, here we go!"

Although the twenty-two-year-old Horn, standing a lanky six-foot-one, didn't look like much, he was already a veteran. Growing up in Omaha, Nebraska, he and his brothers frequently played a game that involved whomping each other with sticks. "The prospect of taking a beating is something I have been faced with since I was five," says Horn.

When Jeremy was thirteen, one of his stick-wielding brothers got him involved in the martial arts, but, not satisfied with the training he was receiving, Jeremy got together half a dozen of his friends and they began working out on their own. "We just watched fights, and I had a knack for seeing things," says Horn. "We'd get together and beat on each other for a few hours."

This informal training ceased, however, once Horn saw his first Ultimate Fighting Championship. He was nineteen, and, determined to compete, he began his formal MMA training. Just a month and a half later, he got a call from an MMA promoter looking for future combatants. "They were giving everyone calls," remembers Horn, "saying, 'Come down and fight for us. We're putting on a no-holds-barred event, and these are trials for it. If you do well, we'll put you in the show.' They were doing this all over, pretty much bullshitting people. I was one of them."

Thinking it was his chance to break into the MMA world, Horn agreed to fight. The promoters flew him to Atlanta and then brought him to a warehouse where fighting was taking place. "They had maybe a twenty-by-twenty area with judo mats thrown down," says Horn. "On one side of the room, they had a bunch of couches, and people were hanging out watching. They also had a half a dozen guys with kicking shields just running around the outside of the mat, so if the two fighters got close to the edge, these guys would get shoulder to shoulder and serve as a wall." The fights were bare-fisted, and everything but biting and eye gouging was legal.

Horn dispensed with his opponent in a minute and a half with an arm bar, but he received no reward for doing so. "We got paid nothing," he says. "They flew us down, they bought us dinner, we fought, and they flew us back the next day. They paid nothing. They were telling everyone these were the trials for their big show. Everyone came down and fought for free, hoping to get a spot on the big show. They told hundreds of people this, and they would film all the fights, and then afterwards we'd all go watch the fights they had already done. They were just using that as a reason to get everyone to come down and fight."

Although the "event" left a bitter taste in his mouth, Horn wasn't through with MMA competition. Shortly after the warehouse gig, he was introduced to Monte Cox and added to the card for Quad City Ultimate 2, where he put away his first opponent, Mike Adsit, with strikes, before losing to Mark Hanssen via arm bar.

Horn had done well in his first true MMA outing, but the best thing to come out of the event was a bond with fellow competitor Pat Miletich. "From then on, I saw him at several fights," says Horn, "because back then it was pretty much local shows. Pat had a group of guys, and I had a group of guys, so we'd fight each other pretty regularly at the Quad City Ultimate. When we ran out of guys—all our guys had fought all of his guys—we said, 'Look, we're done fighting, so how about if we start training together?' I'd come up once or twice a month and train for the weekend at Pat's [in Iowa]. Eventually, I got sick of driving, and I figured I'd just move there."

The move paid off—Horn received the regular training that he needed. He continued fighting for Monte Cox, who was now calling his promotion Extreme Challenge. After nine fights and only one loss, Horn attracted the attention of other promotions, including the UFC.

UFC XVII—Frank Shamrock versus Jeremy Horn

Because of his impressive victories in numerous events, Jeremy Horn was added onto the card of UFC XVII as an alternate for the middleweight tournament. Then, a week before the show, things were changed. Horn would fight Frank Shamrock, the middleweight champion. "I wasn't very nervous," explains Horn, "because all I figured is if I can last a minute then I've done better than anyone else has. I was really relaxed, because I knew I could defend myself for a minute. That's really all I was looking to do—not get beat for at least a minute."

Horn did more than just defend, however. He came hot out of the gate, shot in, took Frank to the mat, and then obtained a mount. For the entire fifteen minutes of the regulation period, he controlled the fight, attempting one submission after another.

But then, two minutes into the overtime period, Horn made a critical mistake. Clinging to Frank's back, eating reverse elbows, Horn grew impatient and pulled the submission fighter to the mat. When they landed, Horn's leg was trapped between both of Frank's. Spotting the potential knee bar, Frank merely reached down, grabbed Horn's heel, and arched back. Horn, who had just given his guaranteed victory away, tapped before his leg was broken. "My mindset was part of the reason why I didn't smoke him like I should have," says Horn. "I was just so concerned with, 'All you got to do is last a minute, all you got to do is last a minute.' Then I go in there and slam him on his head and mount him, and I was just in shock. I couldn't kick it into gear and get the job done. I was just dumbfounded."

Frank had pulled out the victory with only two and a half weeks of training, and with no help from the people of SEG, who appeared to believe that he was invincible. "I'm an athlete, a trained athlete," says Frank, "and I wasn't trained. I pulled that one out with pure mental ability. I didn't have the energy to push the fight. If I had tried to push the fight, I would have lost, because I didn't have the conditioning. So I just had to wait around. Jeremy never tried to win; he just tried to hold me down. Here's a guy who refused to do anything, and me who doesn't have the energy to do anything, and I'm just thinking, 'Oh God, let it end!' But luckily I pulled it out."

UFC XVII—Pete Williams versus Mark Coleman

Although Frank's narrow win over Horn was exciting, it was the main event of the evening that garnered the spotlight. Lion's Den fighter Pete Williams was making his UFC debut, and it was a difficult one. His opponent was Mark "the Hammer" Coleman, who was there for redemption after devastating loss to Maurice Smith eight months before.

The fight started off as everyone had expected it would. Coleman grounded his smaller opponent and then proceeded to pound on him for the first five minutes. A surprise came when the two fighters were made to stand up due to inactivity and Coleman showed some prowess with boxing. But once Williams began landing leg kicks, Coleman decided to stick to what he did best and closed the distance. Williams had practiced defending the takedown, however, and he forced Coleman to work for it, pounding on Coleman with knees and punches as he did so. When the Hammer finally brought Williams to the mat, there was only two minutes left in regulation time. Wasting precious time defending against Williams's submission attempts and upward strikes, Coleman failed to put his opponent away.

When Williams got back to his corner, Bohlander was waiting to coach him. "You've got to move now, you've got to win this! You've got to move!" It sunk in. In overtime, Williams headed back into battle like a man on a mission. He landed a devastating leg kick, a combination of punches, and when Coleman shot in, he sprawled immediately. As Coleman started to rise, Williams cupped the back of his head and delivered a powerful knee to Coleman's face. The Hammer shook his head like a wet dog, throwing punches blindly, unaware that one of the most brutal knockouts the UFC had ever seen was about to occur.

Williams, knowing his opponent was in trouble, stepped forward and threw yet another powerful kick. The top of his wrestling shoe collided solidly with Coleman's face. The muscle-bound wrestler's eyes rolled back, he staggered, and he fell. It was the upset of the year. "I came back from my knee surgery way too soon," says Coleman. "I don't want to make excuses—he kicked me right in the teeth—but I wasn't prepared to go. That really, really shook my confidence."

Coleman was determined to redeem himself at UFC XVIII, held in New Orleans, Louisiana on January 8, 1999. He took on yet another experienced standing fighter, Pedro Rizzo. It was a grueling battle that had to be resolved by the judges, and Coleman lost a controversial decision. "I was out there trying not to lose instead of trying to win," he admits, before adding, "I could've have done more, but I think I did plenty to win. I just needed the win. If I had any idea that I was behind on the scorecard, I would have done a hell of a lot more. I was coasting in for the victory in the end . . . You've got to try to finish the guy off. You've got to do that for the fans, because they're the ones paying, and that's what they want to see."

Coleman would bring that mentality into his next fight, but after three consecutive losses in the octagon, that fight would not be in the UFC. "The Pedro Rizzo loss was a horrible, horrible feeling," says Coleman, "but it was also sort of a blessing in disguise, because the UFC at that time was going way downhill. By losing three times, it opened me up to go over to Japan, where it's just been incredible for the last two years."

UFC Brazil/October 16, 1998
(São Paulo, Brazil)

Frank Shamrock versus John Lober

Coleman had learned a valuable lesson in UFC XVII, as had Frank Shamrock. Frank returned to UFC Brazil, held in São Paulo on October 16, 1998, after his close victory over Jeremy Horn. This time, he had come prepared. His opponent was John "the Machine" Lober, the only competitor ever to have defeated him in MMA competition. There had been some strong words from both combatants in the prefight interviews. Lober had confidently stated that he would be knocking middleweight champion Frank Shamrock repeatedly to the mat, letting him get back up, and repeating the process. He also referred to Frank's three championship title defenses as a "catching up" to his own level of skill. He didn't feel that there was any bad blood between them, but he did sense that he had gotten into Frank's head.

Frank didn't hold Lober in the highest regard, either. After they'd both arrived in Brazil, Lober had taunted Frank with prank phone calls and dirty e-mails; he'd also pounded on Frank's door in the middle of the night and attempted to disrupt Frank's meals by making loud noises. Lober's strategy to get under Frank's skin worked, but it may have worked too well. "That is the only fight I have ever been in where I was actually angry," says Frank.

Just moments into the match, Lober shot in and seized Frank's leg, trying to bring him down. Frank held his ground with an underhook and slid his arm around Lober's neck, sinking in a guillotine choke. "I had the choke," says Frank, "and I said to myself, 'No, not like that. He's not going to get off that easy.'" He slammed Lober down on the mat and took a side mount, grinding his right elbow into Lober's face. But the fight would not remain there for long.

Frank seemed to be in total control of the fight, standing it up and bringing it down as he pleased. And in the end, he chose his feet. He chased Lober with sharp and effective muay Thai kicks. Then he caught Lober with a hard right hand that sent him to the mat. Lober stayed down, wanting Frank to bring it to the ground, but Frank wouldn't go. He glared down at his opponent, and Lober cautiously stood. It was then that Frank turned on the juice, kicking Lober hard enough to send him careening into the fence. Frank followed up with a knee and then a hailstorm of downward strikes. Bleeding from his face, Lober fell to the canvas. Still Frank did not stop. He unloaded on Lober's ribs. "I broke him," says Frank. "We were in the corner, and I beat him until he said he couldn't take any more, and I was like, 'You're going to take it. I'm going to beat you to death in front of all these people.' I told him, 'I want you to say it . . . I want you to say it out loud.'" The Machine got shut down, and he tapped at seven minutes and forty seconds.

Frank had unleashed his fury in the octagon. Later, he felt badly about it. While he was waiting in the airport to return home, a stitched-up Lober approached him and apologized for his prefight disrespect, claiming that the things he'd done to get under Frank's skin had just been part of the game plan.

UFC Brazil—Mikey Burnett versus Pat Miletich

As often happened, two Lion's Den fighters were set to compete along-side Frank, this time at UFC Brazil. Pete Williams took on Tsuyoshi Kohsaka, and although the match went the distance, Williams lost by a unanimous decision.

Mikey Burnett was fighting Pat Miletich for the first-ever lightweight title, and he was no stranger to Brazil. The first time he'd gone there was to serve as Jerry Bohlander's cornerman. "Me and Jerry went to a bar and were pretty intoxicated," Burnett recalls, "and I was talking shit about how I was going to beat Eugenio Tadeau and Renzo Gracie. Everybody was looking at me like, 'This guy has lost his mind.' But being there the second time was odd to me; fighting overseas is definitely harder. The plane trip, the atmosphere—it's totally different and kind of shocks you a little bit."

Miletich was confident, coming off a tournament victory in UFC XVI. In that same UFC, Miletich had seen Burnett fight Eugenio Tadeau, and he figured his best bet would be to tire Burnett out. But this plan didn't take into consideration the superior conditioning of the Lion's Den fighters. The fight went the entire regulation fifteen-minute period, as well as both three-minute overtime periods, resulting in a twenty-one-minute bout.

Burnett was on the attack the whole time. He continuously threw hard knees to Miletich's midsection, and solid elbows to Miletich's back. For most of the fight, Miletich was on the defensive, clinging to Burnett to close the distance and prevent Burnett from unloading his powerful strikes.

"If I had known that he was going to do that, I would have pressed it," maintains Burnett. "I always wait and see what the guy is going to do and then counterattack, and then I cut loose on him. But he shut that down for me. I felt a couple of times like cutting loose, but I was just so tied up. I thought to myself, 'Just relax, he's going to have to cut loose and trade sooner or later.' It just never happened."

Miletich threw some knee strikes as well, but for the most part he was defending himself, both standing and from the guard. He refused to fight Burnett's fight. "I was just trying to accomplish my goal," says Miletich, "which was to put him on his back, and he was trying to accomplish his goal—to stay up on his feet."

The decision went to the judges. Burnett felt confident that he had won. But during the bout he had thrown a knee that landed to Miletich's groin, and referee John McCarthy had declared a foul. In a very surprising split decision, Pat Miletich was declared victorious, and one can only assume that it was the result of the foul. Even Miletich commented that the bout was too close for either of them to deserve the title belt.

"My dad once told me, 'You're going to have to work for everything you get, and you're not going to get everything you work for,'" says Burnett. "And I've learned to live with it." He had planned to get back into fighting right after UFC Brazil, and he returned to Dallas to train with Guy Mezger. But, while there, he suffered a serious illness brought on by a poisonous spider bite and was forced to end his training.

Although he recuperated quickly, Burnett would only compete in one more UFC. His last appearance in the octagon was in UFC XVIII, where he defeated Townsend Saunders. The Lion's Den was moving from Lodi to San Diego, and Burnett returned home to Oklahoma to resume training for a rematch with Pat Miletich—but SEG never gave him the opportunity.

Although his UFC career was short-lived, Burnett went down in many people's books as one of the most exciting fighters to date. "In all of no-holds-barred fighting, there are a couple of fights that were just amazing," says UFC matchmaker John Perretti. "Eugenio Tadeau and Mikey Burnett was an amazing, amazing fight."

Although Mikey Burnett looks forward stepping back into the octagon, he's bogged down these days with responsibilities: "Even though I believe I have the talent, it takes a lot of time. I have two young children right now, and I want to be around. I don't want to be in California training for six weeks and not be able to see my family. I did that with my son when he was a baby, and I didn't know what I was missing. My daughter knows me so much better for not doing that. My biggest thing with fighting is that if I can be as good a father and husband while I'm fighting, and if I can get my fighting level to where I am better, I will do it."

Frank Steps Down

UFC Brazil was a pivotal competition for both the Lion's Den crew and Frank Shamrock. After Frank's victory over John Lober, his contract with SEG was fulfilled, and he was reluctant to sign another three-fight deal. Meyrowitz believed that the show itself was the star, rather than the fighters. Because of this, Frank had been forced to take charge of his own development, even though he was one of the UFC's most powerful draws. He spent twenty-five percent of his own income promoting himself— calling sports clubs and Direct TV, sending out posters, and even paying an advertising firm to promote him. In addition to this, his prize money was dwindling with each fight. "Several times during my career, they had scrapped contracts because they said they couldn't pay me," says Frank. "They said, 'You're the champ, we apologize, but we can't pay you what you're worth. We can't pay you what we told you we were going to pay you. So you can either quit, give up your title, take us to court and try to get the money, or we'll just offer you another contract for less money.' That's how bad things were. So when my fight with Lober was finished, my contract had expired, and I told them that until things got better I wasn't going to fight."

And he didn't fight, at least not competitively. Instead, he turned his focus to his students and his new marriage. He felt that he had conquered the most challenging fighters the sport had to offer, and he didn't think he had anything left to prove—that is, until a bleached-blond brawler possessing both strength and bravado stepped onto the scene and caught the champ's attention . . . in a big way.

CHAPTER 17

Showdown

**UFC XVIII—Road to the Heavyweight Title/January 8, 1999
(New Orleans, Louisiana)**

Jerry Bohlander versus Tito Ortiz

The Huntington Beach Bad Boy, Tito Ortiz, was looking for redemption after his questionable loss to Lion's Den fighter Guy Mezger in Alabama. After sitting on the sidelines for more than a year, he finally got another chance to prove himself, at UFC XVIII. For the second time in his short professional career, he would be taking on a seasoned Lion's Den fighter.

Jerry Bohlander's confidence was high coming off his win over Kevin Jackson in UFC XVI, but shortly after he returned to Lodi to resume his training, the Lion's Den moved to San Diego. Because he was still taking care of his family, Bohlander did not make the move with the team. Instead, he went back home to Livermore to tend to family matters. "I didn't do much training," says Bohlander. "Not much training at all. I was going to go fight Vitor Belfort down in Brazil, and then I hurt my knee when I was training for it. That fight was supposed to be in September, and I had to skip over it. Then SEG contacted me in November or December, and I hadn't been training much at all, a little boxing, a little wrestling, but nothing consistent. Then they called me and asked me if I wanted a fight with Tito. They told me if I fought Tito and beat him that I would get a shot at the title."

An inspired Bohlander made the trip down to San Diego and went right back to his old Lion's Den training regimen—three times a day, five days a week. His motivation was high, and he worked himself harder than he ever had before. He believed that SEG had passed him up for a title shot several times, and now his opportunity to get into the hunt had finally arrived. "The one mistake that I made," he says, "was jumping from not training at all to training really hard."

On fight night, there was plenty of tension. "He's pretty much a one-dimensional fighter," said Bohlander of Ortiz in his prefight interview. "There's nothing he can do that I can't counter . . . I'm basically going in there with the win already." Understandably, Ortiz did not take these comments as a sign of camaraderie, and, in retrospect, Bohlander admits that he came off cocky: "In my interviews, I was just so pissed off at the UFC. I look at my interview and I get kind of embarrassed about the way that I carried myself. I usually carry myself with so much more class."

But when the two stepped into the octagon to go to war, the talking was over. As Bruce Buffer made the introductions, Ortiz paced in his corner, his head angled low, glaring across the ring at Bohlander. Behind Bohlander was his team and family, the Lion's Den.

Just as he had in his bout with Mezger, Ortiz dominated from the outset, taking Bohlander to the mat and striking him with punches. Bohlander attempted countless submissions, but Ortiz had learned much since his encounter with Mezger and was quick to power out of them. When the fight returned to standing position due to inactivity at four minutes and thirty seconds, Bohlander was winded. "Suck it up, Jerry," instructed Ken Shamrock, squatting on the outside of the cage. "Suck it up."

Bohlander began chopping away at Ortiz's legs with kicks, but the brawler's hands proved to be daunting. In a flurry, he rocked Bohlander with rights and lefts, and then a knee to the face. Bohlander, knowing he was in trouble, closed the gap. But it was Ortiz who managed the takedown, landing on top. Ortiz dominated on the ground, and each time they were made to stand back up, he dominated on his feet. Knowing Bohlander was behind on points, Ken Shamrock commanded, "You must try something now!"

But Bohlander was not himself that night. His intensive training had burned him out. Less than a minute into the first overtime, Ortiz wrapped his arms around Bohlander, leaned his weight forward, and buckled Bohlander to the canvas. "Stay strong!" Shamrock bellowed. Bohlander did his best, but the fight was taken out of his hands when Ortiz landed an elbow to his eye, opening a nasty cut. At two and a half minutes into the first overtime, the fight was stopped so the doctors could take a look.

As Bohlander was being examined, Ortiz's smile grew. He wiped Bohlander's blood off his face as he made a lap around the octagon. When the fight was declared over, a few seconds later, Ortiz wasted no time in putting on a shirt that read, "I Just Fucked Your Ass!"

Bohlander had lost his first fight in the UFC since his battle with

Gary "Big Daddy" Goodridge in UFC VIII. After taking some time off for reflection, Bohlander regrouped and began his comeback by defeating Brian Foster in a promotion called King of the Cage. Although he was defeated by Romie Aram in another event, called the Gladiator Challenge, it was by a decision, not a submission or a KO.

UFC XIX—Young Guns/May 3, 1999
(Bay St. Louis, Mississippi)

Guy Mezger versus Tito Ortiz

After defeating Jerry Bohlander in UFC XVIII, Tito Ortiz had no plans to take a leave of absence from the octagon. "I was still young back then," he recalls. "I didn't really know how to train the way I do now. I pretty much just ran and boxed and wrestled, and that was it."

Despite his lack of training, Tito Ortiz had made a powerful impression, and he continued to do so at the very next event—UFC XIX: Young Guns, held in Casino Majic in Bay St. Louis, Mississippi on May 3, 1999—where he took on Guy Mezger for the second time. "He would have been knocked out," says Ortiz, referring to his first encounter with Mezger. "He was in a position of being kneed."

Mezger, who was the reigning king of Pancrase, had given up his belt so that he could avenge the loss of Bohlander, his teammate. He also wanted to prove that his first matchup with Ortiz—during which he pulled out the win with a guillotine choke after taking a beating from his opponent's knees—was not a fluke. It was the UFC's biggest rematch since Ken Shamrock and Royce Gracie.

And, once again, there was plenty of tension leading up to the bout. "He comes in very cocky," said Ortiz in his prefight interview. "A professional fighter shouldn't be like that. I have respect for every other fighter that I fight, but I lost a little respect for him, just because of some of the things that he said."

Ortiz wasted no time in taking the Lion's Den fighter to the mat, but Mezger exploded back to his feet and began to utilize his phenomenal kicks and punches. Ortiz did everything he could to get him down, and his relentless attack finally paid off at two minutes and twenty-eight seconds. But when they went to the ground, Mezger had Ortiz's arm cranked behind his back, looking to lock in a submission hold. "Break it!" shouted an enthusiastic Ken Shamrock, sitting on the sidelines. But Ortiz used his strength to survive the submission attempt; and then he was on top, pounding down with elbows and fists.

Mezger weathered the storm well, and he continued to try to get out from under his opponent, but Ortiz kept dragging him back down. Just as it started to look like Ortiz was dominating, Mezger again trapped Ortiz's arm and cranked it behind his back. Ortiz avoided the submission by gripping his fireball-striped shorts, and when he finally powered out of it at just under seven minutes into the bout, he went back to work with the strikes.

The final moments of the fight saw Mezger on all fours and Ortiz striking him with his knees. "Guy, you're a warrior!" shouted Ken Shamrock. But it was not this warrior's day. With Mezger still stuck on all fours, Ortiz unleashed exhausted punches to his head. When Mezger did not defend himself, referee John McCarthy stopped the bout.

While McCarthy helped Mezger to his feet, Ortiz strutted across the ring, turned towards Ken Shamrock and the rest of the Lion's Den fighters in Mezger's corner, and flipped them not one finger, but two. As if this wasn't enough, he then pulled on a custom T-shirt that read: "Gay Mezger Is My Bitch!"

Ken Shamrock did not see the shirt at first. He was too busy arguing with McCarthy, because he believed that although Mezger hadn't defended himself, the punches Ortiz threw were weak, at best, and they hadn't caused injury. McCarthy's decision, however, stuck.

Then Ken spotted the Bad Boy's blatant disrespect. "Hey, Tito! Tito! Don't let me see you wearing that shirt!" Ortiz, of course, shot back, setting the entire Lion's Den into an uproar. SEG cameras panned away from the pandemonium, and announcer Jeff Blatnick quickly began commenting on the fight. But inside the ring all hell was breaking loose. The crowd began to chant, thinking Ken and Tito were going to go at it. Eventually, Blatnick was drawn back in. "We were all wondering whether or not Ken Shamrock was going to make a return to the UFC," he joked. "I'm not sure if anyone thought it would be here, at UFC XIX."

Even after everything had settled down in the ring, Ortiz continued his assault on the Lion's Den. When asked in his postfight interview what he thought about Ken Shamrock's reaction to his disrespect, he said, "I'd be upset as hell too. I beat up on his two number-one contenders in the room. It's kind of hard—I mean, I kind of beat on his little alley cats and sent them back to the litter box."

Naturally, this only fueled Ken's rage. Bob Shamrock recalls that Ken "threw the table apart in the back dressing room. The security guards came up to him, and Ken looked right at them and said, 'What are you going to do?' They just said, 'Nothing.' They were keeping Tito up in the ring because they were afraid Ken was going to kill him. I went to Ken and said, 'This is stupid. What are you going to do, go out there in the casino and create a ruckus? You'll fall right into his hands.' Then I went back out and waited for Tito. When they brought Tito down the plank, I got right in his face. I said, 'Tito, you are an asshole. Nobody disrespects another fighter. Guy Mezger gave up his Pancrase title to come in here and fight you, and you disrespected him. You beat him, there's no question. But you have no right to disrespect him.'"

In addition to talking outside the ring, the Huntington Beach Bad Boy had done plenty of talking inside the ring. Tito Ortiz seemed invincible. He had defeated two of the best middleweight fighters in contention, and in dramatic fashion. His striking abilities and his superlative strength were undeniable, and his crowd appeal was contagious. Ortiz was the sport's newest and brightest star.

UFC XXII—There Can Be Only One/September 24, 1999 (Lake Charles, Lousiana)

Frank Shamrock versus Tito Ortiz

Ortiz's entrance onto the MMA scene had caught the attention of a dormant Frank Shamrock, who called SEG and asked specifically for the opportunity to fight the phenomenal Bad Boy. "When Tito came along," explains Frank Shamrock, "and I saw what he was doing, and I saw how his popularity was rising, and I saw the fighters he was beating, I thought to myself, 'This guy could beat me! If I wasn't a hundred percent, this guy could beat me.' I actually called the UFC and said, 'I want to fight Tito.'"

SEG smelled a great fight and quickly granted the request. The two would meet in UFC XXII, held in Lake Charles, Louisiana on September 24, 1999, for what would be one of the best fights in UFC history. Ortiz would take this fight—unlike his other two bouts—very seriously, and he would train much harder.

But then so did Frank, focusing on plyometric training to compete with Ortiz's strength. "Plyometric training is all the fast-twitch muscle fibers in your body," he explains, "especially in the lower body. Any kind of sudden jumping, or combination jumping—any full-body explosion starting with your feet can be considered plyometric training. That first explosion starts the power source and the inertia."

On the night of the fight, Ortiz and Shamrock warmed up backstage, preparing to face each other in one of the most highly anticipated bouts in UFC history. Ortiz was found shadowboxing and feeling very confident, while Shamrock, wearing the Alliance's red, white, and blue sweatshirt, donned a pair of blue boxing gloves for his warm-up routine. "I think what you're going to see is two middleweights really going at it," said commentator Jeff Blatnick before the fight. "They don't like each other at all. Ortiz was able to beat stablemates Jerry Bohlander and Guy Mezger, and it really ticked off Ken Shamrock. There seems to be a lot of bad blood here, but Frank has removed himself a lot from the Lion's Den with his Alliance with Maurice Smith and Tsuyoshi Kohsaka . . . I'm really itching to see what will bloom from this metamorphosis we call Frank Shamrock."

The crowd went wild as these two fighters entered the octagon to battle it out for the middleweight belt in a bout that was scheduled for five rounds of five minutes each. The time for talking had come to a close. Both fighters meant business, and both came out swinging. Ortiz connected with a right cross to Frank's face, and Frank landed a kick to Ortiz's midsection. After trading a few more shots, Frank closed the distance. Unable to move his larger opponent, however, he turned his back and attempted a standing arm bar. "He was six-foot-three and easily 220 pounds," recalls Frank. "The strength of him was absolutely amazing. In the first thirty seconds, I give him my back and swing around and go for an arm bar, and he just shrugs his shoulders and rips his arm out. And I was thinking, 'There's no way I can go against that strength. If I try and match him strength-wise, I'm going to lose.' So I went around his strength for twenty or so minutes."

When Frank's arm-bar attempt failed, Ortiz was in the perfect position to suplex the submission fighter. But Frank knew what was coming and wrapped his feet around Ortiz's leg, keeping himself from getting dumped on his head. "I think that working with so many good wrestlers got me conditioned to moving," says Frank. "It got me conditioned to being controlled, but, while I'm being controlled, still making openings."

Giving up on the suplex, Ortiz leaned forward and dragged Frank down. After delivering a few shots, however, Ortiz backed out and got to his feet, apparently looking for the knockout. But Frank had been working on his stand-up with Maurice Smith, and he dropped two solid leg kicks that compelled Ortiz to shoot in. Although Frank was taken down, he made use of his extreme flexibility and spun under Ortiz like a top, attempting an arm bar and then spinning around and securing Ortiz in

FRANK SHAMROCK

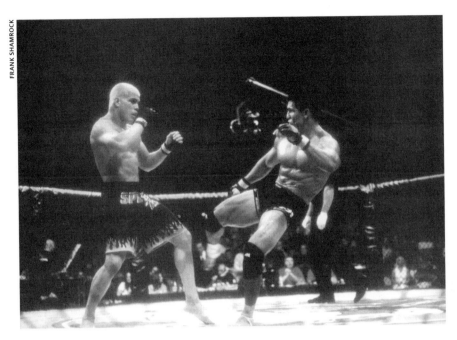

Frank Shamrock throws a Thai kick at the leg of Tito Ortiz in UFC XXII.

FRANK SHAMROCK

Frank Shamrock plays standup with Tito Ortiz at UFC XXII.

FRANK SHAMROCK

Frank Shamrock finishes off Tito Ortiz with crushing blows to the skull.

his guard. Ortiz, not wanting to get caught in a crafty submission hold, dragged Frank over to the fence, hoping to eliminate some of his mobility. It worked, but every time he tried to punch, Frank would attempt to regain his footing, forcing Ortiz to use energy to keep him down.

At the opening of the second round, both fighters again exchanged strikes. Frank even managed to land an impressive head kick. Just as Ortiz was getting the worst of it, he rushed forward and plowed Frank to the canvas. Although Ortiz landed the occasional bomb, Frank stayed active from his back, chopping away at the face and head of his opponent. "We actually had a guy go through and count the strikes in the fight," says Frank, "and I hit Tito three hundred times from the bottom. And when you start adding that up, it's like, 'Man, how much work did I actually do?' He was so strong. He was like this giant table on top of me that I couldn't budge. So I was just scooting out to the side and sitting around and dipping around, and beating on this big giant table in hopes that I could slip out. And I was using all these punches as distractions to get him to lift an arm so I could slip out, or lift his head so I could move away a little bit."

Then, with just thirty seconds left in the second round, Frank made use of his plyometric training and exploded. Securing Ortiz's head under his arm, he popped up to his feet and began dropping ruthless elbows into Ortiz's spine, bringing the round to a close.

At the beginning of the third round, it was Frank's fight. He came out firing, landing a kick to the leg, a cross to the face, and another kick to the liver. Tying up with Ortiz, he was alive with energy, and when they went back to the mat he seized Ortiz's arm and attempted a crucifix. Ortiz squirmed out, however—and, still possessing some strength, he pushed his weight forward and tried to smother his opponent. When that didn't work, Ortiz attained a side mount and tried to choke Frank out with his shoulder. That still didn't work, but it did create an opening that allowed Ortiz to drop a powerful knee to the head. Blood running down his face, Frank once again used his agility and scrambled back to his feet with two minutes left in the round. He paid Ortiz back with several shots before the action went back down.

For the first minute and forty seconds of the fourth round, the fight remained standing, and Frank dominated. He landed kicks to the leg, and a series of punches to both the head and the body. Finally, a fatigued Ortiz shot in and took him down. But that didn't help his situation. Spending most of his energy just holding Frank down, he accepted a continuous barrage of strikes to the ears and the back of the head. After holding on for several minutes, Ortiz launched three elbow strikes at Frank's head—they all missed. Winded, the Huntington Beach Bad Boy collapsed on top his opponent. "Get him off you, Frank!" shouted Maurice Smith. "Get him off you!"

Frank took his trainer's advice. In an explosive move, he rolled Ortiz off and rapidly regained his footing. When Ortiz scrambled back to his feet, Frank unleashed a flurry of kicks and punches to the face. An exhausted Ortiz dove forward and again took his opponent to the mat—but by the time they landed Frank had sunk in a guillotine. Using his last store of energy, Ortiz muscled out. But when he did, Frank hopped to his feet and began raining elbows and fists down on the side of Ortiz's head. The abuse simply became too much, and a damaged Tito Ortiz submitted.

"That fight went exactly as I planned," says Frank. "I told my trainers, this is either going to be a really quick fight—I'm going to catch him, I'm going to finesse him, catch him sleeping—or it's going to be a really long fight, and I'm going to have to get this guy off me. Just beat him down. Everything went exactly by the book. If you see the fight, I'm checking in with my corner; we're checking the time, we burst at the last of every minute, the last thirty seconds I would either go for a hold or go for a huge flurry. Every round, everything, went exactly as planned except for me getting cut, and that was just a freak thing. That was by far one of my best strategies, and one of my most challenging physical confrontations."

While Frank was making his victory walk around the octagon, he took the opportunity to flip off Ortiz's corner. Although he was no longer a part of the Lion's Den, he couldn't help but serve up a little redemption for his former family.

Ortiz knew he had been beaten, and he showed his respect. "He had two T-shirts for this fight," remembers Bob Shamrock. "One was, 'Frank Shamrock: Middleweight Champion.' And the other one was, 'One Shamrock Down, and One to Go,' which was referring to Ken. It was a totally different attitude."

In addition to putting on the first shirt that Bob described, Ortiz walked across the octagon and embraced his worthy opponent. Despite this, he still had some strong opinions about the fight. "The only reason I lost was due to cardio," insists Ortiz—"not working hard enough, not knowing what it takes to make it. That's the reason Frank's been a five-time world champion; he knew the secret, and the secret was cardio."

Tito Ortiz would be back, however, and he would be back with a vengeance. "When I fought Frank, I was still a young kid fighting," says Ortiz. "That was only my fourth pro fight, and I never had any amateur fights before, and that was like his thirteenth fight. It just seems that the more I train, the harder I train, and the older I get in the sport, the better I get." But before Ortiz could become a champion, he would have to face his demons. "Something I had to overcome was the loss to Frank Shamrock. I mean that shit hurt me. It hurt me bad, 'cause I hate losing."

The night belonged to Frank Shamrock. Robert Meyrowitz came out to congratulate the champion with his standard "That's what the UFC is all about!" canned speech, but Frank, convinced that there were no contenders on the scene he couldn't beat, decided to exercise a clause in his contract. "When I fought Tito, I signed a multifight contract, because they would not let me fight Tito without signing a multifight contract. All I cared about was fighting Tito. I knew his ability, and I knew how strong and good he was going to be. That's the only guy I cared about fighting. So I signed this multifight contract, but I put a clause in there that said if at any time I should publicly retire, renounce my title and my belt, that I will no longer be bound by the terms of this contract. So I fought Tito, and I beat him, and I stood up in the ring and said, 'I'm done. You guys keep the belt, I'm retired.'"

Although Frank publicly retired from MMA competition, he never did so in his heart. He stayed involved in fighting and went on to win his first kickboxing bout in under a minute by breaking his opponent's arm

FRANK SHAMROCK

Frank Shamrock with his title belts.

with a kick. These days, however, he devotes most of his energy to training the students on his fighting team, Team Shamrock. "The team is only
three or four years old," Frank says, "but we've already got really good.
The team is all there to support each other, and that's what it's all about.
A team is about a family."

Because of the never-say-die attitude of fighters like Frank Shamrock,
mixed martial arts competition has survived Senator John McCain's campaign to eliminate the sport from the United States. Instead of sitting back
and watching their sport disappear, Frank and a number of other determined fighters worked tirelessly in the gym, cross-training in a number
of martial art styles and developing a system of fighting that would give
promoters a reason to carry on and diehard fans a reason to keep coming
back for more. Their efforts have brought MMA competition back into

the American spotlight. The Ultimate Fighting Championship has finally been sanctioned in key states, and the event that began as a spectacle has returned to cable TV as a sport. The UFC has once again become the leader in the sport, rivaled only by the Japanese MMA organization called the Pride Fighting Championship.

CHAPTER 18

Fighting for Pride

*Fighting for pride has been part of the Japanese culture since the samu-
rai era. The samurai, or fighters, are very respected. Everyone in Japan
wants the fighter to fight for their pride.*
   —Yukino Kanda, cofounder of the Pride Fighting Championships

*The thunderous voice of the announcer echoed throughout Japan's famed Tokyo
Dome, welcoming an audience of over forty thousand to the Pride Fighting Championship Grand Prix 2000. This long-awaited show of shows was being hailed as
the most competitive mixed martial arts tournament in the history of the sport.*

*The event had brought eight of the toughest full-contact fighters in the world
together under one roof, and, one by one, they would clash in a vicious bone-
on-bone MMA single-elimination tournament to crown a champion. Each had a
legitimate shot at winning the competition, and although only one combatant
would triumph over all the others, each would return to his homeland with honor.
In the eyes of the Japanese fans, these fighters were the modern-day equivalent of
the samurai—heroic warriors with the heart and determination to uphold the tra-
ditions of Japan's famed fighting class.*

*Following the announcements and a blaze of pyrotechnic splendor, five beau-
tiful, scantily clad Japanese women entered the roped-off ring. They stood before
the throngs of screaming fans, proudly displaying an enormous trophy, the coveted
Pride championship belt, and the check for twenty million yen (approximately
$160,000) that would be awarded to the victor. The prefight air was charged
with anticipation.*

* * *

But there was also something else happening that night. Besides the
upcoming battle for the belt, the fans were going to witness the return of
two legendary fighters—Ken Shamrock, the former WWF wrestling
superstar, and Royce Gracie, the most famous practitioner of the art of

Brazilian jiu-jitsu. Although these two titans of the sport had, almost single-handedly, put mixed martial arts on the map, the MMA world had evolved so much during their hiatus that many questioned whether they could successfully compete in—let alone win—their respective matches. In a featured "superfight," which wasn't technically a part of the Grand Prix 2000 tournament, Shamrock was scheduled to face Alexander Otsuka, a famous Japanese professional wrestler who was also a tenacious mixed martial artist. Gracie, in a highly anticipated quarterfinal matchup, was pitted against Kazushi Sakuraba, a lightning-quick, unorthodox fighter who, pound-for-pound, was thought to be the best MMA competitor in the world.

Shamrock had been out of the sport for four years, and Gracie had been out of the spotlight for almost five. A victory at the Grand Prix would reestablish Shamrock as the most formidable opponent in MMA competition and secure his reputation as "the World's Most Dangerous Man." Gracie was fighting for the reputation of Brazilian jiu-jitsu, trying to prove that his family's fighting system was still a viable and effective style, despite the evolution of the mixed martial arts disciplines. A loss for either of these competitors would signify a changing of the guard and the end of an era.

The forty-thousand-plus spectators packed into the Tokyo Dome, and the thousands of fight fans watching at home, were clamoring to know whether these two heroes would fall or once again stand as champions. Would superstars Shamrock and Gracie be able to carve their initials even deeper into the history of the sport, or would a new breed of warriors replace them in the spotlight?

Spectacular Pride

Japanese professional wrestlers had been refining their fighting techniques since the days of Karl Gotch, and, eager to test their skills in full-out combat, several wrestlers had turned worked matches into real fights. Although this did not sit well with their unfortunate opponents and with pro wrestling promoters, the evolution could not be stopped, and fight promotions such as Pancrase were formed. These organizations enjoyed tremendous success, and soon MMA competition exploded onto the Japanese scene, prompting the creation of the most popular MMA promotion Japan has ever seen—the Pride Fighting Championship.

The first Pride event was held on October 11, 1997 in the Tokyo

Dome, and the main event featured a bout between Nobuhiko Takada and Rickson Gracie. Takada was an extremely popular Japanese professional wrestler, and his fame, combined with the real-fight angle and the rising popularity of the Gracie family through such events as the UFC, drew forty-seven thousand eager spectators to the show. Rickson wound up defeating Takada via arm bar just four minutes and forty-seven seconds into the bout.

With this kind of response, Pride soon dwarfed other MMA competitions such as Pancrase and RINGS. The Pride organization began holding an event roughly every two months, and although only one company had the capability of airing pay-per-view in Japan, Pride enjoyed an average of sixty thousand buys per show. Approximately a week after the event was aired on pay-per-view, it was broadcast to the mainstream Japanese television networks so millions more could watch their favorite warriors battle it out.

Pride only accepted competitors who had proven their abilities in the ring, and to entice the world's most exciting fighters, it issued contracts ranging from $80,000 to $900,000, depending on the number of fights per contract. It was reported that Ken Shamrock received $700,000 for a three-fight deal. "Pride is not just a competition," says Yukino Kanda, one of the organization's cofounders. "What we are trying to do is show the entertainment of the sport. That doesn't mean staged fights—all fights should be real. For Pride, winning or losing isn't too important. We judge the fighters by how they fight. If the fighter is only concerned about winning—trying to survive until the end of the round then waiting for the decision—they may not fight as tough as they possibly can. The fighters in Pride shouldn't ignore the fact that they are fighting in front of forty or fifty thousand people."

In return for laying it on the line, Pride fighters were not only rewarded with healthy paychecks, but they also enjoyed celebrity status throughout Japan. Their faces were routinely seen in the mainstream media, gracing the pages of newspapers and the covers of magazines. "A fighter may not necessarily be the top fighter, but they can still be very popular if they have a strong character," explains Kanda. "The fans in Japan are very loyal to a fighter. Even if they lose sometimes, as long as they show a good fight, an aggressive fight, the fans will stay with them. Japanese fans are very educated about the sport, and the audience respects the fighters. We think making stars out of our fighters is one of the most important ways to promote our show."

In addition to seeing fighters go to war every time they stepped into the ring, spectators at Pride events were also treated to a unique and spectacular production. The opening show was different each time, as were the stage sets and the fighter introductions. With attendance levels rivaling those for American NFL games or major league baseball, millions of dollars were pumped into each show.

This was the case at the Pride Fighting Championship Grand Prix 2000, but after the fireworks and the big buildup, the crowd became focused and intent as the first fighter of the night, six-foot-three, 230-pound Gary "Big Daddy" Goodridge, made his way towards the ring to take on Igor Vovchanchyn, a five-foot-ten, 230-pound Russian brawler who had one of the most brutal knockout punches in the sport.

Goodridge had stepped onto the MMA scene at UFC VIII, held on February 16, 1998. After he knocked out Paul Herrera in his quarterfinal bout and pummeled Jerry Bohlander in the semifinals, he was asked back to UFC IX. His opponent was Olympic wrestler Mark Schultz, and Goodridge entered the octagon ready to knock him out by throwing heavy leather. Instead, he found himself lying on the canvas, dominated by Schultz's spectacular takedowns and ground-fighting skills. "At the time I fought Schultz, I knew absolutely nothing," says Goodridge. "I didn't know how to stop his shooting. I didn't know how to get him off me. I didn't know nothin'!"

Goodridge continued to have trouble with wrestlers, and after losing to Mark Coleman in UFC X and Don Frye in Ultimate Ultimate '96, he stopped relying solely on his wild strikes and began cross-training and learning submissions. It was a good strategy: when he headed to Brazil to compete in the first International Vale Tudo Championship (IVC), he submitted his first two opponents, taking out Augusto Santos with a crucifix and Cal Worsham with a key lock. These victories landed him in the finals against Pedro Otavio.

Goodridge tied up with Otavio, attempting to slide Otavio's protective jock over to the side to allow for some clean (and legal) groin strikes. When he finally managed to move the cup out of the way, Otavio realized what was about to happen to him and, in a desperate attempt to avoid the impending assault, fell to the ground, claiming that Goodridge had succeeded in his efforts and crushed his testicles. Although Goodridge admitted that this was his intention, he hadn't been able to complete his dastardly plan. Either way, he ended up winning the bout with punches.

A new and improved Goodridge came out of the IVC, and his next opportunity brought him to Japan to compete in the very first Pride

Fighting Championship. "They called me up and wanted me to fight Oleg Taktarov," recalls Goodridge. "I guess they wanted me to be a bum boy for him." But Goodridge refused to be any such thing, and although he broke his foot while landing a kick to Taktarov's head, he continued to fight, and just a few seconds later he unleashed on the Russian sambo master. "Obviously, I was supposed to lose to him, but I ended up knocking him out."

Because of this impressive Pride debut, Goodridge was asked back to fight in the next three consecutive Pride events. After losing to Marco Ruas in Pride 2 via ankle lock, he came back in Pride 3 to knock out Amir Rahnavardi. Then, in Pride's fourth event, he ran up against one of the most powerful fighters in the game, Igor Vovchanchyn. "The first time I went in to fight Igor, I dislocated my shoulder twelve days before the event," says Goodridge. "At that point, I had already done a forecast on my income tax, and this was the last fight of the year, so I was kind of forced to fight even with a dislocated shoulder. So I thought I'd get it to the ground and try really hard for a submission. But I knew I couldn't. I couldn't throw a right punch." Although Goodridge stepped into the ring to give it his all, without adequate use of his hard right hand he could not contend with Vovchanchyn's strikes. After six minutes of battle, Goodridge found himself on the receiving end of a powerful flurry, and the referee ended the fight.

Goodridge now had a record of 2-2 in Pride, but he was far from being abandoned by his Japanese fans. "My fighting style is one that I had to develop in order to be popular within the Japanese market," he explains. "I had to really understand the Japanese culture and what they really wanted. And I had to quickly decide what is important here. Is it important to always win? Is it important to be a flashy, flamboyant character?" Goodridge did his research, and he discovered that although David "Tank" Abbott also had an equal win/loss record, he was one of the biggest stars in the sport. So Goodridge modeled his "fight anyone" attitude on the original Huntington Beach Bad Boy, and the rest is history. "I quickly saw how the Japanese public really didn't care if you lost. They just wanted somebody that they could follow and love. They just wanted a knock-down, drag-out fight."

When Goodridge entered the ring at the Pride Grand Prix 2000, he was determined to give the fans what they were looking for. "I was in great condition," he remembers. "No injuries. There was nothing wrong with me." This was his chance to get revenge on the Ukrainian power puncher, Igor Vovchanchyn.

Vovchanchyn grew up in a small village. Although his early youth was relatively uneventful, during his teens he developed an insatiable appetite for brawling. "I enjoyed street fights and got tremendously excited," he says. "Sometimes I became really aggressive, which was dangerous for my fellow villagers." As Vovchanchyn grew older, his aggressive streak prompted the villagers to hang a metal rail from a tree in the center of town; whenever young Igor would fly into one of his rages, someone would bang on the rail. Hearing the alarm, the villagers would drop what they were doing, hurry home, lock their doors, and remain inside until the hot-headed teen cooled down and it was once again safe to venture outside.

At age seventeen, Vovchanchyn gave his fearful village a break by moving with his family to Kharkov—the second largest city in the Ukraine, after Kiev. While living in the city, Vovchanchyn took up the sport of boxing, at last finding an appropriate release for his violent energy. "I guess my passion for fighting brought me to the boxing gym," says Vovchanchyn, "and it was a good thing for me, because I learned the trick of controlling my feelings and my excessive aggressiveness as a street fighter."

Only a few months after taking up boxing, Vovchanchyn decided to enter the Kharkov boxing championships. His coaches tried to dissuade him, insisting that he wasn't ready, but the young scrapper ignored their advice. "Actually, I KO'd my first opponent very quickly," says Vovchanchyn. "And I liked it! I thought before the fight that I was going to have fun in the ring, but the reality surpassed my expectations. And I definitely enjoyed the atmosphere of the venue. Fighting in the streets, you can't hope to have the right kind of audience."

In 1993, a year after that championship boxing victory, Vovchanchyn decided to take up kickboxing. He met manager Yevgenia Borshevska, who was the general secretary of the sporting organization called the All-Eurasian Kickboxing Federation; she sent him to Denmark as part of the Ukrainian national team to compete in the World Kickboxing Amateur Championships. He won the competition and the title, but during this time Vovchanchyn became aware of a new form of martial arts competition that was beginning to gain worldwide popularity. "I happened to see a video with Ultimate fights, and I immediately fell in love with this martial arts style," he remembers. "It was like street fighting—you were allowed to do next to anything."

Realizing that he'd found the perfect sport for him, Vovchanchyn began pursuing a career in mixed martial arts. But Borshevska and her

Ice Cold Igor Vovchanchyn.

organization did not work with this type of fighting, and Vovchanchyn was temporarily on his own. To advance his career, he moved to Brazil, where the sport was thriving. There he earned the nickname "Ice Cold." "I differed from the highly excitable Brazilian fighters," says Vovchanchyn, "so they gave me this name. I think I lived up to it."

He entered a tournament called the Absolute Fighting Championship (AFC), and although he defeated three opponents with powerful striking, breaking one fighter's arm and another's nose, he ended up losing in the finals when Mikhail Illoukine drove his chin deep into his eye socket, forcing him to submit.

Vovchanchyn continued to fight in mixed martial arts competitions, including the International Fighting Championships, two more AFC events, and the highly competitive World Vale Tudo Championships. From 1996 to 1998, Vovchanchyn fought in twenty-one bouts, and besides losing to Illoukine and drawing with Leonardo Castello Branco in AFC 2, he won every fight.

In 1998, the All-Eurasian Kickboxing Federation changed its focus and became the Professional Association of Martial Arts (PAMA). Vovchanchyn was reunited with manager Yevgenia Borshevska. "I think he definitely has what they call charisma," says Borshevska. "He has much appeal. His image is that of a guy who does not look very tall and very powerful, who enters the ring in a cool way (without roaring or showing his teeth), and then suddenly and magically turns into an aggressive beast. His fans always expect him to win by punching."

When Vovchanchyn made his Pride debut in the fourth show, held on November 10, 1998, he did not disappoint his fans. Stepping into the ring, he demolished Gary "Big Daddy" Goodridge with strikes—making him an instant star in Japan. He continued to fight in Pride, defeating such seasoned competitors as Akira Shoji, Carlos Barreto, and Alexander Otsuka. By the time the Pride Grand Prix 2000 rolled around, Vovchanchyn had an amazing Pride record of 7-0. With his experience and his heavy hands, he felt confident that in his quarterfinal bout he would once again defeat Goodridge and go on to win the entire tournament. There was no doubt in Vovchanchyn's mind—he was going to bring home the most prestigious belt in the history of MMA competition.

After the starting bell chimed, Goodridge and Vovchanchyn met in the center of the ring and briefly touched gloves. Each fighter was aware of the other's powerful striking abilities, and each kept his distance, feeling his opponent out. The fight went back and forth, with Goodridge landing jabs and Vovchanchyn answering back with hard, low kicks. They were giving the crowd a show and going for the knockout with almost every strike. But when Goodridge went for a leg kick of his own, Vovchanchyn leaned forward, his right hand whizzing up high and connecting to his opponent's face. Goodridge's legs turned to rubber. He covered up the best he could as Vovchanchyn came in for the kill, landing right after left to his body and head. After accepting twenty-two hard shots, Goodridge still wasn't out, and with Vovchanchyn now winded, Goodridge closed the gap, tying the Ukrainian up in the clinch and then taking him to the mat. "My weapon is my punches and my ability to stay cool in the ring," says Vovchanchyn. "I never lose my head, and I keep the ability to analyze the situation." Vovchanchyn did just that, and with the massive Goodridge riding his weight on top of him, he remained calm and pressed the attack from his back.

Once Goodridge had recuperated from the blows, he stood the fight back up, looking to end this one on his feet and give the fans something to remember. When Vovchanchyn lunged in for another overhand right, Goodridge answered back with a knee to the face. Although both fighters were exhausted, they gave it their all, exchanging a barrage of knee strikes, kicks, and punches. Just after Goodridge landed yet another knee to his opponent's face, Vovchanchyn connected with a powerful overhand right that sent Goodridge stumbling across the ring. He managed five paces, and then fell to his back. Vovchanchyn leaped on top of him, but before he could administer a beating, the referee stopped the fight.

Although Goodridge was knocked out of the tournament, he retained his superstar status in Japan. He continued to fight in Pride, taking on some of the toughest fighters in the sport, including Ricco Rodriguez, Gilbert Yvel, and Antonio Rodrigo Nogueira. "I don't pick and choose my opponents," maintains Goodridge. "I've never turned down a fight with anybody at any time, regardless of the time I've had to prepare for it."

While Vovchanchyn went backstage to get some rest for his semifinal bout, the next quarterfinal matchup of the evening, Kazushi Sakuraba versus Royce Gracie, got under way. It was billed as the fight of the century—a showdown between an old-school warrior and one of Japan's new samurai. The outcome of this battle was pivotal: it would determine whether Gracie jiu-jitsu could hold up in the contemporary MMA world.

Although this match was a part of the elimination tournament, special rules had been negotiated between the Pride promoters and Rorion Gracie. Rorion knew that Royce was trained to fight for however long it took to achieve victory, and he didn't want his brother's fate put into the hands of judges. In order for Royce to fight, Rorion insisted, there must be no time limit and no judges' decision. Changing the rules was not common practice for Pride, but Sakuraba agreed to the stipulations and the match was made. One man would win, and the other would lose—a draw could not occur.

The bout was evenly matched, with both fighters standing six feet tall, Gracie weighing in at 176 pounds, and Sakuraba at 183 pounds. Although Sakuraba was a Japanese pro wrestler, he was no stranger to MMA. Besides defeating such well-known fighters as Vernon White and Carlos Newton, Sakuraba had also beaten Royce's brother Royler in Pride 8 via kimura (a type of arm lock), and he was not intimidated by Gracie jiu-jitsu in the least.

Dressed in his traditional white gi, Royce Gracie stood in his corner. He watched without emotion as three masked men entered the ring at the opposite side. One of them was his opponent, Kazushi Sakuraba. The three men taunted the crowd with their guessing game until the announcer finally bellowed, "Sakuraba!" With true professional wrestling showman-ship, the real Kazushi Sakuraba whipped off his mask and flung it into the crowd, revealing a mop of dyed red hair.

The crowd went wild as the two fighters stared each other down. After the referee stepped between them to reiterate the rules, the battle began with the clang of the bell. Gracie immediately charged and attacked with a flurry of punches, but Sakuraba was battle-tested, and he remained calm. He was so relaxed, in fact, that later in the first round he took a moment to smile at a camera and shake his head mockingly. The crowd responded enthusiastically as his antics were displayed on giant monitors above.

Gracie was not deterred by his opponent's lack of fear. He pushed his attack during the early rounds of the fight, beating on Sakuraba with his fists and knees and attempting one submission after another. But Sakuraba was a sleeping dragon, biding his time and waiting to strike.

By the third fifteen-minute round, the tide of battle had reversed, and the elusive Sakuraba was now the aggressor. Gracie's gi—which he had used in many battles to choke out his opponents—was now being used against him. Sakuraba pulled it over Gracie's shoulders in an attempt to limit the movement of his arms. He hoisted Gracie by the seat of his pants and rained punches down on his face. But these were only a couple of Sakuraba's tricks. He also attacked Gracie's legs with powerful kicks, steadily chopping the Brazilian down.

With such trademark moves as double-handed strikes and diving punches, Sakuraba dominated Gracie. In the final minute of the sixth round, Gracie was forced to scramble onto his back while Sakuraba circled him, striking whenever an opening presented itself.

After the bell rang, the two fighters retreated to their corners. Gracie sat with his wounded leg extended straight out in front of him; a vile scratch zigzagged down his left cheek. He was surrounded by his family of warriors, many of whom were gazing in wonder across the ring at Sakuraba, who showed no visible signs of fatigue. Before the bell could ring for the seventh time, Royce Gracie's cornerman threw in the towel, ending the hour-and-a-half-long bout. Royce did not protest. He had had enough.

The fans responded with fervor and rose excitedly to their feet. No one could believe that the contest had lasted so long. It was the longest match in MMA history, outside of Brazil. The victorious Sakuraba, who had just advanced to the semifinals, accepted triumph with all the dignity of a sportsman and a warrior. The two contestants met in the center of the ring to exchange words and show their mutual respect. It was power-ful testimony to the level to which MMA had evolved.

Despite the climactic nature of this bout, the night was only getting started. Ground-and-pound specialist Mark "the Hammer" Coleman was set to take on Japanese fighter Akira Shoji in the next quarterfinal bout.

Coleman, standing six-foot-one and weighing 245 pounds, had been fighting in Japan for over a year. After experiencing three consecutive losses in the UFC—first to Maurice Smith, then to Pete Williams, and finally to Pedro Rizzo—he had left the UFC to compete in Pride 5, waged on April 29, 1999. "When you've got three straight losses in the UFC, and they're offering you ten grand, and Japan is offering you fifty grand, it's kind of a no-brainer," says Coleman. He made his Pride debut against none other than the legendary Nobuhiko Takada.

Although Coleman came out strong, the crafty pro wrestler caught him in a heel hook and forced him to submit, chalking up another loss on Coleman's record. "For some people, losses can ruin their career," says Coleman. "But for me, I learn a lot more from my losses than I do from my wins. It never crossed my mind to think about quitting. I just knew I had to learn and get in better shape. There was no doubt in my mind I was going to return to the top."

To ensure that this comeback really happened, Coleman began a rigorous cross-training regimen. "I got real serious with a boxing coach back here in Columbus, Ohio," he recalls. "Doug Owens is his name. He actually worked with Buster Douglas when Buster upset Mike Tyson. I didn't believe that I was a good puncher, but most of my workout partners had said I hit as hard as anybody they've ever held pads for, and I just had a lot of natural instincts on my feet. I think it's always been there, just once you get in the ring it's natural to resort back to what you do best, and what I do best is I take people down and ground and pound."

Feeling confident now that strikes had been added to his arsenal, Coleman returned to Pride on November 21, 1999. He took on Ricardo Morais, and although he won by decision, he wished he could have put his opponent away with a knockout or submission. "You've always got to be trying to finish the fight," says Coleman, "because the fans are paying, and that's what they want to see. They don't want to see 'ground and hug.' But to be able to finish a fight, people need to understand what it really entails. The time we put in to prepare for a fight like this is incredible. I've got no complaints, but there's a lot of work to do. Always. Because everybody is improving so much, if you don't stay with 'em, you're going to be behind 'em."

Coleman trained harder than ever for the Grand Prix 2000: "I knew I was prepared like I've never been prepared before in my fighting career. I'd gotten away from my family and gotten back to six months of training. I went into that tournament knowing I wasn't going to get tired, and knowing I was prepared—so there really wasn't a whole lot of fear. When you know you've done your homework, all you can do is go out there and do your best."

As his quarterfinal bout in Grand Prix 2000 got started, Coleman showed just how much work he had done on his striking. He began landing crosses, jabs, and hooks to the face of the five-foot-eight, 194 pound Akira Shoji. After making his point, he closed the gap, snatched his opponent's legs, and brought him to the mat. Lying on top of his smaller adversary, he unleashed with hooks to the body and head. As Shoji endured dozens of strikes, the skin covering his ribs began to glow a bright red, then a deep purple, and finally a grotesque black. Refusing to give in, he managed to wedge his feet inside and push the Hammer off him—but the abuse Shoji took on his feet was little better. Pinning his opponent against the ropes, Coleman continued his strikes to the ribs. And when Shoji tried to escape, Coleman tripped him and threw his full weight on top of him.

Again Coleman got to work, delivering a hailstorm of hard shots to the body and more than a dozen shots to the head before Shoji, flailing underneath him, could struggle back to his feet. Although the Mark Coleman of yesteryear would have been winded at this point, making him susceptible to a kick or a punch, the current incarnation showed no visible signs of fatigue. For the remainder of the fight, he hunted Shoji with knees and punches, and when the bout fell into the hands of the judges, Coleman won by unanimous decision.

The last quarterfinal bout was between famed Japanese pro wrestler Kazuyuki Fujita and the skilled American amateur wrestler Mark "the Specimen" Kerr. Fujita was fairly large, standing an even six feet and weighing a solid 220 pounds, but at six-foot-three and 255 pounds, Mark Kerr looked enormous in comparison.

The two fighters got right to it, exchanging strikes in the opening seconds of the round before Kerr shot in and put Fujita on his back. Stuck in his opponent's guard, Kerr hammered away at Fujita's body and face with powerful downward strikes. This was not where Fujita wanted to be, but when he escaped to his knees, Kerr planted several knee strikes on his face before he could regain his footing. While Kerr exerted energy trying to take him down, Fujita attacked with his fists. As the fight went back and forth, from one side of the ring to the other, Kerr began to show signs of fatigue. Sensing that he now had his opponent where he wanted him, Fujita shot in, taking Kerr down. Kerr managed to get on all fours, but Fujita rode him, keeping Kerr pinned with his weight and teeing off with countless knees to his liver and ribs. When the fight went to the judges, just a few moments later, Fujita received the unanimous decision.

With the number of competitors narrowed to four, Kazushi Sakuraba reentered the ring to face Igor Vovchanchyn for the first semifinal bout. Vovchanchyn played it safe, and although Sakuraba was able to take the Ukrainian powerhouse to the ground several times, land plenty of strikes, and come close to pulling off numerous submissions, the bout went the distance, and the judges declared it a draw. The fight went into overtime, but before the round could begin, Sakuraba's cornerman threw in the towel. The one-and-a-half-hour war Sakuraba had waged against Royce Gracie had taken its toll, and his trainers knew he'd had enough.

Sakuraba may not have won the Grand Prix Tournament, but he had demonstrated his heart and determination and defeated Royce Gracie. In the very next Pride event, he defeated Renzo Gracie, and in Pride 12 he won a decision over Ryan Gracie. Due to these impressive victories over the legendary Brazilian fighting family, he acquired the nickname "the Gracie Hunter" and became the most popular mixed martial arts fighter in Japan.

The last semifinal matchup in the Grand Prix was between two true powerhouses—Mark "the Hammer" Coleman and Kazuyuki Fujita. Their combined weight was close to five hundred pounds and this battle

The powerful Kazuyuki Fujita.

was expected to be one of the night's most brutal. It did not live up to expectations. Fujita had injured his knee during his fight with Kerr, and although he charged Coleman in the opening seconds of the bout, the move was apparently only for show, for his cornerman threw in the towel before Fujita had traveled halfway across the ring.

Before the Grand Prix 2000 finals got under way, the other major conflict of the night had to be resolved: the Superfight between Ken Shamrock and Japanese pro wrestler Alexander Otsuka. At the age of thirty-six, after four and a half years of participating in the fixed matches of the WWF, Shamrock was stepping back into the ring to put it all on the line. "The training was hard," he says. "My body was rejecting the training. My body had all kinds of injuries. I didn't have one good week of training for when I fought Alexander. But I got through it." And there was no question that both fighters were there to win.

With the tolling of a bell, a hooded Ken Shamrock entered the ring, his face stern. On the other side of the arena, Alexander Otsuka strutted past the rows of fans, sporting a cleanly shaven head. Both fighters stood six-foot-one, but Shamrock, at 235 pounds, outweighed Otsuka by thirty-two pounds.

Both fighters came out swinging, and both landed solid punches and hard kicks. Otsuka rallied the crowd with a couple of tricky pro wrestling moves, bouncing off the ropes and stomping his feet. But Shamrock was unimpressed, and he continued to attack Otsuka with crushing overhand rights.

The two wound up in the clinch, and Shamrock quickly took Otsuka to the mat, where he climbed into the mount. He delivered a continuous barrage of strikes before locking up Otsuka's arm with a submission hold. But Otsuka was well versed in the submission game, and he managed to free himself.

The fighters were now back on their feet. Shamrock's intensity was overwhelming; he unleashed on the gasping Otsuka. There was a brief exchange of fists, and then, in a mechanically powerful blur, Shamrock threw a combination of hooks and crosses that knocked Otsuka to the canvas. Shamrock stepped forward, dropped one more strike to his opponent's head for good measure, and the bout was over. The match had ended Shamrock style.

The World's Most Dangerous Man was back. Having worked out the cobwebs, he returned to Pride 10 to take on Kazuyuki Fujita. He pressed the attack in the early minutes of the fight, avoiding Fujita's takedowns and beating on him with punches and kicks. But just when Shamrock

*Vanderlei "the Axe Murderer" Silva lands a powerful knee
to the face of Kazushi Sakuraba.*

seemed to have Fujita right where he wanted him, Shamrock suddenly
stopped fighting. Pressed up against the ropes and battling exhaustion,
Shamrock spoke to his cornerman, and a few seconds later his towel was
thrown in. He had lost due to improper conditioning. To ensure that this
didn't happen again, he returned to the Lion's Den in San Diego and
began training hard for his next Pride event.

After a number of epic battles, the Grand Prix was down to two fighters: Mark "the Hammer" Coleman and Igor "Ice Cold" Vovchanchyn.
Coleman had only fought one true fight going into the finals. He was in
the shape of his life, and he'd had plenty of time to replenish his strength
after his showdown with Akira Shoji—but still he was on edge. "The day
before the fight," he remembers, "they let us know that the final was
going to be a no-time-limit fight. Immediately I was kind of shook up,
because I kind of figured it was going to be me and Vovchanchyn in the
finals, and I knew I wasn't going to knock him out. And I knew my
submission skills weren't the greatest, so I was really concerned about
how I was going to finish him off. I knew if it was a twenty-minute time
limit, I was going to ground and pound him for twenty minutes and get the
decision, but now I had to find a way to finish him off. Quite honestly, I
really didn't know how that was going to happen."

Igor Vovchanchyn had reached the finals by first trading blows with
Gary Goodridge and then scrambling after the elusive Kazushi Sakuraba.
But, despite his earlier battles, he knew that the fight with Coleman

would be his most grueling of the night. "My toughest opponent in Pride was Coleman," he says. "He is very strong physically and has an excellent command of ground technique."

Although Vovchanchyn came into the match appearing as if he were about to keel over, when the bell chimed he headed straight into combat. When Coleman shot in and took him to his back only seconds into the match, Vovchanchyn not only defended, but also launched powerful upward strikes that connected with Coleman's jaw. This, however, did not stop Coleman from engaging in his usual ground-and-pound technique. While beating on Vovchanchyn's ribs and head, he looked for some way to put the Ukrainian away, first trying an ineffective neck crank and later snatching Vovchanchyn's arm and attempting a key lock. But Vovchanchyn seemed immune to pain and held on, waiting for Coleman to get tired.

As the bout went on, Coleman grew more and more worried that he wouldn't be able to finish off his opponent. He continued to chop at Vovchanchyn's body and head, looking for an opening. Finally, one came when he escaped from between his opponent's legs and spun into a side mount. Leaning all his weight on Vovchanchyn's midsection, he let loose with eighteen knees to the head. "In the middle of that knee flurry, I'm really getting nervous because I can't believe the guy is not tapping," says Coleman, "and I figure, 'If he survives this, I'm in some trouble.' Igor almost seemed inhuman to me. I really don't see how somebody can take eighteen knees, even if he did partially block half of them. He's an incredibly tough man who, when he's in shape, gets the best out of himself."

Vovchanchyn had fought hard, but the knees Coleman delivered finally proved too much, and he was forced to submit. The loss was extremely disappointing for the Ukrainian brawler. In his heart, he had been counting on emerging victorious from the event: "My ultimate goal as a fighter is to be a Grand Prix winner. Unfortunately, I lost. Coleman was the champion."

Mark "the Hammer" Coleman had won the Pride Fighting Championship Grand Prix 2000, and he was once again on top of the MMA world. Instantly, he became a superstar in Japan, and he went on to compete in Pride 13, where he beat Allan Goes with devastating knee strikes. But in Pride 16, held in the Osaka Castle Hall on September 24, 2001, Coleman suffered a devastating loss when Antonio Rodrigo Nogueira caught him in an arm bar. "My mother-in-law was diagnosed with ovarian cancer thirty days prior to my fight with Noguiera," says Coleman. "I don't want to sound like I'm a big excuse maker, but if you don't have some sort of reason for getting beat, then basically you just got your ass kicked. So I always try to find some kind of reason, something I could have done differently, and then do it differently when I come back. If I just sit here and tell you, 'He beat me, and he's better than me' ... well, then I'm done."

Coleman was far from done, and he knew just what he had to do to take his game to the next level. "I haven't really had anybody slap a real fuckin' nice knee bar on me, or a triangle choke on me," he says. "I've had people try to, but for the most part anybody who was ever skilled enough to do these things, normally I was fifty or twenty or thirty pounds heavier than they were. Now I'm running across people who are my size, who can move like a hundred-and-fifty-pound snake. It's time for me to get out and get some serious training in. I'm confident I can pick it up quickly. Nothing against my teammates around here, but nobody can move like a Nogueira, a Josh Barnett, or a Matt Hume. Nobody in my camp can really move like that, so I need to travel and get the quality of training partners that I need to fight with these guys these days."

Because of the tremendous heart and skill of fighters like Mark Coleman, the Pride Fighting Championship Grand Prix 2000 was a resounding success. As the fans filed out into the streets, their heads still spinning with the sights and sounds of the night, they knew that they had just witnessed one of the most spectacular competitions ever. One of their Japanese champions had triumphed over a Gracie, while the other had been struck down by a Shamrock. Heroes had been born, and a champion had been crowned. Fortunately for the Japanese fans, who adore the thrill of dramatic conflict, there were still many epic confrontations to come. Another Pride would be fought.

New Warrior Class

The new UFC logo.

The Pride Fighting Championships Logo.

CHAPTER 19

The New UFC

Back in the U.S.A., the UFC had managed to set up many classic confrontations, but the cable ban was bleeding SEG dry, and even the live events were limited to a few select states that allowed MMA competition. Robert Meyrowitz hadn't been able to make much headway in securing sanctioning for the event, and the extravaganza that had so drastically changed the face of martial arts was becoming a financial burden. Meyrowitz knew that without sanctioning the UFC was doomed, so he turned his attention to the state of Nevada, which was the boxing center of the West and a key state for combative sporting promotions. He invited the members of the Nevada State Athletic Commission to Iowa to check out UFC XXI, hoping to instill in them a greater understanding of the sport and gain their support for its legalization. One of the commissioners who attended the event was casino tycoon Lorenzo Fertitta.

Growing up in Las Vegas, Fertitta was a huge fan of boxing. Over the years, he learned the industry inside and out, and in November of 1996, Governor Bob Miller appointed him to the Nevada State Athletic Commission. Although many commissioners seemed to have a bias towards boxing and frowned upon mixed martial arts, Fertitta was intrigued by the sport, and when Meyrowitz approached the commission about sanctioning MMA events, Fertitta kept an open mind. At that point, the only knowledge the commissioners had about MMA competition was from the UFC's early "No Rules" marketing campaign, and Fertitta wanted to learn more before forming an opinion on the sport. "I headed up a team of people to study it," he says, "and we went out and watched some events."

The first event they attended was UFC XXI. While at the show, Fertitta met fighters such as Frank Shamrock, Tito Ortiz, Chuck Liddell, and John Lewis. He was impressed by their professionalism, and when he learned that Lewis, a renowned jiu-jitsu tactician, happened to have a training facility in Las Vegas, he arranged for private lessons. Fertitta became hooked on MMA. Thrilled about what he was learning, he invited his friend Dana White, who had left the Boston boxing world to pursue a career as a boxing promoter in Vegas, to come and study jiu-jitsu with Lewis. White also fell in love with the sport, and he soon found himself managing MMA fighters, including Tito Ortiz and Chuck Liddell.

While Fertitta and White were studying jiu-jitsu, Meyrowitz struggled on. He was not able, however, to obtain further sanctioning for his event. Knowing he couldn't keep the show afloat on his own, Meyrowitz put out the word that he was looking for a partner to help relieve some of the financial pressure. "I think he just felt like he had taken it as far as he could, and he was looking to just move on," says Fertitta.

At about the time of UFC XXIX—held in Tokyo on December 16, 2000—Dana White, who had been negotiating his fighters' contracts with SEG, learned of Meyrowitz's intentions. He contacted Fertitta, who had stepped down from his post at the State Athletic Commission in the summer of 2000 to take on a full-time job as president of Station Casinos. Fertitta's interest was immediately piqued. But instead of partnering up with Meyrowitz and the battle-weary SEG, Fertitta wanted to purchase the UFC outright. Meyrowitz conceded, and a month later Lorenzo Fertitta and his brother, Frank, formed Zuffa Sports Entertainment and began proceedings to buy the UFC. Dana White, who had been instrumental in coordinating the deal, was appointed president of the company, and SEG's matchmaker John Paretti was replaced by Joe Silva—a MMA stratagest who had been orchestrating matches behind the scenes practically from the UFC's inception.

The sale to Zuffa was finalized several weeks before UFC XXX, which was named Battle on the Bordwalk. The event played out on February 23, 2001 in Atlantic City, New Jersey, and it boasted a star-studded card, including Tito Ortiz, Pedro Rizzo, Jeremy Horn, and rising stars Jens Pulver and Josh Barnett.

Dana White set out to restore the UFC to its former glory. He began by implementing an aggressive public relations and marketing campaign. The first step in the plan was to educate the various athletic commissions about MMA as a legitimate sport—and it didn't hurt that one of the new owners was a former commissioner. "Lorenzo has a lot of credibility," says White. "He's a stand-up guy and a great businessman, with a lot of respect from a lot of people. Rather than butt heads with the commissions, we went in and sat down with them and said, 'Hey, listen,' and they listened."

Along with educating the athletic commissions, Zuffa also altered some of the UFC rules to make the sport more acceptable to those who thought it too violent. In the words of Josh Hedges, Zuffa's public relations coordinator: "Sports do have rules, and we can't have it just be a barroom brawl like it used to be, with two or three rules and that's it. We try to give the hardcore fans as few rules as is possible, but then again we have to have the rules for it to be recognized as the sport that it is, and to be as safe as it is." In addition to making the sport safer, Zuffa also adopted the same weight classes as professional boxing. "We really tried to formulate the set of rules to be very close to sports such as boxing and wrestling and Olympic judo," says Lorenzo Fertitta. These weight classes consist of five divisions: lightweight, welterweight, middleweight, light heavyweight, and heavyweight.

Zuffa also recognized the absolute necessity of getting the UFC back on cable; so, while they were educating the politicians, they also began to educate the cable providers. They did this by taking their fighters to the cable call centers to sign autographs and talk about the sport. "In the early days, it was promoted as a blood sport," says Hedges. "It was promoted all wrong. That's not what we're about; we're about the sport. These guys are real athletes, and we want them to be respected as real athletes. We want people to understand that these people are trained just as hard as NFL football players, or baseball players in the World Series— like any other mainstream sport. They just chose a different sport to utilize their talents."

Another of Zuffa's tasks was to bring the UFC back into the public eye. Many of the fans hadn't seen the show since the days of Royce Gracie, and some still thought he was competing in the event. To promote the new UFC, Zuffa produced spots for radio and television and even took out full-page ads in magazines such as *Maxim* and *Playboy*. They also brought in the ever-popular Carmen Elektra as spokeswoman for the UFC. "People have no idea what Carmen Elektra has done for us," says Dana White. "If you went to UFC XXX's press conference, there was nobody there. Now, fast-forward to the UFC XXXIII press conference at ESPN Zone with Carmen Elektra. *Entertainment Tonight, Extra*—all the Hollywood press was there."

The Zuffa team knew what they were doing. Not only did they get MMA sanctioned by the Nevada State Athletic Commission, but they also succeeded in getting the major cable companies to lift their ban. UFC XXXIII was the first event since UFC XII to be aired on mainstream cable, and it was made available through On Demand, the most popular pay-per-view provider. The show was held on September 28, 2001 at the Mandalay Bay Hotel and Casino in Las Vegas, Nevada. The night's main event was slated to be a contest between the new UFC poster boy Tito Ortiz and the Brazilian sensation Vitor Belfort. But the bout never happened—Belfort cut himself in a freak accident and couldn't fight. Vladimir Matyushenko was brought in as an alternate. The fight went the distance, with Ortiz winning by unanimous decision; but although Ortiz considered the fight one of his toughest yet, the match was visually unimpressive.

The rest of the fights went much the same way, with very little explosive action. For the niche submission fan, the event offered a great display of technique, but for the general public, the people who would ultimately make or break the new venture, it was a long and dull program. "It was devastating," admits White. "I don't know how it happened, but it will never happen again. First of all, they bomb us on September 11. Vitor gets hurt, pulls out. Then they put the Hopkins/Trinidad fight the night after us. There were just so many things that went wrong that were beyond our control it was insane—and things that were within our control! It was just a bad month." To top it off, the event ran overtime. Viewers who had paid to watch the return of the UFC were cut off halfway through the main event.

Zuffa, however, was undaunted, and the company's next event, High Voltage, was held on November 2, 2001. The show went off without a hitch in the Las Vegas MGM Grand, and the fighters gave it their all, treating the fans to some of the most dramatic bouts the UFC had seen in quite some time. Matt Hughes snared the welterweight title belt when he slammed Carlos Newton in the second round, knocking him out cold. Lightweight competitor B.J. Penn destroyed Caol Uno in just eleven seconds with a flurry of strikes, and heavyweight champion Randy Couture took out Pedro Rizzo in the main event.

Zuffa and the UFC were back on track. With most cable companies now carrying the event—AT&T Broadband, Cox Communications, and Comcast, to name a few—MMA competition was basking in the limelight. The sport was recognized by key state athletic commissions such as those of Nevada and New Jersey, and Zuffa's commitment to a long-term plan promised to create an atmosphere where both the UFC and MMA could thrive. But, even with the education of politicians and the media, the marketing campaign, and the improved production values, Zuffa still understood that it was the fighters who would keep the fans coming back for more. They drew up a budget to entice world-class athletes, and built a new stable of fighters who would lead the charge into the next phase of the Ultimate Fighting Championship.

CHAPTER 20

The Lightweights
(154.9 pounds and below)

It was being called the grudge match of 2001—the UFC XXXI bout between reigning lightweight champion Jens "Little Evil" Pulver and challenger Dennis "Superman" Hallman. The two had gone to high school together in Washington, but after Hallman put away Pulver's teammate Matt Hughes in under twenty seconds during UFC XXIX, harsh words had flown back and forth between the two. Now it was time to settle the score in the cage.

Hallman came out hot. Running across the octagon, he landed a front kick to Pulver's midsection and worked for a takedown, eventually pulling Little Evil into his guard. Although Pulver played it safe, Hallman was crafty, and in one deft move he seized Pulver's arm, looking to lock it out. But Pulver wouldn't go that easily. Feeling the submission immediately, he spun on top of his opponent, gaining the leverage to tug his arm free. Then he dropped a bomb to Hallman's face before leaping to his feet. As the first round came to a close, neither fighter seemed the worse for wear.

Having cleared out the cobwebs, Pulver came out strong for the second round—and he remained strong for the remainder of the fight. While stuck in Hallman's guard and avoiding submissions, he punched away at his opponent's body and head before working his way back to his feet. Hallman tried to throw head kicks, but each time he did, Pulver retaliated with his hard left hand. Pulver did everything he could to keep the fight standing, and Hallman finally grew frustrated. He repeatedly fell to the mat, wanting Pulver to join him. At one point, Hallman even scooted after his opponent, hoping to coax him down. When nothing else seemed to work, Superman jumped into the air and tried knocking Little Evil over by kicking him with both feet at the same time. Pulver backed up and then fended off Hallman with his own piece of kryptonite—his heavy left.

The last action of the fight—before it was put into the hands of the judges—was Pulver landing right after left to Hallman's face. It didn't come as a surprise to many when Pulver was awarded the win by unanimous decision.

*   *   *

Jens Pulver had retained the lightweight championship title, something that meant the world to him. "I wasn't supposed to amount to much. I was beaten as a child and watched my mother get punched on by a grown-ass man," he says. "But I proved them all wrong, and that's something I will continue to do until the day I die."

Bleeding and sweating to be his best was nothing new to the Seattle-born wrestler. At five-foot-seven and 150 pounds, he was a two-time state champion and a four-time All-American while at Tacoma High School. After again becoming an All-American wrestler at Highline Junior College, Pulver was recruited by Boise State; but he suffered three concussions during his senior year, which ended his season. To fulfill his need for physical exercise, he began training as a fighter. He had watched the UFC while growing up, and, knowing that it was only a matter of time before they introduced weight classes, he set his sights on competing in the event.

As his trainer, Pulver employed Lowell Anderson, a jiu-jitsu expert he had met while wrestling at Boise State. They worked on his ground game, and just a few months later Pulver found himself facing competitor Curtis Hill in his first MMA event—the Bas Rutten Invitational, held on April 24, 1999 in Littleton, Colorado. Pulver was competing in the 170-pound-and-under division, and although he only weighed in at 150 pounds, he showed just what a terror he could be. "Lowell told me if I wanted to impress John Perretti, the UFC matchmaker, that I needed to stand up and show him my all-around game," says Pulver. "Up until that point, I had always shot for the takedown and would fight on the ground. But this time was different. I stood up the whole time and kept him from taking me down. I knocked him out and knew that I was going to fight on my feet from that point on."

Pulver had beaten down his first opponent, but he still had David Harris to get through to earn the division tournament title. "I beat that man from one end of the cage to the other," recalls Pulver, "but I could not put him away because I didn't know submissions. We lasted for about twenty minutes, and then I found myself in a position where he had my legs and then my foot. He applied pressure, and it hurt. I had no idea until later what it was he actually did—that he got me in a toehold. I didn't know anything about submissions, but after that I started to pay more attention to them."

*Jens Pulver tearing into Dennis Hallman in
their UFC XXXIII Lightweight Championship bout.*

Although he lost his fight, Pulver had done what he'd set out to do: he had made an impression on John Perretti. The two talked after the event, and Pulver said he was going to work on his finishing moves. He did just that, and at the next Bas Rutten Invitational he submitted his first opponent with a choke and then scored a one-punch KO in the finals. Perretti could not ignore the rising star. He told Pulver that he was going to add him to the card of UFC XXII—to be held on September 24, 1999 in Lake Charles, Louisiana—and he would be competing in the first-ever bantamweight bout.

Although the fight would not be aired on cable, it was an opportunity Pulver took very seriously. "I stopped training with Lowell because he was too one-dimensional," he explains. "He only wanted things done his way, and he was not willing to cross-train with the stand-up aspect of fighting." Pulver went looking for a more complete gym, and his search took him to California, where he found himself under the tutelage of Bob Shamrock and his newly established team, Shamrock 2000. With teammates Jason Peitz, Steve Heath, Valeri Ignatov, and (coauthor of this book) Erich Krauss, Pulver cross-trained in muay Thai and submission. When he arrived at UFC XXII, he felt more than prepared.

Standing backstage, waiting to do battle with kickboxer Alfonso Alcarez, Pulver could hardly believe where he was: "I was awestruck when

I met all the fighters, especially Pat Miletich and his camp. That was the first time I met Monte Cox, Jeremy Horn, or Pat. They helped me out in the locker room before the fight. Pat helped me gain my composure and told me to take it easy and not to burn myself out."

Pulver took Miletich's advice to heart, and he fully intended to remain composed. But once he'd set foot in the octagon, he says, "My heart was pounding and I was nervous. But I was also having fun. I mean, I got to fight in front of the biggest crowd I had ever been in front of, and I just let it all go."

Pulver shot in on Alcarez right away, taking him to the mat. Alcarez managed to scramble to all fours, but Pulver leaned his weight down on him, unleashing a series of knee strikes to the head before sinking in a guillotine choke. Although Alcarez was able to power out, Pulver immediately fired upon him with uppercuts and jabs. Pulver was clearly getting the better of Alcarez, but Bob Shamrock, sitting in Pulver's corner, had studied countless tapes of the kickboxer in action, and he knew he was a dangerous striker. "Tie up," shouted Bob. "Tie up with him!"

Pulver did just that, and, cupping the back of Alcarez's head, he delivered knee after knee to his opponent's midsection. When his shots buckled Alcarez, Pulver snatched his head, using it as a target for more knees until the first round came to an end. But delivering all those shots had taken its toll on Pulver, and at the beginning of the second round Alcarez came out strong, landing several uppercuts before a fatigued Pulver could close the gap and press his opponent up against the fence. Again Pulver began chopping away at Alcarez with his knees, but Alcarez was now fighting back, hooking to the body and head. At one point, he even managed to pick Pulver up and throw him over his back. Then, after they'd both regained their footing, all hell broke loose—Pulver landing knees, and Alcarez throwing hooks to the face. After several minutes of this, Alcarez ducked low and snatched Pulver's legs, putting him on his back. The end of the fight saw Alcarez swinging wildly, and Pulver jabbing upward.

When Pulver came back to his corner, John Perretti was there to greet him. "Oh man, incredible fight," said Perretti. "What a great fight!" The crowd agreed, and when the word came in from the judges, Bruce Buffer announced that Jens Pulver was the winner. But that decision would not stick. Shortly after the fight, the outcome was officially changed to a draw. Pulver comments, "I felt that they changed the decision later to a draw for the simple fact that it was a good fight and they wanted to showcase a rematch when they unveiled the new bantamweight division. I still feel that I won that fight."

*Jens Pulver deals a stern left cross to Caol Uno
in their UFC XXX Lightweight Championship bout.*

Uno lands a high Thai kick to Pulver's head.

After his impressive octagon debut, Pulver was guaranteed another shot in the UFC. But because the financial troubles created by the cable ban were trickling down to the various teams, Shamrock 2000 was unable to survive, and again Pulver needed to find a place to train. "I called Monte Cox [Pat Miletich's manager], and he told me to come to Iowa and see what I thought," says Pulver. It would be a huge transition—he'd have to leave his friends and family—but he also understood that it was necessary to achieve his goal of being pound for pound the best fighter in the world.

So, carrying only two bags, Jens Pulver hopped onto a train and traveled two days to Iowa with plans to become a world champion. "It was the best decision I have ever made," he insists. "Miletich's gym was perfect for me, and the fighters in there were at a level I had never seen before. It was an oasis for fighters." Not only did Pulver receive world-class training in Iowa, but he also found a second family: "I am very close with the fighters and they are some of my best friends. We watch out for each other and we are there every day to push each other for the fights."

Backed by this inseparable crew, Pulver felt invincible when he stepped back into the octagon to do battle with Dave Velasquez in UFC XXIV. This time, he refused to put his fate into the hands of the judges. "I went in there with the intentions of roughing him up and beating the hell out of him with constant pressure and a lot of punches," says Pulver. "He could not stand with me, and I already knew that I would beat him on the ground. So I went in there to just beat him in every way possible. And that is what I did." Pulver dominated Velasquez for two minutes and forty-one seconds before the referee stopped the bout and put an end to the abuse.

This victory only fueled Pulver's determination to win the soon-to-be-introduced bantamweight title. After earning a judges' decision over Joao Roque in UFC XXVI, held on September 6, 2000 in Cedar Rapids, Iowa, he faced off in UFC XXVIII against John Lewis, a dangerous and experienced lightweight jiu-jitsu competitor who had dropped weight for the fight. "I was really nervous fighting John because of all his experience and because of his size," says Pulver. "I knew it would be a test for me, and that a title was in the making if I won. I knew that I would knock him out if I let my hands go and hit him the way I trained to. We worked really hard on getting inside his lazy jab and connecting the big left hand on the inside of his reach." That's exactly what Pulver did on November 17, 2000 in Atlantic City, New Jersey. Just seconds into the bout, Pulver slipped Lewis's jab, stepped forward, and connected with a huge left hook to the chin. "I hit him as hard as I have ever hit anyone," says Pulver. Lewis fell to the canvas and did not get back up. The fight was over in thirty-five seconds.

After chopping down a legend in the sport, Pulver returned to the octagon, in UFC XXX, to fight for his dream—a title belt. It would not be for the bantamweight title, however. With Zuffa's takeover of the UFC, the weight divisions used in boxing had been introduced, and now Pulver was considered a lightweight. His opponent was Caol Uno, a shooto competitor who was famous throughout Japan. But nothing would stop Little Evil, and after a full-out war on February 23, 2001 in Atlantic City, he won by judges' decision. With this momentum, he sailed into UFC XXXIII to dispatch Dennis Hallman.

Although Pulver was on top of his game, there was no time for relaxation. An up-and-coming jiu-jitsu expert by the name of B.J. Penn was hot on his heels, and the two would meet in UFC XXXV.

The Prodigy

Growing up in Hilo, Hawaii, Penn was introduced to the fight game at an early age. "Everyone over there is into boxing or kickboxing," he says. "Although I never boxed anywhere, I was into sparring everyone. I actually wanted to fight amateur when I was thirteen, but I was stubborn and wanted to train myself. So that never really went through, because it was kind of ridiculous for a thirteen year old to train himself."

Penn's formal training in the martial arts began in high school, shortly after a tae kwon do instructor named Tom Callis moved into the neighborhood and came to Penn's door in search of sparring partners. "He had taken some private lessons from Cesar and Ralph Gracie up in California," says Penn. "He didn't want to teach tae kwon do; he just wanted some grappling partners. My father told me I should go down there and wrestle with him, but I thought it would be a waste of my time. Finally my dad said, 'You have to go—this guy won't leave me alone. Just go down there one time and you won't have to go down there ever again.' He tapped me out and arm barred me. From that point on, I got addicted to it and just kept doing it every day."

Penn excelled in the sport, and in no time at all he was able to defeat his instructor. So when Callis went to the mainland to test for his black belt in tae kwon do, Penn went with him. "He told me we were going to be right by Ralph Gracie's school. He asked me if I wanted to go up and just see how it is," Penn says. "I was thinking I was going to go there and tap everyone out. I thought I was good, but I really didn't know anything. When I went there, everyone beat me. But I was doing pretty good, seeing that it was my first time out there at a real school."

Penn had made an impression, and Ralph Gracie told Callis that the boy had a future in the sport. Callis reported this to Penn's father. "Back home," says Penn, "I wasn't doing anything. I was just hanging out—going to the beach, partying, doing stupid things. I wasn't working; I wasn't doing anything. My dad wanted me off the island, but I didn't want to go. [When I was] seventeen, my dad told me that in six months he was going to send me to the mainland to check out the school and train. To make him happy, I agreed, not thinking the day would ever come. But when that day did come, I almost wanted to cry. He forced me to go, and so I came to the mainland to train."

Penn moved to Mountain View, California, and he found a place to live only a few blocks from Ralph Gracie's academy. He began training three times a day, six days a week. "That's all I did. I didn't even really like it," says Penn. "I liked it to a point, but I wasn't in love with it. I just did it because my dad wanted me to be up here."

Despite his initial lukewarm reaction to the sport, training in jiu-jitsu eventually changed Penn's life. "I would still be doing the same things if my dad hadn't sent me over here. Who knows if I would have shaped up? I probably would have still been drinking and getting into fights at the beach. When I first came up here, I only thought that jiu-jitsu was sport fighting. Everything with me was always fight-oriented. I was always into boxing and getting into a lot of fights. I probably had sixty or seventy street fights. Everything I did in jiu-jitsu I wanted to use for the street. I never wanted to train with a gi."

Penn got to see just how effective his new techniques were when he entered his first competition as a white belt and defeated everyone—not only in his weight division, but also in the entire open-weight tournament. Having tasted victory, he entered another competition, this time Joe Moreira's Blue Belt International. Although Penn was still a white belt, he once again ran through the competition.

After scoring a string of tournament victories in the United States, Penn entered the big time and traveled to Brazil to compete with the best athletes in the sport. Although he initially found it difficult to get a fair judges' decision because he wasn't Brazilian, he eventually won his

ZUFFA SPORTS ENTERTAINMENT

B.J. Penn dismantles Joe Gilbert from the mount in their UFC XXXI Lightweight bout.

hosts over with his superlative skill, and he became the first American to win the Jiu-Jitsu World Championships.

Penn's skills were improving every day, thanks, in part, to training partners like Frank Shamrock. "We both train at the American Kickboxing Academy," says Penn. "There is a time when all the fighters train, and a lot of people stop in. There are so many different fighters there all the time. It's a big help with Frank there—his charisma, being a UFC champion. He knows how to train for cardiovascular strength. He's got good workouts and drills."

Another champion Penn had the pleasure of training with was jiu-jitsu competitor and UFC veteran John Lewis. "I got into the UFC through John Lewis," Penn maintains. "He pulled some strings and got me in, and so I owe him for that. He knew Dana White and Lorenzo Fertitta before they bought the UFC. I met those two and rolled around with them, so they knew my ground and pounding. But they didn't know how I would do as a fighter. Nobody really knew that I was really fighting all my life, all the time. So it translated pretty well for me. No one knew how it would translate, because they all thought of me as a jiu-jitsu guy."

Penn showed just how well rounded a fighter he was in his octagon debut, against Joey Gilbert, at UFC XXXI—held on May 4, 2001 in Atlantic City. "I didn't know what to expect. When they called my name

*B.J. Penn attempts an armbar on Din Thomas
in their UFC XXXIII Lightweight bout.*

Penn lands a knockout knee to Thomas's face.

backstage, people were like, 'B.J., let's get out there!' Although I didn't know what was going to happen, I was happy, because I wanted to know where I stood in the fight world. It went pretty smooth. Right as I walked out, I almost felt like I wanted to cry. Everyone around me was getting pumped, but none of them knew I felt like breaking down and crying. It was like losing your virginity. No time will ever be like that one."

Penn came out strong and began dismantling Gilbert with strikes. With only seconds left in the first round, Gilbert found himself belly down on the canvas, Penn's weight riding on his back. All he could do was lie there as Penn batted his head back and forth with eleven punches to the temple. Just as Gilbert freed his arms to cover his head, referee John McCarthy ended the bout and put a stop to the punishment.

To prove that his victory wasn't a fluke, Penn stepped back into the octagon at the very next show—UFC XXXII, held on June 29, 2001 in East Rutherford, New Jersey—to take on Din Thomas, a fighter who had once defeated the reigning champ, Jens Pulver, in a competition called World Extreme Fighting.

Penn went for the takedown right away. When Thomas countered with a sprawl, Penn resorted to the clinch, softening up his opponent with knee strikes and punches before pulling him down into his guard. He took his time, and when the moment was right he went for an arm bar. But Thomas was well versed in submission, and he powered out, regaining his footing.

Both fighters stood sizing each other up for a few moments before Thomas came forward to swing a huge right hook. Penn slipped it, and with his opponent overextended he stepped in, gripped the back of Thomas's head, and brought up a knee that collided with Thomas's chin, dropping him. Penn followed him down, landing three hard shots to the face before referee John McCarthy realized that Thomas was out cold and stopped the fight.

The jiu-jitsu expert had done something no one expected—won his first two bouts with strikes. Penn had showed the world what he already knew—that he liked to hit people. Although he was always on the look-out for a submission, he simply enjoyed hitting his opponents.

Penn proved just how much he liked to strike in UFC XXXIV, when he returned to the octagon to fight Caol Uno, the shooto competitor whom Jens Pulver had gone to war with for twenty-five minutes. Just after the bout started, Uno dashed across the ring and dealt a flying kick. Penn stepped to the side, then dropped a straight right cross to Uno's face that grounded him on the canvas. Penn seized the opportunity and rushed forward. With his victim lying motionless, he dropped five more punches to Uno's face before the referee intervened. He had won in an amazing eleven seconds.

UFC XXXV—Throwdown/January 11, 2002
(Uncasville, Connecticut)

Lightweight Title Bout—Jens Pulver versus B.J. Penn

With three decisive wins in the octagon, Penn had not only earned his shot at Jens Pulver for the lightweight belt, but he'd also become the crowd favorite. When the two met in UFC XXXV, held on January 11, 2002 in Uncasville, Connecticut, Penn's lightning-quick punches and stealthy ground game made him a three-to-one favorite in Las Vegas betting circles. It was the main event of the evening, and the most anticipated lightweight bout in UFC history.

"This one, to me, is a fight," said Pulver in his prefight interview. "I'm fighting against all those people who said that I'm just going to get trucked over, that I'm going to be helpless, that Penn's too good standing up and too good on the ground."

When Pulver came out jabbing, Penn shot underneath and brought him to the mat, working for a submission to end the bout quickly. But, although Pulver was a proficient wrestler, he wanted the fight standing. After defending himself for over a minute from his back, he used his feet to push Penn off him. Then Pulver jumped up, but Penn rushed forward, hooked an arm around Pulver's head, and wrapped his legs around him, cinching down on the guillotine choke.

Pulver remained calm. "Patience is the key," he has insisted. "Keeping a level head at all times and not panicking in a bad situation." Once he had broken Penn's hold on his neck, he took three steps forward and slammed his opponent to the mat. Yet it would take more than that to take out the Hawaiian jiu-jitsu expert. As Pulver chopped away at his body with short punches, Penn continued to hunt for submissions from his back. Both warriors had come prepared for battle, and the fight went up and down. It wasn't until the middle of the second five-minute round that one of them found a dominant position. Having sent Pulver onto his back, Penn scooted around his opponent's legs and obtained a mount. At first Pulver clung on for dear life, but once Penn began landing shots he did everything he could to get the jiu-jitsu expert off him. Penn rode out

ZUFFA SPORTS ENTERTAINMENT

B.J. Penn finishes off Caol Uno in their UFC XXXIV Lightweight bout.

his thrashing, and then, with just five seconds remaining in the round, he snatched Pulver's arm, swung around to the side, and went for the arm bar. Just as he was extending it, the buzzer sounded.

When Pulver returned to his corner, his trainers were there to coach him. "Be ready for the sprawl," said Jeremy Horn. "You're hurting him with those punches, and he's scared of you." Having narrowly escaped defeat, Pulver listened to his trainers' advice and came out with jab/cross combinations. Again the fight went up and down, but Pulver was becoming more familiar with Penn's takedowns, and although he didn't find a way to avoid them entirely, he consistently came out on top, punching his opponent's ribs and face before escaping back to his feet. His tactics began to wear on the Hawaiian, who became more and more reluctant to fight Pulver on the ground. By the fifth round, the bout had turned into a stand-up war. Despite Penn's knockout history, it became evident that this was Pulver's territory as he repeatedly landed rights and lefts.

The last seconds of the fight saw Pulver delivering a kick to Penn's head. The bout's outcome went into the hands of the judges. Despite his dominance, Pulver didn't seem confident that he had won. When Bruce Buffer announced, "And winner, by majority decision, and *still . . .*" a very emotional Jens Pulver broke into tears. "That was, without a doubt, the hardest fight I have ever been in in my life," he admits.

Pulver had once again retained his title. As his teammates poured into the ring to congratulate him, it was obvious to all that Little Evil had attained his ultimate goal. "I have much to accomplish," says Pulver, "but none as important as gaining the recognition from my peers. I am just a kid who grew up with many obstacles in my way. I have overcome some things that would make most crumble. I have given a lot to being a better person, and I will continue to give back to help in any way that I can. I came to Iowa with two bags on a train ride that lasted two and a half days just to be a world champion. I train like I am going to fight the devil himself. I have sacrificed much to be here and would do it all again if it got me to this moment in time once again."

CHAPTER 21

The Welterweights
(155 pounds to 169.9 pounds)

After a long, grueling bout with Townsend Saunders, Pat Miletich, standing five-foot-ten and weighing in at 169 pounds, entered the octagon for the second time at UFC XVI to do battle with jiu-jitsu expert Chris Brennan, an alternate who had won his qualifying bout in under two minutes. Brennan was no chump fighter, and no one knew this better than Miletich, who had fought him in the Extreme Challenge 9, just a few months earlier. The two had gone to war, and after thirty exhausting minutes, the bout was declared a draw. Miletich needed to do better than that tonight; he needed to push himself harder and bring home the win. The lightweight division was 170 pounds and under, and the lightweight tournament title was on the line.

Miletich played it safe, picking his shots while backpedaling. But Brennan was hungry for the title, and when Miletich dropped a kick to his leg, Brennan snatched Miletich's leg, tugged him to the mat, and jumped on him. Stuck in Miletich's guard, however, Brennan couldn't mount an effective attack. While trying to better his position, Miletich escaped and popped to his feet. Brennan joined him, and while the two worked in the clinch, Brennan saw an opening. Wrapping an arm around Miletich's head, Brennan dropped to the mat, pulling his opponent between his legs and cinching down on his neck.

After a few dangerous moments, Miletich powered out of the choke, and for the next six minutes, he beat on his opponent with punches to the body and face, all the while slowly dragging Brennan towards the fence. Once there, Miletich managed to free one of his legs and, using the added leverage, he sunk his shoulder deep into Brennan's throat. In seconds, the exhausted jiu-jitsu expert tapped.

*   *   *

Pat Miletich was one of the original proponents of MMA in his home state of Iowa and throughout the Midwest. He was the premier fighter at the Quad City Ultimate and participated in the battle to make the sport legal in Iowa. Miletich was a wrestler turned kickboxer turned MMA

*From his guard, Pat Miletich lands a hard hook to the face of
Townsend Saunders in their UFC XVI bout.*

competitor, and after winning the UFC XVI lightweight tournament
title, he went on to defeat Mikey Burnett in UFC Brazil and win the first-
ever 170-pound-and-under lightweight championship title.

In possession of a championship belt, Miletich ran the gauntlet much
like Frank Shamrock had. He focused on conditioning and intense workouts, training seven to nine hours a day, six days a week. In addition to
this, he found time to oversee one of the most impressive mixed martial
arts camps—a camp that now boasts champions such as Jens Pulver and
Matt Hughes.

After successfully defending his UFC title four times, as well as competing in other events such as Superbrawl and Extreme Challenge, Miletich
entered the octagon at UFC XXXI for his most publicized matchup yet.
The UFC had been sold to Zuffa, there was talk of the show going back
on pay-per-view, and finally Miletich was going to get the attention he
deserved. But to remain the champion he first had to beat the technically
renowned jiu-jitsu practitioner Carlos Newton.

Newton was a warrior on all fronts. Growing up in the British Virgin
Islands, he excelled not only in karate, but also in his schoolwork. His
single mother, hoping to improve the quality of his education, sent him
to Canada to live with his aunt when he was just ten years old. "Coming
here to Canada when I was younger," says Newton, "there was a period

when I thought anything could happen to me. I don't know how I did it. It was like I was one of those little baby turtles that hatch on the beach, and they have to make that perilous journey from the sand to the water. With all those birds swooping overhead and picking away, I don't know how I made it. I just saw the water and kept going."

Although he was captain of both the swim team and the gymnastics team in high school, Newton's true passion was the martial arts. He began studying jiu-jitsu at the age of fifteen, and, not always having a place to live, he spent much of his time traveling to different dojos around Canada. "I approached each learning experience I had pretty much like a baby," he recalls. "I don't react to egos. When a person was actually able to beat me, I would always cling to that person. I did not care at all about winning; it was just the sheer pursuit of learning the art in every facet."

At sixteen, Newton began competing in both karate point-sparring and demo tournaments, and then, just three years later, on April 26, 1996, he entered Extreme Fighting 2, his first MMA tournament. He took on MMA veteran Jean Riviere. "I weighed 180 pounds, and he weighed 286 pounds," says Newton. "We really rock and rolled. I got exhausted and I almost passed out. The referee gave me a stop-fight, but it caught the public's attention that I was able to do that well with a big weight advantage to my opponent. Riviere had fought in the Brazil show and knocked out all his opponents. I was the only guy who walked out of there in one piece."

With this impressive debut, Newton returned to Extreme Fighting and found a home among other the fighters there. "That was the old show that had Maurice Smith, Conan Silveira—all the guys," he says. "I was pretty much invited back all the time, mostly as an alternate. That's where I met all the other guys, like Frank Shamrock. I was pretty much just a kid; everyone called me 'kid.' All the other guys looked out for me—like Maurice, John Lewis, and Igor Zinoviev. They all really encouraged me and always corrected me. They were such a big help—especially Maurice."

Being an Extreme Fighting competitor opened doors, and Newton got the chance to go to Japan and compete in shooto. It was his second true MMA bout, and he fought none other than Erik Paulson, the shooto world champion. Newton remained composed during that bout, and when Paulson came forward throwing punches, he ducked under them, shot in, and took his opponent down. Taking the mount, Newton landed a few punches of his own and then spun into an arm bar. He won the bout in forty-seven seconds.

The victory was inspiring, but it was Japan that made the biggest impression on Newton. "I feel that in Japan there is a bigger presence of the martial arts spirit, the 'budo,'" he says. "There is a bigger sense of the samurai. In the U.S., everyone loves the winner, but in Japan, everyone loves the warrior. Sometimes the winner is not always the true warrior. In Japan, they started calling me 'the ronan' because many of the Japanese know my idol, Musashi, who was a famous ronan. He won sixty-four duels to the death. Japan was one of the places where I have taken up a lot of my philosophy. It has served as a foundation for a lot of my thoughts."

After winning one more shooto competition, Newton was asked by newly appointed UFC matchmaker John Perretti, the man who had put together the Extreme Fighting cards, to display his skills in UFC XVII, held in Mobile, Alabama on May 15, 1998. Not only was this a bigger show than Newton was used to, but he would also be fighting in an elimination tournament for SEG's middleweight tournament title.

When the five-foot-nine, 169 pound Newton stepped into the octagon to take on his first opponent—six-foot-two, 199-pound submission fighter Bob Gilstrap—he was stunned by his opponent's size. "I just had to use my skill," says Newton. "I knew in MMA size isn't going to matter all that much, and so I wasn't discouraged." In addition to having a size advantage, Gilstrap also had world-class training partners, including Maurice Smith, Frank Shamrock, and Tsuyoshi Kohsaka. The matchup promised to turn into an epic battle.

Newton shot right in, lifted his opponent off the canvas, and then slammed him down. He had a side mount on Gilstrap when they landed, but he quickly slid into the full mount and went for an arm bar. He was unable to lock it in, however, and Gilstrap reversed him. But instead of backing out, Gilstrap remained on the ground and tried to drop a downward blow. Wrong move. Now Newton had Gilstrap's other arm secured between his legs and was applying pressure. Gilstrap managed to roll out of it, but Newton had another submission waiting. Wrapping his legs around his opponent's head, he applied a triangle choke that forced Gilstrap to submit.

In just fifty seconds, Newton had put away his first opponent and displayed flawless submission skills. His next opponent, however—world-class wrestler Dan Henderson—would be a far greater challenge. Instead of shooting in, Newton decided to fight the wrestler on his feet. "I ducked to the side and hit him with a body shot," remembers Newton. "I heard him go 'Oop!' and I came upstairs right away. I heard his jaw go 'crack.' I looked at my hand, thinking it was my hand. I broke his jaw, and he just did the Ickey Shuffle and came right back. I wasn't sure what happened, and then my coaches were like, 'Get him!'"

Newton took his trainers' advice and delivered a flurry of punches and kicks that rocked Henderson. Looking as if he was going to finish off his opponent right then and there, Henderson did what he did best and seized Newton's legs, taking him to the mat. From his back, Newton attempted one submission after another to no avail, all the while eating serious blows. And there was a problem—Newton had forgotten to put in his mouthpiece before the fight. John McCarthy finally stood them up so Newton could retrieve the necessary piece of protective gear.

When the fight was restarted, Henderson was throwing blows, and this time Newton took him to the ground. But he could not keep the wrestler down, and when they finally worked their way back to their feet, both fighters were gassed. Henderson pressed the fight, however, and took Newton to the mat, brought him back up, and rocked him with more strikes, including fifteen knees to the face and head. Somehow, Newton seemed unaffected, and when the fight returned to the mat, he continued with his submission attempts from his back.

After beating on Newton for several minutes, Henderson stood up. Both of them were exhausted, and they picked their shots carefully. Henderson landed a solid right, and Newton worked his leg kicks. Then, after nine minutes of battle, Newton opened up and rushed forward, fists swinging. Henderson ate several shots to the face, and his legs went out from under him. He grabbed blindly at the advancing Newton, and, capturing his legs, managed to pull him to the canvas. After twelve exhausting minutes, the regulation time came to an end.

The opening of overtime saw Newton bursting forth with a flurry of kicks and punches, and Henderson letting loose with power punches. But it wasn't until two minutes in that Newton got the break he was looking for, turning the wrestler's legs to rubber with a wicked hook to Henderson's already broken jaw. Newton rushed in for the kill, and a wobbly Henderson shot in to save himself, taking Newton to the mat once again.

Riding on top of Newton, Henderson recuperated quickly. The fight came to a close with Henderson chopping away, and the decision went to the judges. After a brutal fifteen-minute wait, it was announced that Dan Henderson had won by split decision. "Dan was the toughest guy I have faced, for sure," claims Newton. "He was tough as hell."

The loss was a huge disappointment to Newton, but he bounced back. Taking some time off from the UFC, he returned to Japan and fought

Kazushi Sakuraba—the Japanese submission master who would later be named "the Gracie Hunter"—before twenty thousand spectators in the Pride Fighting Championship's third event on June 24, 1998. "It was a great fight," recalls Newton. "It went back and forth, and I learned a lot in that fight." But Sakuraba prevailed, catching Newton in a knee bar at five minutes and nineteen seconds into the second fifteen-minute round.

UFC XXXI/May 4, 2001
(Atlantic City, New Jersey)

Welterweight Title Bout—Pat Miletich versus Carlos Newton

After competing in three more Pride competitions, winning one by decision and the other two with arm bars, Newton returned to the octagon to take on Pat Miletich for the welterweight title in UFC XXXI. "I tried to see it as just another fight," says Newton, "and not get carried away because it was a big title match—didn't want to screw up my head. I tried not to think the fight was going to put me on top of the pile and keep me there for a while. I just wanted to go out there and do a good job. I felt strongly that I could beat him, but I knew my strategy going in was that I was going to have to beat him. He's such an experienced fighter. For me, still growing up as a fighter, experience is what I fear most. I don't care about the young guys like myself who can do ten back flips. Experience and brains always overcome brawn. I felt Pat, if anything, would have more of that than I do. I counted on that."

Both fighters came out striking, but, knowing that Miletich had an advantage on his feet, Newton made several attempts to take his opponent to the ground. Miletich countered perfectly, tying up with Newton and landing knees and punches before pushing him away. The fight turned into a kickboxing match until Newton shot in with thirty seconds left in the round, taking Miletich to the mat. Although he finally had his opponent where he wanted him, Newton only managed to throw a few shots before the round came to an end.

When Miletich came out firing at the opening of the second round, Newton shot in on a single leg and hauled him to the ground. After several reversals, both fighters popped to their feet and exchanged a barrage of blows; Miletich came out of that exchange ahead. Again Newton worked tirelessly to drag Miletich down, but when he finally accomplished this task, the second round was almost over.

ZUFFA SPORTS ENTERTAINMENT

*Pat Miletich throws a Thai kick to the midsection of Carlos Newton
in their UFC XXXI Welterweight Championship bout.*

ZUFFA SPORTS ENTERTAINMENT

Newton takes Miletich to the canvas.

Carlos Newton with the UFC Welterweight Championship belt.

It wasn't until the middle of the third round that Newton found an opening. As Miletich came forward punching, Newton ducked low and executed a flawless double-leg takedown. Once on the ground, he moved Miletich slowly towards the fence, hoping the chain-link would take away Miletich's mobility and allow him to lock in a submission. Determined to prevent this, Miletich turned a hip and tried to scoot out from underneath Newton. In the process, he turned his back to his opponent. Newton flipped around to the side and secured Miletich in a headlock. With his own arm digging into his throat and Newton applying more and more

ZUFFA SPORTS ENTERTAINMENT

*Pat Miletich lands a knockout Thai kick to the head of Shonie Carter
in their UFC XXXII Welterweight bout.*

pressure, Miletich tapped out, knowing it was only a matter of time before he lost consciousness. "I got to a point where I felt there was nothing he could do to hurt me," says Miletich, "and I got lazy and got caught. Lesson learned. He did a good job of taking advantage of the mistake that I made."

Fighting for the Title Shot

Miletich took the loss in stride, but he was eager to return to the octagon and earn another shot at the title he had held for so long. In UFC XXXII, he took on Shonie Carter, a wild striker whom Miletich had defeated once before, in Extreme Challenge 27.

Although Carter came out blasting, Miletich took him down fast and obtained a mount. He was unable to put Carter away before the round came to a close, however, and when the action started up in round two, Carter again came out firing. Miletich weathered the storm, going on the defensive and picking his shots. He landed several punches to Carter's ribs, and a couple of kicks to his legs. And then, when the time was right, he went up high, delivering his shin to the side of Carter's head. "I was just trying to set him up with low kicks," explains Miletich, "getting him to drop his hands. I just threw it. I tried taking his head off with it, and it just landed. I got lucky."

With Carter crumpled on the canvas, Miletich was declared the victor. "Everyone said that he was a dangerous person to be fighting in this UFC after that loss," says announcer Jeff Blatnick. "Miletich came out and showed everyone the kind of talent he has, and that he was certainly looking for that title opportunity again."

It looked like the opportunity would come in UFC XXXIV. Just one month before the event, Miletich received a call asking if he wanted a rematch with Newton for the title. Not sure if he could prepare himself in time, Pat didn't commit to the fight right away. He first wanted to ask his trainers for their opinions. But before he could get back to the people at Zuffa, they called him to say that they had confirmed a rematch between the Heavyweight Champion Randy Couture and his rival from UFC XXXI, Pedro Rizzo. The two had fought in the same UFC in which Miletich had lost to Newton, and Zuffa didn't feel that it was good business to put the same two main events on the card for XXXIV. Instead, Matt Hughes—one of the members of the growing Miletich fighting camp and next in line for the title shot—was given the opportunity to face Newton for the welterweight belt.

UFC XXXIV—High Voltage/November 2, 2001 (Las Vegas, Nevada)

Welterweight Title Bout—Carlos Newton versus Matt Hughes

Newton understood that Hughes was a world-class wrestler known for his power slams, and he did not take the match lightly. He trained harder than ever leading up to the bout, but despite his seriousness in the gym, his entrance into the octagon on fight night was all showmanship. With a beautiful model on his arm, he danced his way down the aisle wearing sunglasses and a massive Afro-style wig. There was no doubt that he was confident he could take out Matt Hughes.

The first five-minute round was a back-and-forth battle. Both fighters demonstrated superlative takedowns and skillful escapes. But since neither of them landed any serious shots, it was still anyone's fight. The opening of the second round saw Hughes closing the distance, picking Newton up off the mat and slamming him down. But when they landed, Hughes found himself stuck in Newton's guard. Making the best of the situation, Hughes began dropping bombs, opening himself up for a submission.

The crafty Newton seized the wrestler's outstretched arm and wrapped

*Matt Hughes attempts to choke Carlos Newton from the mount
in their UFC XXXIV Welterweight Championship bout . . .*

. . . then slams him.

his legs around his head, locking in a triangle choke. It looked grim for Hughes, but he was far from ready to give in. Not able to pull his arm free, he displayed his tremendous strength by picking Newton up off the mat and carrying the jiu-jitsu practitioner on his shoulders over to the fence.

Pressed against the cage, five feet off the canvas, Newton continued to grip Hughes's head tightly with his legs. He could feel his opponent slowly losing consciousness, and he was sure victory would be his. Then came the slam.

When the fighters hit the canvas, they were both out cold—Newton as a result of the five-foot fall, and Hughes due to the choke. Newton lay on his back, Hughes on top of him. John McCarthy rushed forward to separate them. He couldn't see Hughes's face, so he didn't know that he was also out cold. All he could see was Newton sprawled unconscious on the canvas. And just as McCarthy was pulling the fighters apart, Hughes woke up.

"I feel it was a tough break," says Newton. "I felt like I was too good of a boy and should have just held onto the fence and not took the slam. Big John was saying, 'Let go of the fence.' And I was like, 'He's going to pass out.' I knew I was going to take a ride—I thought that the whole time. I was like, 'Here it comes.' I should have held on, because I knew he was passing out; and he did pass out. When I hit, the first thing I thought was, 'Oh, that was hard.' I must have thought that at the same time I was going out. Then I was coming to. I asked John who won, and he told me I lost. I thought, 'How can that be?' It was not the type of disappointment where you feel like you've let yourself down—you just feel like it was a tough break. It was like flipping a coin, that's what it felt like."

The fight was given to Hughes, and despite the controversy the decision stood. Millions of dollars had been bet on the fight in the Las Vegas casinos, and if the decision were reversed, then reimbursements would have to be made.

It was a tough break for Newton, but the loss only made him stronger. "I'm getting better because I'm getting more experience," he says. "I'm not 35-0, like some of the fighters, because all of my fights have been against top opponents right from the beginning. If you give your training your all, you're going to get something from it. I always remember that I do it for me. I did martial arts as a kid before I ever entered the octagon. I always wanted to be a great fighter, and this is just a way of helping me achieve that dream."

CHAPTER 22

The Middleweights
(170 pounds to 184.9 pounds)

After winning a fifteen-minute back-and-forth contest against Ken Parham, Dave Menne entered the cage for the second time that night to face Mike McClure. Although both fighters had gone the distance in their quarterfinal bouts, they were raring to go—the Extreme Challenge middleweight title was on the line.

Menne had a strong background in muay Thai, and when he advanced kicking, McClure rushed forward and tied up with him, hoping to take him down and eliminate his strikes. He attempted a hip throw, but Menne's balance was keen, and when they came down Menne landed on top. For several minutes, Menne pounded on his opponent, but when neither fighter went for a submission hold, the referee had them return to their feet.

Menne began utilizing the jab, and when his opponent tried to take him down again, he pushed him away with ease and then unloaded with his right hand. Eventually, McClure was able to close the gap, but Menne came out on top once more. The fight went up and down, and all the while Menne thrashed his opponent. "I typically try to go out there until I don't got any more," insists Menne, "and I try to push the fight and push the fight. I try to bring it to the point where it's uncomfortable for my opponent, because that's where you start to see people make mistakes and question themselves. I try to keep pressure on my opponent, and make him make mistakes, and make him doubt himself." His strategy was working well with McClure. Each time the ref returned the fighters to the standing position, it took longer and longer for McClure to rise.

After taking several hard kicks to the leg, McClure made one last push to win. He rushed forward and, undaunted by a solid knee to the face, he drove Menne across the enclosure. When they finally hit the fence, Menne had locked in a guillotine choke. McClure hooked Menne's leg and put him on his back.

Menne's technique was flawless. With his opponent riding his weight on top of him, he hooked his legs around McClure's head and locked in a triangle choke. When McClure raised his weight up to try and escape, Menne rolled backwards, flipping his gasping victim over onto his back. Now Menne sat on top of his opponent, his legs still wrapped around McClure's head. McClure's unprotected face was staring up at him—a perfect target.

With Menne raining punches down on his cheeks and skull, McClure had no choice but to submit. In front of the thousands of fans in attendance, Dave Menne was awarded the 170-pound-and-under championship belt. He had come a long way in his fighting career.

* * *

Growing up in Forest Lake, Minnesota, Dave Menne never planned on becoming a professional fighter. But while traveling across the U.S. on a mission to see his country, he settled for a time in Santa Fe and began training in muay Thai. He was instantly hooked, and when he returned home he continued his training at the Minnesota Martial Arts Academy. There, he not only worked on his striking skills, but he also became a proficient grappler. Wanting to see where he stood, he decided to enter a MMA competition.

His first tournament was nothing like the Extreme Challenge or the UFC—both of which he would one day dominate. "There was supposed to be an event at this small town in Wisconsin, at a gymnasium," says Menne. "But they basically backed out of it because the people in the town didn't want it to happen. The fight got transferred into an abandoned house and there was no heat; it was the middle of winter. That was basically my first fight—in an abandoned house with no heat. We had three fights each, and I won all three of my fights by arm bar. The fights were quick, but in almost every one my feet went numb because of the cold."

Liking the feel of competition, Menne brought his talents to the small but well-respected promotion Hook 'n Shoot. After securing three victories there, two by submission and one by technical knockout, Menne was added to the card of Monte Cox's Extreme Challenge 5, held on April 18, 1997 in Iowa. His first opponent, however, was the dangerous competitor LaVerne Clark. "I think I'd only trained about six months in submission grappling by then," says Menne, "but I won by a triangle choke." Although Clark was also relatively new to MMA, after this fight he would go on to defeat numerous names in the sport, including UFC competitors Fabiano Iha and John Lewis. It was a huge victory for Menne. "That's where I started taking it more seriously and training harder," he says.

His next fight of the night was against Shonie Carter, who would also go on to secure wins in the UFC. Despite the fact that Menne had only trained in grappling for a few months, he abandoned strikes and went for one submission after another. "I was just basically winging it," he explains. "I would have changed my game plan a little bit if I'd realized you need to win on points if you don't get the submission." Menne gave it his all and survived the entire bout, but in the end Carter was awarded the decision. "That was my first loss up to that point," says Menne.

Yet Menne was not discouraged, and he continued on in the Extreme Challenge (EC). After winning both his bouts at EC 19, he was awarded a rematch with Shonie Carter in EC 20. This time, Menne not only relied on his submission skills, but he also put his devastating strikes to use. When the grueling battle ended, it was declared a draw. "Most people said that I should have won the fight," says Menne. "At the time, in Iowa, you couldn't get a decision. I felt like it was a hard-fought fight. Shonie always puts on a good fight, but afterwards they took him away on a stretcher to the hospital. It was a lot of stand-up, a lot of striking."

After this, Menne stayed busy in the fight world. "For a while, I was probably fighting about three to four times a month," he says. "I had beaten some top opponents and some people who had already been in the UFC." Some of these competitors included Dennis Hallman and LaVerne Clark, whom Menne again defeated in a rematch via guillotine choke. These impressive victories began to catch the attention not just of local promoters but also of UFC matchmaker John Perretti.

After he defeated Kiyoshi Tamura in the Japanese promotion RINGS, Dave Menne was added onto the card of UFC XXIV, slated for October 3, 2000. He defeated his opponent, the technically renowned jiu-jitsu practitioner Fabiano Iha. "I was actually really calm going into the Iha fight—to a point where I didn't know if it was good," recalls Menne. "I felt so relaxed that I didn't know if I should feel more nervous. But I'd had a lot of fights under my belt, and I just kind of went in. I had good presence. I felt good when I was in there. You never really know until the first fifteen, twenty seconds in there, but after the first fifteen, twenty seconds, my confidence kept on getting better, and I felt at home in there. I was able to listen to my corner, and I was able to think when I was in there. Think and try to do what I needed to do; and I kept control of myself, and thus controlled the fight. I won a decision, but I pretty much dominated the fight for three rounds. Striking on the ground, and striking on the feet. Iha was trying to get me down. He was in kind of survival mode for pretty much the last two rounds of the fight."

Although Menne took some time off from the UFC at this point to return to RINGS, he would reemerge in the octagon in UFC XXXIII for the biggest fight of his life. He would be taking on Gil Castillo for the UFC's middleweight title belt, which was up for grabs.

Grabbing for the Title

Like many MMA competitors, Gil Castillo had come from a strong wrestling background. After wrestling at California State University, Long Beach, he competed in the 1988 Olympic trials at 147 pounds. "I had four matches, and I went 2-2," says Castillo. "If I would have won the fourth, I would have been on the squad that trains for the alternate team. But, as luck would have it, I had this freak beat me on points. I competed until '89, and then I stopped. You just start to go, 'Why am I doing this? I'm not getting paid.' So you start getting a career—that type of thing."

Castillo became a licensed stockbroker and dropped out of the competitive sports world for five years. Then, in 1995, he visited the school of Ralph and Cesar Gracie, and he was captivated by Gracie jiu-jitsu. Castillo began training with the world-renowned fighters at the school, and he and Ralph became very close friends. Just two years later, Ralph told Castillo he was ready for his first MMA competition. Castillo's instructor entered him in the promotion called Stockton Extreme Fighting. "Cesar and Ralph thought I was good enough to go into a no-holds-barred match," says Castillo. "It's not that they wanted me to go in one, really—it's just that they knew I was scared. But it was kind of a scary thing to do. It wasn't anything like jiu-jitsu—in no-holds-barred, you're getting punched in the face. So it kind of brings back memories of old street fights, when you're kind of scared of confrontations, that kind of thing. So it was a scary thing for me to do, and they knew I was scared of it, and they knew I kind of wanted to face my fear."

When the team arrived at the event, however, Castillo found himself in a state of denial. "It was kind of funny because we went in this thing," says Castillo, "and I thought we were just going to watch. The promoter comes up to Cesar soon as we get there and says, 'Is Gil ready?' And I was like, 'What are you talking about?' And they said, 'You're fighting.' And I said, 'Holy shit.' This was January of 1998. It was actually a tournament—back when tournaments were still going—where you fight two or three times on the night. So I made every excuse I could to not fight, and they said, 'Don't worry about it. We brought your shorts, we brought your cup, your mouthpiece . . .' My first fight was against some West Coast karate champion—I don't know who he was. There were no weight classes in this thing, and so he was 220 pounds, or something like that. I beat him in about forty seconds with a rear naked choke. In the first minute of my second fight, the guy broke his wrist somehow and had to quit. The match was called a forfeit."

Thinking that his participation was over, Castillo got ready to leave. He was quickly informed, however, that even though he had won his semifinal bout by forfeit, he was still eligible to continue on to the finals to face Lion's Den fighter Vernon White for the tournament title. This did not sit well with Castillo. "Keep in mind, Vernon had already fought in Japan and Brazil," he says. "I'm sitting there going, 'Holy shit—on my first night!'"

Castillo steeled his nerves and rose to the challenge. He was not timid in the least, and he gave it to White right from the start. "I was on top of him mounted and had the rear naked choke," he recalls. "He rolled me over, I got him in my guard, and then I tapped him from an arm bar." Castillo had taken out one of the most dangerous MMA competitors in just three minutes.

"I was on a high from that whole thing because I just kind of faced my fear," says Castillo. Having accomplished this, he pulled back from competition; "I never really wanted to go any further with it," he explains. But about a year later, while on vacation in Canada, Castillo got a call from Cesar Gracie asking when he was going to return home. When Castillo told him that he would be back in a couple of days, Cesar told him he would once again be fighting. Although Castillo wasn't in shape, he agreed to compete because this time he would only have to fight in a single bout.

"I went in that and won it," he says, "and then all of a sudden I just kind of kept entering competitions." In no time at all, Castillo had chalked up an amazing record of fourteen wins and no losses. Feeling confident in his skills, he set himself the goal of competing in either the UFC or Pride. To catch the attention of these promotions, he fought in a popular new promotion called King of the Cage. In the eighth King of the Cage event, held on April 29, 2001 in Williams, California, he took on Lion's Den fighter and reigning welterweight champion Joe Hurley. Although it was a seesaw battle, Castillo managed to take Hurley to the mat seven times throughout the fight, racking up enough points to earn a judges' decision.

In possession of the King of the Cage title belt, Castillo talked to Paul Smith of the IFC. Smith arranged a fight for Castillo with famous Pancrase competitor Nathan Marquardt for the world IFC welterweight title. "People have called it the most technical fight they've ever seen," says Castillo. "The Pancrase organization came over to support Nathan—they kind of wanted to say their fighters are better than yours, that type of thing. So they came over, and I won a unanimous decision. I won four rounds, and he won one. We were going all out with submissions and passing guard, all kinds of stuff like that on the ground. And we did some good stand-up, too. That's where the UFC saw me, and they hunted me down later that night. They saw me at a restaurant—Dana White and Joe Silva—and asked me if I would fight Dave Menne in the UFC."

Castillo did not agree to the fight right away. "Dave had just fought two months before in Kuwait at 204 pounds," says Castillo, "and I just fought at 168 pounds against Nathan. So I said, 'You know what? It's an honor to have you guys offer that to me, but I would like to stay in my own weight class (welterweight) and try to get a title shot somewhere in there.' So they said, 'Think about it.' A couple weeks later, we were thinking, and I thought, 'You know, it's going to take me over a year to get a title shot in the UFC at welterweight.' Dana and Joe said, 'Yeah, we want you in the UFC either way. At welterweight, we're going to have you fight a few fights, though, before we can give you a title shot; but right now we can get you Dave Menne for the middleweight title.' So we just thought about it, and we just said, 'Hey, this guy's the best in the world. I know he's a little heavier than me, but let's see what we can do.'"

Training to fight a middleweight, however, would not be easy—especially since there was only six weeks left to prepare. Castillo wanted to bulk up to be as heavy as possible, but he also wanted to have strong cardio to ensure that he wouldn't gas out during the five five-minute rounds. After putting on almost ten pounds, he decided to drop back down to his normal weight (180 pounds) when his sparring partners said he looked slow and sloppy. If he couldn't overcome Menne with his strength, then he'd just have to finesse him.

UFC XXXIII—Victory in Vegas/September 28, 2001
(Las Vegas, Nevada)

Middleweight Championship Bout—Dave Menne versus Gil Castillo

Immediately after John McCarthy waved his hand to signal the beginning of the bout, Castillo rushed forward, looking to take Menne to the mat. "I'm very, very comfortable with takedowns and wrestling," says Castillo. "I trained with the best in the world for wrestling."

Menne, however, wanted to keep the fight standing and go for a knockout. He landed several kicks to the leg, and when Castillo came barreling forward, he tied him up in the clinch, refusing to let his opponent take him down. The two remained pinned against the fence for several minutes before Castillo dropped low and pulled Menne's legs out from under him. Once they hit the ground, they scrambled for position, and after several reversals Menne came out on top. By the time Castillo could capture his opponent in his guard and bring the round to a close, Menne had dropped a series of punches and elbows to his face.

Menne continued to strike for the next three rounds, and Castillo continued his takedown attempts. Although Castillo managed to ground his opponent numerous times, Menne kept coming out on top. "I took him down five or six times," remembers Castillo, "but I couldn't do anything when I got down there. That was the problem. He beat me with the knees, basically, against the fence." By the fourth round, things looked grim for Castillo. A cut had opened under his eye, and his leg was stiffening from repeated kicks. Having no luck doing damage to his opponent on the mat, and with only thirty seconds left in the fourth round, Castillo began trading blows on his feet. He landed several shots, but it was Menne who fared best in the exchange. Wrapping his arms around Castillo's head, he let loose with knees.

When Castillo reverted to takedown attempts in the fifth round, Menne laid on the strikes. "My corner was yelling at me the entire last round," says Castillo. "They said don't take him down at all, just do all stand-up. They said just go for it in the fifth round. I didn't listen to them. It's a funny thing that happens to you in the octagon . . . Even though that was my seventeenth fight, I was a bit overwhelmed by the UFC—fighting in front of ten thousand people, and the whole pay-per-view thing. So I guess I just didn't pay attention to my corner and went ahead trying to take him down. The fifth round is where he really took it

*Dave Menne attacks Gil Castillo with kicks
in their UFC XXXIV Middleweight Championship bout.*

Menne tries put away Castillo with a series of devastating knees.

to me, and he beat me pretty good. I didn't listen, but it happens. Sometimes you get a little stage fright." The end of the fight saw Menne pinned against the fence, taking a much-needed breather. There was no doubt in his mind that he had won the fight, and when official word came in from the judges, his assumption was proven correct.

"Castillo was tough," says Menne. "He put on a good fight. He stayed in there for the five rounds, and I was surprised that he actually stayed in there a few of the times, because he took some heavy shots. I felt like I controlled the fight and maybe came inches away from finishing it a couple times."

Either way, Menne had won, and Castillo had lost a bout for the first time in his fighting career. He wasn't too disappointed, however; after all, he had moved up a weight division to face Menne. "At least now people can't say that I pick my opponents," says Castillo, "or that I don't fight tough people. Because I went in there and banged out a little war. And I did a good job. There were a lot of true middleweight guys that Menne beat that didn't do as well as I did."

At UFC XXXV, Castillo was given another chance to show his skills in the octagon—this time in the welterweight division. Despite a severe muscle pull in his thigh, he dominated opponent Chris Brennan for the entire fight and won by judges' decision, positioning himself for a shot at the welterweight title.

UFC XXXIV—Dave Menne versus Murilo Bustamante

After earning the middleweight championship belt in UFC XXXIII, Dave Menne went to UFC XXXV to defend his title against Murilo Bustamante, a world-class jiu-jitsu expert who had secured victories all over the world. Bustamante himself was no stranger to the octagon—he had defeated Yoji Anjo in UFC XXV and Chuck Liddell in UFC XXXIII.

Menne knew he had his hands full. Unlike Castillo, who had come up from the welterweights, Bustamante had dropped down from the light heavyweights. So Menne trained harder than ever for this fight; still, he was under the weather on fight night. Just a few hours before his match, he came down with a stomach bug that had already hit many of the fighters. "I had diarrhea and was throwing up," he recalls. "It basically hit me that afternoon, around one or two. I was taking Imodium tablets before my fight so I could try to keep all my liquids in my body during the bout."

ZUFFA SPORTS ENTERTAINMENT

*Gil Castillo struggles to break free from Dave Menne's choke
in their UFC XXXIV Middleweight Championship bout.*

Despite his sickness, Menne came ready for war. As he'd done during his fight with Castillo, he did everything in his power to keep the fight standing. At the opening of the first round, he attacked Bustamante with kicks to the leg and jabs. Although Bustamante kept timing his shots and ducking under for the takedown, Menne kept finding his way back to his feet.

It looked as if Menne's strategy was going to work when he landed several hard shots at the opening of the second round. But then, in reaction, Bustamante changed his strategy. Moving towards Menne, he suddenly threw a jab and then a strong right hook. The hook landed on Menne's cheek, and it dropped him. Bustamante jumped on his downed foe and began manically striking the side of his head. John McCarthy, realizing that Menne was not defending himself, ended the bout right away. "I definitely wasn't in my game," says Menne. "I was daydreaming in the middle of the fight. I started thinking about other things completely off from the fight."

Menne had lost the belt he had fought so hard to earn, but he wouldn't allow himself to feel discouraged. For him, just being out there fighting was a dream come true. "I like to push myself, and I like to push the envelope," he maintains. "There is a certain amount of freedom that you're allowed when you're fighting, because it's you and your opponent in there. When it's just you and him in the ring, there isn't a lot of politics. Occasionally, there can be with the judges; but usually there isn't, and you can always overcome that by finishing the guy. There's an amount of freedom from it, a certain kind of reward that doesn't always occur in everyday life. A lot of times it's a matter of who you know, or who your dad knows. In our sport, it is what you accomplish. You just have to weather the storm. Sometimes it's a battle of attrition, but you can always be a master of your destiny."

With the addition of Murilo Bustamante to the middleweight division and the confirmation in January 2002 that former welterweight champion Pat Miletich was officially moving up to the middleweights, Dave Menne found himself in the company of some of MMA's most serious competitors. This, however, did not intimidate Menne, and he once again set his sights on the middleweight title and dreamed of one day being considered the best fighter ever to have competed in his division.

CHAPTER 23

The Light Heavyweights
(185 pounds to 204.9 pounds)

After losing to Frank Shamrock in UFC XXII, Tito Ortiz realized that if he was going to be a world champion, then his training would have to change. He stopped partying and hanging out with his friends at night. He dedicated himself completely to the sport, focusing on weight training and developing his submission skills. He even swallowed his pride and went to train with his conqueror, Frank Shamrock, hoping to discover his secret to success. "That's when I realized that the only reason I lost was due to cardio," says Ortiz. "Not working hard enough; not knowing what it takes to make it. Frank knew the secret, and the secret was cardio."

Ortiz reinvented himself as a fighter. "I put everything together in cross-training," he says, "trying to do everything with the kickboxing, the boxing, and wrestling. Besides one or two other fighters, I'm one of the most well-rounded fighters. I do everything. People can't take me down. People haven't seen me in my guard—there's no reason to be in my guard!"

This new and improved Tito Ortiz stepped back into the octagon to take on the dangerous Brazilian Vanderlei "the Axe Murderer" Silva in UFC XXV—Ultimate Japan. Because Frank Shamrock had retired the belt after his win over Ortiz, SEG's middleweight title was up for grabs. Many expected Silva to take it, but few knew how hard Ortiz had been training, or how ruthless he had become.

Ortiz dominated the fight from the get-go, ducking Silva's punches and taking him to the mat. Despite turning his back in the third round after getting rocked by a punch in the face, Ortiz remained composed and stuck to his ground-and-pound game plan. After five rounds spent picking his shots while trapped in Silva's guard and exploding in a flurry of downward strikes when there were just seconds left in each, Ortiz was given the judges' decision.

He had stunned millions, and he strutted around the octagon wearing a T-shirt that read, "I Just Killed the Axe Murderer." Tito Ortiz had climbed the mountain, and he had no intention of coming down. As others struggled to reach him, he beat them back one by one. Among the first victims he claimed while at the top was the cunning Evan Tanner.

* * *

Evan Tanner was born in Amarillo, Texas. He spent much of his unsettled youth philosophizing about the world as he followed his parents from state to state on their perpetual quest to find work. It wasn't until Evan was in high school that his mother and father finally returned to Amarillo and settled down. Having a home base, Evan felt free to pursue a more physical lifestyle through a broad range of sports. Although he became an accomplished pole-vaulter, it was wrestling in which he excelled, winning the state championships in both his junior and senior years. Tanner also dabbled in kenpo karate, intrigued by the discipline, focus, and control that it seemed to demand, unaware that one day he would put these skills to use in the octagon.

Tanner went on to college, but the demons of his turbulent childhood caught up with him. Angry at the world, he grew his hair long and dropped out of school. "I got a motorcycle and a tattoo and took off exploring," he remembers. "I got rid of all my stuff and took off. Nothing was real well planned, and I didn't have a lot of money to work with. I wanted to go to Montana and get a job at a ski resort."

Tanner's Zen adventure lasted almost a decade, and from it he gained practical and worldly wisdom. During this time, while doing some cable TV contract work in Hartford, Connecticut, he was contacted by a friend who said there were going to be some UFC-type fights in Amarillo. Tanner looked into it further and discovered that one of the local high school coaches, Steve Nelson, had started a local shoot-fighting company called the United Shoot Wrestling Federation (USWF), and a lot of Tanner's friends were going to compete in its events. Tanner was planning to move to California to do some surfing, and he decided he would stop in Amarillo on his way to the Coast to see what the USWF was all about. "I stopped in town, saw one of the fights, and kind of talked myself into staying and trying it out," he says. "The next show was a heavyweight tournament, and I thought I was pretty much the toughest guy in town. I thought, 'What better way to prove it than fight the biggest and toughest guys in town?'"

Tanner didn't bother cutting his hair, which he had finally grown past the "ugly stage." Thinking he would only be in town for a short while, he simply braided his long locks. He only weighed in at 190 pounds—most of his competitors weighed well over two hundred pounds—but he still ended up winning the tournament. It gave him a feeling like no other, and he realized he had fighting in his blood. "I couldn't quite get away from it," he recalls. "I got invited back to fight for the heavyweight title later in the year, and once again I was like, 'Well, might as well get the heavyweight belt. Then that will be it. I won't fight anymore.' It just kept going from there."

In the beginning, he pretty much taught himself how to fight. "The majority of what I've learned has been off technique videos," says Tanner. "I learn things pretty quickly, and so I'd watch the tapes and then go practice what I saw. I'd set aside the few moves I was going to practice that day, then go to practice and try to work on those moves. Then it started slowly developing into a system where the moves were interconnected, like chain wrestling." As Tanner's submissions improved, he began to work on his stand-up fighting skills as well, learning how to deliver devastating kicks, elbows, and knees. He excelled so quickly at striking, in fact, that he soon considered it his forte.

While he was training for his fights, Tanner could be found in the gym twice a day. In the mornings, he did three hours of weight lifting, conditioning, and stretching. In the afternoons, he put in another three hours, focusing on drilling techniques and sparring. To test himself and his skills, he sparred with people from a variety of disciplines, including judo practitioners, jiu-jitsu practitioners, and boxers.

After demonstrating his prowess in several more small events, Tanner caught the eye of promoter Monte Cox, who asked him if he would like to compete in his Extreme Challenge. This was the opportunity Tanner had been waiting for, a chance to make an impact in an event that was well run and moving towards full legitimacy. As usual, he tore through the competition, and he brought home the heavyweight title. But his victory did more than just put him on the MMA map; it also attracted the attention of Phyllis Lee, Dan Severn's former manager, who was scouting fighters to compete in the Japanese organization Pancrase. Tanner signed on.

He fought five times in Pancrase, winning all of his bouts—four by submission, and one by decision. "It was really enjoyable to go over to Japan," he says. "They basically cover everything, so you get to compete in your sport and then have a free trip to a new place. But it is really difficult to compete over there because the flight is so long and the time change. I prefer competing in the United States because of those things."

Tanner's chance to fight again in America came on August 1, 1999— only this time it wouldn't be in the USWF, or even the Extreme Challenge. His numerous victories had pushed him into the fight world's center stage, and he was added to the card of UFC XVIII—The Road to the Heavyweight Title. His opponent was two-time national Greco-Roman wrestling champ Darrel Gholar, whose strength would make the fight one of the toughest of Tanner's career.

Tanner began by landing two hard kicks to the leg, but when he went for a third, Gholar snatched his leg, yanked it into the air, and brought him to the mat. Gholar found himself trapped in the guard. Tanner stealthily wrapped his legs around Gholar's head, tightening down a triangle choke. Feeling the pressure, Gholar used his strength to his advantage and stood up with Tanner's legs still wrapped around his neck. He stood there for a moment, and then slammed Tanner to his back. But Tanner refused to let go, forcing Gholar to use all his energy to power out.

Gholar's effort temporarily landed him in a side mount, but all the grappling videotapes Tanner had watched paid off, and he was able to keep trapping the wrestler in his guard. As Gholar pounded away with his fists, Tanner kept working for a submission. When nothing presented itself after six minutes of battle, Tanner escaped to his feet with blood running from a cut under his eye. He trapped Gholar against the fence and brought up a hard knee that connected with his opponent's head.

Dazed, Gholar ran out to the center of the octagon on wobbly legs. Tanner chased him, delivering leg kicks, and once again trapped him against the fence, where he landed another three knees to the face. Gholar turned his back to run, but Tanner wouldn't let him go. In a devastating flurry, he landed punch after elbow after knee. Still Gholar refused to go down, but when he turned his back a second time, Tanner saw the submission he had been waiting for and wrapped his arm around his opponent's neck, pulling him to the mat. Gholar held on for a few more seconds and then tapped.

Tanner had been victorious in his UFC debut, but he did not sprint across the octagon or scream triumphantly into the camera. He was so calm, in fact, that if it wasn't for the cut under his eye, one would think he hadn't fought at all, let alone been involved in an eight-minute war. "You might say I'm kind of a shy guy," says Tanner. "I'm going to accomplish what I set out to do, but I might not be as flamboyant as another person might be. But I'm extremely stubborn, and I'm going to get the job done. When I get in there to fight, most likely I'm not going to explode on the guy, because that's not my approach to anything. It's more of a slow and methodical approach. I'm out there to finish—I don't just want to get a decision. I'm going to beat the guy, but I have a more conservative approach to it."

Tanner had shown what he could do in the octagon, and he was invited back to the next show, UFC XIX, held on May 3, 1999 in Bay St. Louis, Mississippi. He faced Valeri Ignatov, a nine-time Bulgarian sambo champion hailing from the Shamrock 2000 team.

Tanner dominated from the start, chasing Ignatov down and beating on him with jabs, elbows, and knees to the face, before taking him to the canvas. Once there, he quickly obtained the mount and delivered ten powerful elbows to Ignatov's face, forcing referee McCarthy to intervene. Securing this, his second octagon victory in under three minutes, Tanner proved he was a worthy competitor at the highest level of competition. Still, he would not participate in the next ten UFC shows.

Shortly after the fight with Ignatov, Tanner returned to Japan to compete in a Pancrase event. He faced Leon Dijk, and he would experience one of the only losses in his career. Tanner believed that his defeat was his own fault—he'd allowed himself to slip into the wrong lifestyle. He took some time off to decide whether he truly wanted to pursue the sport further and began studying Buddhism. "My greatest challenge was trying to conquer the enemy within," says Tanner. "To gain discipline and control over myself. I think we all have a beast within us that needs to be controlled so the reasonable can come out." While making plans to join a monastery, Tanner came to the conclusion that the best method of correcting his problems was to tackle them head on.

His love for the sport of MMA drew him back to Amarillo and the event in which he'd first competed, the USWF. The original owner of the show was going to sell it because the Texas State Athletic Commission was planning to step in. To prevent out-of-state interests from running the event into the ground or taking it elsewhere, Tanner bought the USWF himself. He soon ran into problems. Aware that the athletic commission would eventually step in and regulate MMA in Texas, he asked the commission for all the necessary paperwork. He was told that the intervention wouldn't happen for some time, and that the commission would notify him as soon as the plans were made.

Thinking everything was in order, Tanner began organizing his first show, which was to take place on November 25, 2000. He reserved the arena and made all the arrangements, and then, in October, after he'd poured almost twenty thousand dollars into advertising, the commission announced that it was imposing regulations. There would be no grace period. Tanner had to get each of the fighters licensed and insured, and he had to have a financial statement prepared by a CPA that showed he had ten thousand dollars in liquid assets. He also had to pay a thousand-dollar application fee and a five-hundred-dollar event fee; all his judges had to be insured, which cost two hundred dollars each; he had to get his time-keeper licensed; and the fighters had to go through intensive medical examinations, at a cost of $250 each. "It was a mess," declares Tanner. "I had to spend an extra twenty or thirty thousand just to meet the licensing requirements. But I pulled it off, and that show turned out really well."

Tanner would put on two shows before calling it quits. "I decided to move on to other things," he explains. "It didn't really work out for me. I wanted to do more with it, but it kind of got taken out of my hands."

He was not ready to leave the fight world behind, however. "It was not something that was a dream of mine, or something I set out to do. It's just something that kind of happened to me and kind of took on a life of its own. I never saw myself as a fighter. I saw myself more as a surfer, a poet, a philosopher, or a writer. It's kind of strange for me to watch some of my videos and see myself out there. I don't consider myself a mean, hateful person. I'm a competitor, and fighting, for right now, is my forum."

Tanner returned to the octagon in UFC XXIX, which took place in the Diffa Ariake Arena in Tokyo, Japan on December 16, 2000. He knocked opponent Lance Gibson out with strikes, and it was as if he had never left. Having proved that he was still a top contender, he got a shot at Tito Ortiz and the title belt at the very next show. It was the main event of the evening, and the biggest fight of Evan Tanner's career.

After Ortiz began the fight by landing a hard kick to the leg, Tanner rushed forward and tied up with him, hoping to do damage in the clinch. But Ortiz showed just how much strength he possessed, manhandling Tanner and landing a knee to the gut and several hooks to the head before cupping his hands behind Tanner's back and lifting him off his feet. Holding his opponent in the air, Ortiz twisted his body and slammed Tanner down onto the mat so hard that he was knocked unconscious. Ortiz did not stop there, however. He landed two hard punches to Tanner's slack jaw before McCarthy pulled him off. Ortiz had won in under thirty seconds.

Tanner did not take the loss well: "I put way too much pressure on myself. I'm probably my own worst critic. My losses, in my own opinion, were my own fault. Not training properly, not paying attention to the things I should have been paying attention to. Not controlling myself enough." He understood that something had to change. "I'd been inde-pendent for a long time, but within the last year the sport evolved so much that I realized it wasn't realistic anymore, and that I wouldn't be able to compete effectively training by myself or with one or two guys. I

ZUFFA SPORTS ENTERTAINMENT

Evan Tanner captures Homer Moore in an armbar
in their UFC XXXIV Light Heavyweight bout.

feel that to compete at this level you have to train with high-level sparring partners and coaches. You have to have a group of people you're working with to be successful now. It's gone to that level."

To achieve the level of training he required, Tanner made the move from Texas to Portland, Oregon. There he joined Team Quest, which was comprised of MMA champions Randy Couture, Matt Lindland, and Dan Henderson. He also trained with Maurice Smith, Josh Barnett, and Matt Hume, all of whom resided and trained in the Northwest. "It took my fighting to a new level," says Tanner. "There're things you learn, little ways to position your body, that you can't learn from tapes or even mid-level sparring partners. You've got to be going against top-level guys to learn these things." His new style of training was evident during his comeback, in UFC XXXIV, where he defeated the skillful wrestler Homer Moore with an arm bar.

Once again, Tanner locked his sights on Ortiz's belt; he was determined to work his way back up to number one. Ortiz, however, was riding high. After his dramatic defeat of Tanner, he had taken on the crafty Australian Elvis Sinosic in UFC XXXII, and bloodied him so badly that the fight had to be stopped. He was set to take on Vitor Belfort in

ZUFFA SPORTS ENTERTAINMENT

*Vladimir Matyushenko attempting to take off Tito Ortiz's head
in their UFC XXXIII Light Heavyweight bout.*

ZUFFA SPORTS ENTERTAINMENT

*Elvis Sinosic aggressively attacking Tito Ortiz with kicks
in their UFC XXXII Light Heavyweight bout.*

UFC XXXIII, but when the Brazilian phenom dropped out shortly before the event, Ortiz found himself stepping into the octagon with Russian Olympic wrestler Vladimir Matyushenko. "I took him down at will," says Ortiz, "and he's an Olympic wrestler, which really tripped me out—which means I'm just getting better and better." The fight went the distance, and Ortiz won by judges' decision.

Ortiz attributed much of his success to the world-class fighters of his camp, Team Punishment. Team members pushed each other to the limit and made sure no compatriot went into battle unprepared. "That's why I think we are so tough," says Ortiz. "Sometimes I'm the leader; sometimes Ricco [Rodriguez] is the leader. I need someone to push me, and at the same time they need someone to push them—someone who will say, 'Come on motherfuckers, let's go train!' This isn't a game. You don't pick up a ball and throw it through a hoop. This is a fight, and you're fighting for your life. That's just the ferocity that I bring into the ring, and everybody who trains on my team thinks the same way."

One MMA competitor who shares Ortiz's training philosophy, commuting several hours to take part in Team Punishment's grueling workouts, is the devastating kickboxer Chuck Liddell.

The Iceman

Growing up in Santa Barbara, California, Chuck Liddell was a huge fan of the television show *Kung Fu Theater*, and at twelve years of age he enrolled in koei-kan karate do classes to see what fighting was all about. Discovering that he liked contact sports, he tried out for the football team in high school. He also wrestled, because it was mandatory for all football players to be involved in an off-season sport. Wrestling became his favorite pursuit, and he continued to train and compete on the mat at Cal Poly, San Luis Obispo, from which he obtained a degree in business accounting.

But Liddell didn't forget his *Kung Fu Theater* days. While in college, he met a trainer named John Hackleman and began studying kenpo karate with him. A competitor through and through, Liddell began entering local kickboxing matches, and his cool-headed toughness soon earned him the nickname "the Iceman."

Twenty-two bouts later, a promoter approached Liddell and asked if he would be interested in competing in an MMA competition. To Liddell, it seemed like a natural progression. "It combined everything I did in one sport," he says. "I had started learning some submission stuff, and I was really excited about that. The arm bars and the triangles—it was all so new."

His first MMA fight was in Las Vegas, and although his opponent was dubbed a submission expert, that didn't stop Liddell from knocking him out with a kick to the head. Due to this victory and his superlative kickboxing skills, he was added as an alternate to the card of UFC XVII, where he took on Noe Hernandez. Liddell made use of his strikes, boxing Hernandez's face and making his eyes swell up. Although he couldn't get the knockout, after twelve tough minutes, he was awarded the decision.

His next bout in the octagon came in UFC XIX, where he went toe to toe with Jeremy Horn, the sharp jiu-jitsu fighter who had given Frank Shamrock a run for his money in UFC XVII. Liddell, sporting his usual Mohawk and goatee, came out swinging. But Horn had been studying kickboxing since his bout with Shamrock, and after chopping away at Liddell's legs, he threw a high kick that connected with Liddell's head. To keep Liddell from retaliating, Horn closed the gap and went for the takedown. After several minutes of struggling in the clinch and eating more than a few punches, Horn captured the kickboxer in his guard and seized his leg, looking for the ankle lock.

A perilous minute passed, and Liddell managed to free his leg. He resumed beating on his foe. Then Horn, in one deft move, took the kickboxer down, and Liddell found himself on his back, guarding against a series of dangerous submission attempts. After several strategic minutes, the action grew stagnant, and referee John McCarthy made them stand back up. This was Liddell's game, but he only managed to throw a few kicks to Horn's legs before once again being put on his back. Liddell managed to roll Horn at just over eleven minutes into the match, but when he landed in Horn's guard, he found that Horn was gripping his head. Liddell's arm was trapped against his own throat, shutting down the blood flow to his brain. He refused to tap, but when the bell rang thirty seconds later, signaling the end of the round, Liddell did not rise. He was out cold. "I didn't think he had the choke," says Liddell. "I knew there were only fifteen seconds left, and I was waiting for time to run out." But the bell sounded too late.

This was Chuck Liddell's first loss in MMA competition, and he would make sure it was his last. He performed a string of brutal knock-outs. He began in UFC XXII by splitting open the face of shoot fighter Paul Jones and provoking a referee stoppage at just under four minutes.

*Chuck Liddell lands blows on Kevin Randleman
in their UFC XXXI Light Heavyweight bout.*

Next, he competed in the IFC against jiu-jitsu expert Steve Heath, who was knocked out cold for several minutes after eating a hard right hand and a brutal kick to the head. Then it was back into the octagon for Liddell—in UFC XXIX, he was awarded a judges' decision after landing continuous leg kicks to Jeff Monson. He fought world-class wrestler Kevin Randleman in UFC XXXI and sent him to la-la land with a single right cross. He knocked out Guy Mezger in Pride 14. And he defeated Murilo Bustamante in UFC XXXIII before securing a judges' decision over Amar Suloev in UFC XXXV.

But even with all these stunning victories under his belt, Liddell has refused to let his guard down. "MMA is constantly evolving, and now you need to be more of a balanced fighter," he says. "I've been working on submission and jiu-jitsu since I started no-holds-barred, and over time I'm getting better. I had the wrestling background as well as the striking. I think that's where it's going—you're going to find guys who are going to be more proficient at all stages of the game: takedowns, takedown defense, striking, submission. I think it's exciting. I like watching the sport evolve."

Encompassing the broad-based fighting abilities of competitors like Tito Ortiz and Evan Tanner, and the hard-hitting power of strikers like

Chuck Liddell, the light-heavyweight division is one of the toughest in the game. Hordes of challengers clamor to knock these fighters out of contention and claim the title belt. And as less-experienced fighters work their way up through the rankings, those on top are stepping up their training, pushing the sport to an even higher level of competition.

CHAPTER 24

The Heavyweights
(205 pounds and up)

A year and a half after relinquishing his UFC heavyweight title belt due to contract disputes with SEG, Randy "the Natural" Couture reentered the octagon in UFC XXVIII, held on November 17, 2000 in Atlantic City, New Jersey. His skills were far from rusty. Like many former UFC competitors, he had gone east and competed in events such as Japan Vale Tudo and RINGS. Although he had suffered his first MMA losses overseas, in the octagon he was still undefeated. And he was a new man coming into the show. Since defeating Maurice Smith in UFC Japan, he had eliminated his only weakness—fighting from his back—by training tirelessly in the guard. This new skill would come in handy when he faced his next opponent, fellow world-class wrestler and UFC champion Kevin Randleman, who was a machine when it came to grounding and pounding his opponents.

On fight night, Couture was composed, but he also knew how important this fight was. "SEG allowed me to fight right out of the cannon for the title," he explains. The outcome of this bout could make or break him.

Couture came out cautiously, feeling his opponent out before closing the gap. But Randleman wanted nothing to do with Couture's "dirty boxing," and once they were in the clinch he lifted Couture off his feet and dropped him to his back. Couture secured the muscle-bound wrestler in his guard, and shortly after Randleman's cornerman, Mark "the Hammer" Coleman, shouted, "Watch the arm bar!" Couture snatched Randleman's arm and then wrapped his legs around his head, trying to lock out the elbow. Randleman had been coached on how to avoid submissions from the Hammer, however, and instead of trying to tug his arm free, he applied downward pressure and eventually powered out. He played it safe for the rest of the round, pounding away at Couture's ribs.

Apparently angered at how the fight was going, Randleman came out swinging in the second round, landing two hard shots to Couture's face. Although Couture was quick to tie him up in the clinch, Randleman broke free and delivered four more hard shots to the face. Couture's legs were wobbly, and he staggered towards his opponent, looking to immobilize Randleman's swinging fists. But *once the two locked arms, Randleman put Couture on his back, beating on his ribs until the second-round clock ran out.*

Looking to make up lost points, Couture used his takedown abilities in the third, and while clinching with his beefy opponent he hooked a leg and grounded Randleman flat on his back. On top at last, Couture went wild with downward strikes. "Randleman hadn't been down there at all," he maintains. "He basically did the dying cockroach and didn't really know what to do with his legs or his hips or anything, and that allowed me to land some elbows and pretty hard shots to his face." Those hard shots opened a cut on Randleman's face, and the blood streamed down his cheeks. When it was clear that Randleman was unable to defend himself against the assault of whirling fists, referee John McCarthy shoved Couture off and ended the abuse.

*   *   *

Randy Couture was once again the heavyweight champion of the UFC. He had demonstrated his superior wrestling ability and done something no fighter had done to date: put Kevin Randleman on his back. In addition to this, he had shown just how proficient he had become at striking and grappling. To many, the man referred to as "the Natural" seemed to embody absolute supremacy. This, of course, was before UFC XXXI— before Couture stepped into the octagon with Pedro Rizzo, a dangerous Brazilian striker who was not only hungry for the title belt but also prepared for full-out combat.

Pedro Rizzo was born to fight. Even as a child growing up in Rio de Janiero, he dreamed of scrapping professionally. He began learning judo from his father at three years of age, and at eight he started studying capoeira, a Brazilian martial art. Although these fighting styles improved his agility, they were too tame for the Brazilian boy with big dreams. He told his parents of his desire to learn kickboxing, but they wouldn't allow him to try it. They both had professions, and they wanted their boy to follow in their footsteps, not spend his time punching people in the head. Pedro did not bring the subject of fighting up again, but his dream remained firmly embedded in his heart. Then, at fifteen, he secretly began looking for an instructor who could teach him the full-contact fighting skills he craved. His search brought him to vale tudo fighter Marco Ruas, the man who would change his life.

Awed by Ruas's skills, Rizzo used his school lunch money to pay for the classes. Every day after school, he'd wait on a street corner, and Ruas would pick him up and take him to the gym. There Rizzo was schooled in the fighting arts, and although he excelled in both wrestling and submission, it was kickboxing that captured his heart. He trained six hours a day and followed his teacher's every movement. "Marco means everything to me," insists Rizzo. "Sometimes he's my dad, sometimes he's my friend, sometimes he's my trainer, and sometimes he's my coach. He is everything to me."

After only two years of training, Rizzo jumped right into competition, entering the Rio de Janeiro Kickboxing Championships. His opponent was a two-time state champion and as tough as they come. Rizzo made use of his powerful kicks and began hacking away at his opponent's legs. By the second round, his foe could barely stand, and Rizzo won by KO.

It was one of the greatest moments of his life, but at the same time he was worried about how his father would react. During the bout, he had received a cut under his eye, and he knew that he could no longer hide the fact that he was fighting from his parents. Deciding to face them head on, he returned home with his trophy in hand and pronounced his victory to his father. Again he met with disapproval and the speech about the importance of becoming a professional. But this reaction only made Pedro train harder; he was determined to please his father by becoming the best fighter in the world.

Just one week after winning his first tournament, Rizzo reentered the ring and won again with low kicks. With two bouts and two victories under his belt, he traveled to São Paulo to do battle once more, this time against an unknown fighter. It was there that he learned never to underestimate an opponent. He got knocked down twice in the first round and then ate a punch to the jaw. The next thing he remembers was waking up in the shower. He asked Marco Ruas what had happened, and upon hearing that he'd been knocked out, he began to weep, thinking his career was over. Ruas assured his young fighter that his career was just getting started.

And he was right. Just a few months later, when one of Holland's best muay Thai teachers came to Brazil, Ruas took Rizzo to meet him. Rizzo demonstrated some of his skills for the man, and he invited the young Brazilian to travel overseas to improve his game.

It was an honor and a huge opportunity, but Rizzo was reluctant to accept. He had his family to think of, and his schooling. But he also knew that if he was going to become the best fighter in the world, it was a necessary move. So he dropped out of college, where he was studying to become a veterinarian, and he left his homeland behind. He moved to Holland and lived in the gym, cleaning the dojo and working as a door-man in various nightclubs to survive.

After eight months and thirteen professional fights, Rizzo decided to take a break from kickboxing and visit Ruas, who had moved to Los Angeles after winning UFC VII. It was on this trip that Ruas made his intentions known: he wanted Rizzo to become an MMA champion. Rizzo recalls, "When I started training kickboxing, Marco said, 'Pedro, no-holds-barred is going to be the sport of the future, so you have to start training on the ground, too.' So I'd been training on the ground since I was fifteen. I saw Marco training, competing in no-holds-barred competitions, and so for me it was very, very natural to become a no-holds-barred fighter."

With the understanding that Rizzo was going to devote himself en-tirely to MMA, Ruas took him to the Beverly Hills Jiu-Jitsu Club to meet John Perretti, the UFC matchmaker. "I said to Mr. Perretti, 'I really want to fight in the UFC. I spent already so much time with kickboxing, and I want to become a professional MMA fighter,'" says Rizzo. "I asked John Perretti to give me a chance, and a few days later he gives me a call and says, 'Pedro, do you want to fight in UFC Brazil?' I said of course—the pleasure of fighting in my country in the first UFC Brazil would be perfect. He said, 'Okay, I'm going to give you Tank Abbott. Do you think you can beat him?' I didn't care; I just came from Europe, and I fought with the best kickboxers in the world. If Tank tried to come and exchange punches and kicks with me, it would be no problem."

UFC Brazil—Pedro Rizzo versus David Abbott

Once again, Rizzo was training with his mentor, Marco Ruas. Ruas him-self was scheduled to fight Alexander Otsuka in Pride just a few days before Rizzo's UFC debut. The two worked harder than they'd ever worked before, and although they would be fighting on opposite sides of the world, they would be together in spirit. Rizzo was sure that nothing would stand in his way of going into the most important fight of his life.

His assumption was incorrect, however. A week before he was to fight Tank in his homeland, Rizzo heard that Ruas had lost his fight. Then, only four days before the UFC, Rizzo was sparring with training partner Ebenezer Braga when he took an unintentional head butt. He felt blood running down his face and stopped to check the wound. He saw that it was deep, and his mind shut down. First, Ruas had been defeated, and

now he was injured just days before his match with the heavy hitter Tank
Abbott.

Rizzo sat down and began to cry; Braga started to pray loudly. Rizzo
soon joined the prayer, and it soothed him. Then he went to the hospital,
where he received four stitches. He asked the doctor if his skin would
close up in four days, and the doctor told him it wouldn't. So Rizzo went
home and made a very important decision: not only would he go through
with the fight, but he would also win it for Ruas.

When Rizzo arrived at the event, he ran into Phyllis Lee, who
suggested that he Superglue the cut closed. He took her advice, hoping
that referee John McCarthy wouldn't see the glue on his face. After passing the prefight physical, Rizzo entered the octagon and stood before
thousands of his countrymen. Across from him stood the infamous Tank
Abbott. "I was very, very nervous, of course," says Rizzo. "It was my
country, everybody cheering for me. There was a lot of responsibility
because it was my debut. I had to make a very good fight because I had
just signed up for that one fight. If I beat him, they would come to sign
more fights for me. I was nervous, but not about fighting against Tank.
It's a competition, and everybody is going to get nervous. Even if you're
going to play golf, you're going to get nervous."

So, with his countrymen backing him up, Rizzo went to war. As was
his custom, the 268-pound Tank bull-rushed his opponent—who
weighed in at 228 pounds. After throwing four hard jabs that sent Rizzo
scrambling backwards, Tank got to work with his right hand, landing
bombs that forced the retreating Rizzo against the fence. The Brazilian's
head jolted back and forth, but he stayed composed. Between Tank's
shots, he slipped out and once again began backpedaling. Tank was right
on him, his heavy fists swinging. Timing his shot perfectly, Rizzo landed
a single right hand that dropped the charging Tank to the canvas.

Tank rested on all fours, his glassy eyes staring upward. Rizzo stepped
in and landed another powerful shot to the face. Tank tried to lumber to
his feet, but Rizzo kept him down by shoving him onto his back and
leaping on top of him. He landed several more shots before Tank muscled
his way back up.

"Now the bear is mad," said commentator Jeff Blatnick. "How will
Rizzo handle that?" He handled it by counterfighting, backing up and
picking his shots. Despite Rizzo's clever strategy, Tank managed to land a
huge right just over a minute into the bout. The shot rocked Rizzo,
distorting his vision. Now he could only see Tank from his feet to his
hips—although he looked for the top part of the heavy-handed brawler,

he could not see it. Because of this, Rizzo had to resort to his devastating leg kicks. The crowd chanted, "Rizzo" as the tired Abbott summoned up the last of his energy and rushed forward, plowing Rizzo to the canvas. Trapped in Rizzo's guard, Tank took a much-needed breather, unleashing with an occasional flurry and reopening the cut under Rizzo's eye. McCarthy separated the two, and the doctor examined the wound.

The fight was allowed to continue, and Rizzo came out strong, delivering leg kick after leg kick. The crowd was in an uproar, cheering every crushing connection. Rizzo knocked Tank to the mat; he powered back onto his feet and then missed with a big uppercut. Administering one last brutal kick, Rizzo followed up with a hard right cross that put Abbott away.

As the crowd went wild, the octagon filled with Rizzo's cornermen. "All my friends were supporting me," says Rizzo, "all my team. For me it was a dream to fight Tank in UFC Brazil. To beat Tank, one of the biggest guys they had in the UFC, was really great. Everyone knows Tank Abbott. He had so many losses, but he always gives an exciting show. He knocked out many, many people and gave a hard time to everyone he'd fought. So it was great."

Right away, Rizzo began celebrating with those who mattered most to him. Rizzo comments, "All the partners I train with are like my brothers, and Marco is like my dad. When I win, I love to stay with them and my family. We try to put everyone together in the same house. My father, in the beginning, was very, very against me fighting. My father is an engineer. My brother is an engineer. My sister is a journalist. We are a really straight family. But today they really love me, and they support me very much. They are my biggest fans. For me my fight life always walks together with my personal life."

The victory over Tank Abbott gave Pedro Rizzo the respect he had been looking for. "When people started to recognize my work, everybody started to recognize me more. I got more respect from everybody, but it didn't change myself. I'm the same family guy. Like my father always said to me, 'You're always going to be that boy who loves martial arts.' I'm the same humble guy who is going to learn every day. But I also worked very hard. I'm a fighter. Everybody is the same—a doctor or an engineer—we're all professionals in our jobs."

UFC XVIII—Pedro Rizzo versus Mark Coleman

After chalking up an impressive win over Abbott, Rizzo was ready to take five months off and relax. But John Perretti and the UFC had different plans for him. They invited him to UFC XVIII to take on yet another octagon veteran: Mark "the Hammer" Coleman.

"Coleman was a great challenge for me," says Rizzo. "Everyone said Coleman was finished, because he had just lost to Pete Williams and Maurice Smith. They said, 'You're going to knock him out.' I didn't agree. He lost his last two fights, and he was going to come into his third fight trying to kill anyone who stepped in front of him. I was nervous about the fight, but I'm a fighter, and I can't avoid any fights. I can't choose the opponents. I have to fight against anyone they put in the ring with me. If you want to be the best, if you want to be the world champion, you have to beat everyone. So I said, 'Okay—Coleman. It will be a great challenge. It will be hard. He will give me a hard time, I know he will. I'm going to work guard, I'm going to work my sprawls, and we will see what will happen in the ring.'"

Although Rizzo's second appearance in the UFC wasn't as dramatic as his first, the strikes he landed both from his back and on his feet were enough to win him a judges' decision over the the Hammer. "I did more than two hundred sprawls a day for that fight," remembers Rizzo. "I worked a lot on my guard. I improved my ground skills and my wrestling skills and tried to stop him. It was a very, very hard fight that time. It was my toughest fight."

After his victory over Coleman, Rizzo went on to fight in UFC XX and XXIII, gaining wins over Lion's Den fighter Tre Telligman and Japanese submission master Tsuyoshi Kohsaka. But when Rizzo went to UFC XXVI—held in Cedar Rapids, Iowa on September 6, 2000—where he would face off with Kevin Randleman, he entered one of the most demanding contests he'd ever endured.

UFC XXVI—Pedro Rizzo versus Kevin Randleman

After the two competitors sized each other up, Randleman rushed forward to subdue Rizzo's deadly strikes. He tied up with the Brazilian, and after a powerful struggle he finally managed to put him on his back. Instantly, Randleman got to work, trying to choke out his opponent by forcing Rizzo's chin to his chest. When that didn't work, he went to work with heavy strikes. Rizzo remained calm and deflected most of the shots. And when he got back to his feet at the beginning of the second round, he continued to play it safe. With no action occurring for several minutes, McCarthy stepped between the two and reminded them that they were in a fight.

Rizzo began picking his shots, well aware that if he made a mistake Randleman would again take him down. He worked the jab, and then, with just thirty seconds left in the round, he landed a high kick to Randleman's head. The crowd booed, but Rizzo was unfazed. When the second round came to a close, it seemed clear that his game plan was working. "At the beginning of the fight, I was waiting for him to get tired because I knew his conditioning wasn't that good," says Rizzo. "I had a strategy: for the first and second round I was going to fight slow, and then the third round I was going to fight hard. When I finished with the second round, I went to my corner and said, 'Marco, I'm going to knock him out in the fourth round.' I had killed his leg already. Marco said, 'Okay, you're fine, everything's fine. Just keep going.'"

At the opening of the third, Rizzo began chopping away at his opponent. But when Randleman rushed forward to close the gap, his head collided with Rizzo's face, opening a deep cut. Rizzo took a moment to complain to McCarthy about the illegal strike, but when he realized it was unintentional he got back into the fight. Although he managed to stop Randleman's takedown, for Rizzo the fight was over. "In the first minute of the third round I took the head butt," he explains. "It wasn't intentional, but after that I just don't remember anything. I just woke up when I was in the dressing room. Marco was beside me, and I looked at him and asked him what happened. I asked him if I lost, and he said I had. I thought Randleman had knocked me out, because I didn't remember how I got into the dressing room. I said, 'What the hell's going on here,' sitting in the dressing room with Marco beside me. I asked everyone how I lost, and they told me on points. I said, 'On points?' The last thing I remember is complaining to John McCarthy about the head butt. He said it wasn't intentional, so I kept on going. I fought almost fourteen minutes, and I wasn't there."

In those fourteen minutes, Rizzo was somehow able to keep Randleman from taking him down by using his jab. But it was obvious that Rizzo was not in the fight, and when the fifth round came to a close the fans saw fit to throw trash into the octagon. It came as no surprise to most observers that Randleman was given the judges' decision.

After this fight, Rizzo wasted no time getting back into the octagon.

He took on legendary wrestler Dan Severn at the very next event, UFC XXVII, held in New Orleans on September 22, 2000. "I am a big fan of Dan," says Rizzo. "I saw him the first time when he fought Royce Gracie in UFC IV. I saw him in UFC V and then in Ultimate Ultimate, beating all the guys. My biggest idol is Marco Ruas, and I thought Marco could beat him. But they never had the chance to fight against each other. And now someone called me after the Randleman fight and asked me if I would fight against Dan Severn. Dan is a legend, one of the greatest I have seen, but he was just one more competitor. I had to beat him. I had to beat him that time."

The bout did not turn out to be the epic battle that many fans expected. Shortly after the first round got under way, Rizzo landed one of his famous leg kicks, which buckled the large wrestler. Leaning against the fence and gripping his knee, Severn forfeited. The match ended almost before it had begun. "When he fell down after that kick," says Rizzo, "I walked over to him, shook his hand, and said, 'I'm one of your biggest fans. It is a pleasure to fight against you.'"

Coming out of his speedy victory over Severn, Rizzo stepped back into the octagon in UFC XXX. But his match with Josh "the Baby-Faced Assassin" Barnett would not be so one-sided.

The Baby-Faced Assassin

Josh Barnett had wanted to compete in the event ever since he saw UFC II at age fifteen. He was no stranger to physical confrontation. Growing up near Seattle, in the quiet community of Ballard, Washington, he was known for his short fuse. "I really enjoyed fighting," he admits. "I was not necessarily supposed to, but I did. I didn't play much sports, but fighting for me was always fun. My dad used to always roughhouse with me. He'd show me little street-fighting moves and things like that. He taught me how to fight at a young age, and I really picked up on it."

During his sophomore year in high school, Barnett joined the wrestling team, and after placing in the state championships, he went on to claim two Greco-Roman state titles. At eighteen, he learned that an Asian security guard at his high school taught Thai boxing. From him, Barnett picked up a series of kicks and strikes to add to his arsenal. It was a perfect sport for Barnett—considering that he enjoyed hitting people and getting hit himself. Yet he never saw fighting as a violent spectacle. He saw it as the highest level of competition and a way of just being himself.

*Josh Barnett attempting to chop down the enormous Gan McGee
in their UFC XXVIII Heavyweight bout.*

Over the years, Barnett discarded the things that weren't important to him in his life, and he was left with fighting. Believing that God had given him a natural talent, he embarked on a quest to better himself.

He was eager to put his skills to the test, seeking out competition opportunities wherever he could. "I would find anybody who thought they were tough—wrestlers, martial artists, anybody in a gi—and asked them if they wanted to do a fight," says Barnett. "If they said yes, we'd get it on right down on these old wrestling mats in a basketball gym. There were like six or seven games going on at the same time. People would stop playing basketball and start cheering us on."

Barnett continued to improve his game at the University of Montana, studying both boxing and judo. When he came home for the winter break in his freshman year, he got a call from his old high school wrestling coach. Local MMA fighter Matt Hume, who owned AMC Pankration in Seattle, was putting on a show in just eleven days and needed a replacement to fight Chris Charnos, an experienced MMA competitor who had fought in the Hawaiian Superbrawl. Barnett jumped at the chance. With less than two weeks to train for the event, he got busy.

"When I stepped into the ring, we dabbled around a little bit," says Barnett. "I caught him in a front choke at about two minutes, and at two minutes and nineteen seconds he passed out. I was nineteen years old."

Shortly after returning to college, Barnett received an e-mail from Matt Hume's organization saying that they were going to match him up against Bob Gilstrap, yet another experienced competitor. Knowing that the young Barnett would need proper training for the fight, Hume offered him the opportunity to work out at his gym before the match. "I got there a week before the fight," recalls Barnett, "and I trained at AMC. It wasn't so much training there. I was allowed to roll with everyone and work out with them, but it was more that they were trying to see what I knew and how good I actually was. I was able to hold my own against most of them. Then I went out there and fought my fight against Bob. I fought a really cautious match, because I wasn't exactly sure how good he was. I probably could have caught him in something. He gave up a lot of stuff I probably should have taken, but I was fighting cautious. It was a unanimous decision in my favor."

After this fight, Barnett made the decision to follow the path of a fighter, and he dropped out of college. "The money was running out, and I didn't want to go back to Montana," he says. "I thought I should stay home and do something with this. So I decided to start training at AMC full time. I would take a bus ride every day for an hour and a half to get there. I wouldn't get home until almost eleven o'clock."

Despite the lengthy commute, Barnett had found his niche. "I talk about fighting most of the time," he admits. "When I'm not doing it, I'm always watching it. Being around it, training. Training other people. It's really a complete effort when it comes to fighting. It's pretty much what I do. I don't know what I would do without it."

With a school of experts on his team, Barnett moved up to the big time and entered the Hawaiian Superbrawl, where he disposed of two giants in the sport, John Marsh and Bobby Hoffman. "I just go out and fight," says Barnett. "Before my fight, I'm just thinking that I want to kill him. I'm going to go out there and cripple him. I'm one of the few people I know who doesn't get nervous or scared before their fight. I just hang out, look around, and relax. It's not even a big deal. And then I get ready, start training. I focus and concentrate on doing damage and punching through them. That's what I do to get ready. Every punch is going to go right through his skull. Every submission is going to break a limb right away. I do some work on the Thai pads, and by the time I get out there I'm just an animal. I just want to get inside there and tear someone's head off. The mentality is, 'I'm pissed this person thinks they can fight me. They don't even have a chance in this to possibly win.' If someone tried to jump out of the cage and not fight me, I'd be pissed off that they tried to disrespect me by leaving. Either way they're fucked."

This die-hard mentality, and his victories over Marsh and Hoffman, got Barnett invited to Superbrawl 16. His opponent was none other than Dan "the Beast" Severn. "It was great to fight Dan Severn," says Barnett. "In retrospect, it was an honor, because he was one of the people who got me interested in wanting to be in the UFC. I had watched Dan go out there and suplex people with his wrestling ability and just go off. He was the Beast. He was one of the people I looked up to and idolized. So to go in there and fight him was an honor, but during the little preparation I did do for it, and while I was there to fight him, for me he was just dog meat. I'd fight friends; I'd fight family—I'd fight anybody if they'd get into the ring with me. Afterwards I can have all the thought about it I want, but beforehand all I can think about is, 'He's going to die.'"

Barnett's victory over the Beast attracted the attention of UFC matchmakers, and he was added to the card of UFC XXVIII. He would take on the six-foot-one, 312-pound Gan McGee in the first-ever super-heavyweight UFC bout.

Although in the first round Barnett found himself on the receiving end of McGee's punches, he lived up to his "I never give up" motto and came back strong in the second. Worn to exhaustion and ignoring the burning pain in his gut, Barnett laid into his massive opponent with brutal strikes, forcing the referee to end the bout.

Barnett had won his first fight in the UFC. Having proved both his skill and his heart, he was called back for UFC XXX, where he would take on his most skillful adversary to date: Pedro Rizzo.

UFC XXX—Pedro Rizzo versus Josh Barnett

Despite Barnett's proven grappling ability, the fight remained standing. It was a back-and-forth battle, with Barnett pressing the attack with huge knockout punches, and Rizzo stepping back to counter with straight-in jabs and crosses. For the first round, the two exchanged a barrage of strikes. Barnett landed several over-the-head elbows, and Rizzo continued to land kicks to the leg. Both fighters laid it all on the line, holding nothing back.

In the second round, Rizzo's counterfighting began to wear on Barnett, who was now bleeding from the nose. Barnett kept stepping in, and Rizzo kept stepping back, landing hard hooks to the head. Frustrated, Barnett threw a hard left hand with forty-five seconds left in the round.

*Josh Barnett and Pedro Rizzo exchanging blows
in their UFC XXX Heavyweight bout.*

Barnett pounds Schilt from the mount.

*Josh Barnett attempting an armbar on Bobby Hoffman
in their UFC XXXIV Heavyweight bout.*

Once again, Rizzo stepped out, throwing a right-handed hook that collided with Barnett's face. It stunned Barnett completely and left him standing there with his hands down. Knowing his opponent was in trouble, Rizzo followed up with a straight right that sunk Barnett's ship.

It was one of the most dramatic knockouts in UFC history—so dramatic, in fact, that the UFC used footage of it on a promotional video that was broadcast in the main lobby of the MGM Grand weeks before UFC XXXIV. "If I ever get a rematch with Pedro, I'd go out there to kill," says Barnett, "just like every other time. There may be a little extra incentive on that. Normally, I don't dwell on losses, but man, when I'm at the UFC and I see that promo eight thousand times, and I keep seeing myself get hit like that, I just want to start a fight with him right there. We'll end up squaring off against each other. Then I'm going to be completely looking forward to my revenge. I take all losses personal."

To earn his shot at a rematch, or a shot at the title, Barnett kept busy in the octagon, securing victories over Sammy Schilt in UFC XXXII, and once again defeating Bobby Hoffman, in UFC XXXIV. "As a fighter, I'm dedicated. I'm focused with one purpose in mind. I'm unrelenting; I will not give up. I don't ever want to give up. If I get knocked down and can get back up, I will."

While Barnett worked his way back up the ladder, Rizzo was preparing for the biggest fight of his life. His loss to Randleman had been redeemed, and he was given a shot at Randy Couture for the heavyweight title belt in UFC XXXI.

UFC XXXI Heavyweight Title Bout—Pedro Rizzo versus Randy Couture

Both fighters stepped into the octagon ready for combat. Rizzo started with his usual barrage of kicks and punches, and, surprisingly, the wrestler answered with kicks and punches of his own. But, not wanting to play the Brazilian's game all night long, Couture eventually shot in and hauled Rizzo to his back. Then, pinning him against the fence, Couture went wild with punches and elbows. He even thought it necessary to drive his shoulder into Rizzo's face, opening a cut on his nose. For the last two minutes of the first round, Couture unleashed with everything he had in an attempt to put Rizzo away. "People said to me, 'Oh, your guard is not that good, you never try to get him into an arm lock,'" says Rizzo. "But try fighting when they put you up against the fence. All the wrestlers do the same thing. When they put you against the fence, you can't move your hips very well."

Rizzo's face may have been thoroughly bloodied, but he was far from being out of the fight. At the beginning of round two, he advanced upon a winded Couture and dropped him with a kick to the midsection. When Couture regained his footing, it was obvious that the kick had hurt him. Again he tried to take his opponent down, but now Rizzo stepped back and grabbed the opportunity to launch effective combinations. He landed punches to Couture's face and devastating kicks to his legs. He avoided takedown attempt after takedown attempt. He spun a high kick that crashed into Couture's nose and made it gush blood. "Couture has heart," said commentator Jeff Blatnick, "but it now seems Rizzo is in his world." With only five seconds left in the round, Rizzo again dropped his opponent, this time with a punch to the face.

After taking another two minutes of grueling abuse in the third round, Couture finally found an opening and put Rizzo on his back. Although he was unable to muster the strikes to put his opponent away, he did get a much-needed rest and came out stronger for the fourth round. Tying up with Rizzo, he landed a series of uppercuts. When Rizzo broke away, a determined Couture rushed forward and brought him down once more, bringing the round to a close.

In the fifth round, Couture tried to take Rizzo down, but Rizzo defended flawlessly, following up with kicks to the leg and punches. The last seconds of the fight saw Rizzo pounding away at his opponent. Despite this, when the word came back from the judges, Couture was awarded a very controversial unanimous decision. "I really had to suck it up and find a way to even finish that fight," he says. "And that, more than anything, I attribute to Pedro. He withstood a whole barrage of punishment in the first round and was able to come back and be pretty effective in the second round. That was certainly the toughest fight."

Couture had taken the win from Rizzo, but barely. The fight had been one of the best the UFC had seen, and because of this, and the controversy, a rematch was rapidly arranged. Although Couture thought that there were other worthy competitors who deserved a shot, he agreed to face off against Rizzo once more—in UFC XXXIV, at the MGM Grand in Las Vegas.

To avoid being subjected to the kind of abuse he had withstood in their first bout, Couture worked to improve his standing skills. He asked kickboxer Maurice Smith to coach him, and in the time they trained together Couture learned how to block the Brazilian's crippling leg kicks and, perhaps most important, how to be patient and not fall victim to Rizzo's counterfighting style.

UFC XXXIV Heavyweight Title Bout—Pedro Rizzo versus Randy Couture (rematch)

Rizzo was the first to emerge from the smoke and lasers, and he worked his way towards the octagon to his own blaring theme song, "You Can't Stop the Rock!" He was in better shape than he'd ever been in before, and his mentor, Marco Ruas, was working his corner. But all the hype leading up to the rematch and his earlier loss to Couture had worn on the Brazilian's confidence. He had stayed up into the wee hours of the morning, pacing in the MGM casino, trying to unwind. "I had too much pressure on my shoulders," remembers Rizzo, "from the promoters and the show. Everyone thought I couldn't beat him, and so I thought, 'I can't do it, I can't do it.'"

Couture, on the other hand, seemed to possess plenty of confidence. With a Jimi Hendrix-style American national anthem sounding throughout the arena, he appeared out of a shower of fireworks and saluted the throng before joining Rizzo in the cage.

After the two fighters had respectfully touched gloves, the action began, surprisingly, with Couture landing several kicks to Rizzo's leg. But after taking a few punches from the Brazilian, Couture closed the distance and secured Rizzo in the clinch. The Natural dropped some knees to the thigh and dealt a series of short uppercuts before seizing both of Rizzo's legs and bringing him down. Once in Rizzo's guard, Couture got to work with punches, elbows, and even a few shoulder slams to the face. With only thirty seconds left in the round, Couture hopped to his feet but did not back off from the still-grounded Rizzo. Instead, he threw a series of crushing downward blows.

The second round saw Rizzo holding his ground, waiting for Couture to advance so he could counterstrike. But Couture had learned much since their last encounter, and he stayed on the outside. The round got rolling at last when Couture made a brave move: he rushed forward and collided with Rizzo. The two staggered halfway across the octagon before they finally fell. Couture came out on top, and, after dragging Rizzo over to the fence to immobilize him, he attacked, dropping shoulder strikes,

*Pedro Rizzo attacking Randy Couture with knees
in their UFC XXXI Heavyweight Championship bout.*

Rizzo brutalizes Couture's leg with Thai kicks.

more elbows, and inside punches. Rizzo made one attempt to escape, but that only allowed Couture to free one of his legs. In this position, Couture had all the leverage he needed to make his elbow strikes count. He split the Brazilian's face wide open, and blood dripped onto the canvas. Referee McCarthy separated the two so the doctors could take a look.

Although the fight was allowed to continue, Rizzo did not look good going into the third round. He was behind on points, yet he did not attempt to mount an offensive. He stood there, waiting for Couture, who refused to play his game. The stalling tactic finally ran out for Rizzo when Couture landed a stiff right cross and closed the gap, taking him to the ground. Once again, Couture dragged Rizzo over to the fence, and this time he went wild, dropping punch after punch after punch, forcing McCarthy to jump between them.

There was no controversy this time. Randy Couture had stopped "the Rock" with authority. But this was not the last of Pedro Rizzo, who clearly had not been himself that evening. "I didn't try to land any punches or kicks, and so I lost to myself," says Rizzo. "I really never thought I could lose to Randy, because I really think I'm a better fighter than him. But I didn't fight, and so I lost to myself. I am really confident who I am right now, and really think I can fight anyone in MMA sport. I can give a great show, and think I can beat any heavyweight in the world. But you never know, the ring is the ring. In this sport, the level is so high, if you make even the smallest mistake you're going to pay for that. And I did. I paid for it that night. What can I do? I have to forget about what happened, and I have to learn from my mistakes and become a better fighter than I am right now. I know now I have to start again—beat one, two, three guys. No problem, I'm a fighter. Now the next opponent who steps into the ring with me, I'm going to fight very, very hard. I don't know what's going to happen, but I'm a hundred percent sure I'm really going to try to knock him out in the first seconds of the fight."

At thirty-eight, Randy Couture had again successfully defended his heavyweight title. "I think my alter ego kind of comes out," he admits. "The real competitive side of me comes out in the competition. I'm one of those kind of people who internalizes a lot of things, and I think I let a lot of those things out when I compete. The biggest challenge for me is that I feel that I'm racing against the clock. I'm thirty-eight, and I probably don't have a lot of competitive years left, so it's important for me to live properly, to take care of my body, and really try to get the most out of it. I'm still trying to ride that wave."

ZUFFA SPORTS ENTERTAINMENT

*Randy Couture wears Pedro Rizzo down on the ground
in their UFC XXXI Heavyweight Championship bout.*

Randy Couture, Pedro Rizzo, and Josh Barnett are just three fighters in a weight class laden with extremely talented competitors. With both power and technique, the heavyweights have given fight fans some of the most exciting bouts in the sport. Whether the fighters hail from wrestling, kickboxing, or the streets, this classically popular weight division has all the punch necessary to push the UFC to the top of the MMA world.

A Parting Shot

In 1993, the first UFC changed the martial arts world forever. When grapplers such as Royce Gracie and Ken Shamrock began to dominate the early MMA scene, the traditional martial arts community was first shocked, then intrigued. The UFC became a tremendous hit, but along with this success came some unwanted attention. Politicians latched on to the UFC's sensationalist marketing efforts, and they launched a campaign that nearly succeeded in wiping the sport out of existence in the United States. But, due to the tenacity of promotions like the UFC, the IFC, and the Extreme Challenge, along with the tremendous heart of the fighters involved, MMA returned from the brink of extinction and slowly but surely developed a strong and loyal fan base.

As the sport of mixed martial arts grew in popularity, fighters opened schools of their own to train the growing hordes of MMA enthusiasts. Inspired by the success of such establishments as the Gracie Academy in Torrance, California, and Ken Shamrock's Lion's Den in San Diego, other schools began focusing on competitive combat, making MMA training available to the public. Even schools teaching traditional styles began offering instruction in submission skills, muay Thai, and boxing. And the sport of MMA became increasingly competitive as a new generation of fighters who saw MMA as the norm came of age. The paradigm shift had occurred, and everyone was trying to keep pace with the sport's evolution.

The sale of the UFC to the Las Vegas-based promotion Zuffa in 2001 heralded a new era for MMA. With the money and the political influence necessary to mount successful competitions, Zuffa laid the groundwork for the introduction of MMA, and the UFC, to the mainstream audience via cable television. New promotions such as King of the Cage, Caged Combat, and the Gladiator Challenge gained nationwide recognition. Even the fighters themselves got involved in event production. Ken Shamrock held his first event, Shamrock Mega Fights, on

August 10, 2001 in Atlantic City, New Jersey, and Dan Severn kicked off
his own promotion, Dangerzone, in Mahnomen, Minnesota on June 19,
1999.

Then jiu-jitsu expert John Lewis got into the promotion game with a
revolutionary new concept. He sought to break into a new demographic
with his organization—called World Fighting Alliance (WFA)—which
would combine aspects of the Las Vegas nightclub scene with the excitement of a live fighting competition. Lewis joined forces with respected
Vegas event promoter John Huntington, who'd hit it big with his Pimp
'n Ho and Club Rubber productions. The two put their heads together,
and the idea for the WFA event called Where the Fight Club Meets the
Nightclub was born. The show's card featured well-known MMA competitors such as kickboxer Alfonso Alcarez, world-class wrestler Frank Trigg,
and veteran brawler LaVerne Clark. The event was staged at the Hard
Rock Cafe in Las Vegas on November 3, 2001, and it was a resounding
success. In one of the most exciting bouts of the evening, Trigg pounded
Clark into submission in front of a capacity crowd. With this promising
kickoff, Lewis immediately began planning to make the next WFA competition a pay-per-view event.

The International Fighting Championship also pressed on. The
promotion had collected fight footage for several years, and in 2002 it
signed the deal with Microsoft to create an all-MMA cable channel. Not
to be outdone, Zuffa added a weekly fight show to its long-range strategy. "We're working with a number of networks," said Zuffa's Lorenzo
Fertitta, "trying to get distribution on free TV to continue to increase
the awareness level and popularity of the sport."

*   *   *

And the phenomenon just keeps growing. Although the IFC and the
UFC have always been competitors, they now realize the necessity of
creating an MMA culture within the United States, and they are open to
working together to further the interests of the sport.

The overwhelmingly popular Japanese promotion Pride, which has
been broadcasting its events on Japanese network television for years, has
decided that it's time to bring its production to America—its first U.S.
event was to be held in Honolulu, Hawaii at the Aloha Arena in August
of 2002. Pride has also developed a business association with Zuffa, and the
two organizations occasionally share fighters; they have even opened talks
on possible unified Pride/UFC titles. With the two most well-known

promotions understanding the necessity of working together, MMA is poised for worldwide recognition.

Further acceptance of MMA as a legitimate sport will come in 2004, when pankration—one of the original Olympic sports—is reintroduced to the Olympics as an exhibition sport. The 2004 games will be held in pankration's birthplace: Athens, Greece.

MMA has survived a near-death experience, and it is positioned to become the number-one combative sport in the world. As fight fans and politicians alike learn more about this tremendous sport, the warriors and the colorful cast who drive MMA will continue in their efforts and take their rightful place in contemporary sports culture.